Spanish Influence on
the Old Southwest

ALSO BY JEREMY AGNEW
AND FROM MCFARLAND

The Creation of the Cowboy Hero: Fiction, Film and Fact (2015)

Alcohol and Opium in the Old West: Use, Abuse and Influence (2014)

The Old West in Fact and Film: History Versus Hollywood (2012)

Entertainment in the Old West: Theater, Music, Circuses, Medicine Shows, Prizefighting and Other Popular Amusements (2011)

Medicine in the Old West: A History, 1850–1900 (2010)

Spanish Influence on the Old Southwest

A Collision of Cultures

JEREMY AGNEW

McFarland & Company, Inc., Publishers
Jefferson, North Carolina

Photographs are from the author's collection unless otherwise credited.

LIBRARY OF CONGRESS CATALOGUING-IN-PUBLICATION DATA [new form]
Names: Agnew, Jeremy, author.
Title: Spanish influence on the old southwest : a collision of cultures / Jeremy Agnew.
Description: Jefferson, North Carolina : McFarland & Company, Inc., Publishers, 2016. | Includes bibliographical references and index.
Identifiers: LCCN 2015039124| ISBN 9780786497409 (softcover : acid free paper) | ISBN 9781476623276 (ebook)
Subjects: LCSH: Southwest, New—History. | Spanish—Southwest, New—History. | Southwest, New—Civilization—Spanish influences.
Classification: LCC F786 .A36 2016 | DDC 979—dc23
LC record available at http://lccn.loc.gov/2015039124

BRITISH LIBRARY CATALOGUING DATA ARE AVAILABLE

© 2016 Jeremy Agnew. All rights reserved

No part of this book may be reproduced or transmitted in any form or by any means, electronic or mechanical, including photocopying or recording, or by any information storage and retrieval system, without permission in writing from the publisher.

Front cover photograph of Kiva and Spanish Mission, Pecos Ruins © 2016 iStock/David Parsons

Printed in the United States of America

*McFarland & Company, Inc., Publishers
Box 611, Jefferson, North Carolina 28640
www.mcfarlandpub.com*

For my wife, Sylvia,
who shares my passion for history and
the allure of Spanish New Mexico

Table of Contents

Preface	1
Chronology	5
One. The Beginning	7
Two. Anasazi Descendants	27
Three. Pushing North from New Spain	45
Four. The City of the Holy Faith	66
Five. A Clash of Beliefs	84
Six. New Spain Expands	99
Seven. The Lure of Pacific Shores	116
Eight. Indian Horseman and Spanish Cowboys	135
Nine. The Spanish Falter	154
Ten. New Trails to Santa Fe	167
Eleven. The Americans Take Over	186
Postscript	205
Appendix 1: Glossary	209
Appendix 2: Outstanding Examples of Anasazi Ruins in the Southwest	211
Appendix 3: The California Mission Trail	212
Chapter Notes	215
Bibliography	223
Index	225

Preface

First-time visitors to the American Southwest, particularly New Mexico, are often surprised to note the strong historic Hispanic influence that exists there today. Indeed, most Americans do not understand the tremendous influence that Spain had on the formation of the United States. This influence has had a major effect on the people, the culture, the architecture and the cuisine of the Southwest. This book traces the origins of this influence, from its beginnings with Spanish explorers to the American takeover and surge of colonists after the settlement of war with Mexico in 1848.

The traditional view of the settling of the American West is that the frontier was settled by Anglo-American colonists emigrating from the East to the West, from the Atlantic Coast to the Pacific shore. Indeed, the early colonies founded in Jamestown, Virginia, in 1607 and Plymouth, Massachusetts, in 1620 by settlers who originated primarily in Europe did eventually result in a population surge across the Appalachian Mountains and into the Midwest. This westward movement later expanded into the settlement of the Great Plains, the Southwest, coastal Oregon and the Rocky Mountains, until restless emigrants ultimately caused a population boom in California during the 1849 gold rush. In spite of this common view, however, several other important streams of migrants had entered the United States much earlier.

One group consisted of British and French trappers and explorers who pushed southwards from Canada during the 1600s and 1700s to catch beaver and other fur-bearing animals in the Rocky Mountains. A second flow consisted of Spanish explorers from the Caribbean who landed in Florida in the 1500s and traveled as far north as the Carolinas and Virginia. Though chronologically early, the Spanish influence in Florida consisted of relatively minor attempts at exploration and settlement that resulted in varying degrees of success.

The more significant impact of Spanish colonization took place in a triangular section of the Far West, south of an imaginary line running between Nacogdoches in eastern Texas and San Francisco in northern California. Though this third flow of migration is often overlooked, it had a significant impact on the history of the southwestern part of the United States. Spanish conquistadors pushed north from Mexico seeking the fabled riches that they were convinced were ripe for the taking somewhere in the western part of North America. The Spanish penetrated the Americas long before the influx of European settlers. In the process they colonized the American Southwest over 250 years before the Anglo-American invasion of settlers in the mid–1800s.

Some chroniclers, however, have disagreed about the importance of the Spanish settlement of the Southwest. They feel that it was minor and not particularly relevant to understanding the history of the United States.[1] Differing viewpoints have evolved among historians and some have even become contradictory. Regardless of viewpoint, the Hispanic culture and legacy is still strongly evident in the Southwest. Much of the culture and many of the traditions brought by the Spanish have influenced what is present and visible today.

This book discusses the collision of cultures, those existing and those of the Spanish colonizers of the Old World and the New, and the results of that meeting. It is not intended to be a detailed history of New Mexico, Arizona, Colorado, California, or the other states impacted by Spanish colonization, but traces the results of their appearance and their efforts that are still evident today.

The Spanish provinces established in Texas and California were weak in colonial times compared to New Mexico. Spanish settlements in Texas were soon reduced to a cluster of missions around San Antonio due to harassment of missionaries and settlers by nomadic tribes in the southern part of the state. Spanish settlement in California evolved into a thin string of missions and presidios that stretched up the California Coast from San Diego to just north of San Francisco.

The strongest Spanish area of influence was their penetration north from Mexico into New Mexico. There, three cultures, the native American Indians, the Spanish and the Anglo-Americans, successively influenced what would become the American Southwest.

The story of the colonization of the Southwest started when the Spanish landed on the North American continent in Central America, 150 years before the Pilgrims landed at Plymouth Rock. Before the West was explored and settled by French trappers and traders, then by American settlers and gold-seekers, the Spanish had investigated parts of Florida, Georgia, Alabama, Mississippi, Arkansas, Kansas, Texas, Oklahoma, New Mexico, Arizona, California, Colorado, Nevada, and Utah. Long before Anglo emigrants set out on the Oregon Trail and California Trail, Spanish settlers spread north from Mexico to settle in the upper Rio Grande valley of New Mexico, and then seeped into southern Colorado, southern Arizona and California. To put this in perspective, in 1607, as Governor Juan de Oñate was leaving New Mexico after almost seventy years of Spanish exploration, Englishmen from the Virginia Company were just starting to erect their palisade on the James River. The following year, in 1608, the French erected a fur-trading post at Quebec on the St. Lawrence River.[2]

The wave of conquerors, soldiers, settlers, and men of the church that flowed north from Mexico during the 1600s and 1700s eventually populated a vast area. Spanish explorers established settlements over a broad section extending over the Southwest from Texas to California as they searched for riches in the form of gold and silver. Along with the original Spanish conquistadors came missionaries who valiantly tried to convert the existing native population to Christianity. This forced conversion of the Pueblo and Plains Indians, and suppression of their native religious beliefs, led to cultural clashes that eventually resulted in outright rebellion.

A strong Anglo presence in the Southwest did not start until the early 1820s, when bold pioneer entrepreneurs traveled from St. Louis, Missouri, to Santa Fe, New Mexico, along the perilous and difficult Santa Fe Trail, carrying the first trade goods between the United States and Mexico. By doing so, these merchants and teamsters linked the American East to the Spanish Southwest, thereby again changing the political and cultural landscape of the Mexican and Indian people living there. The primary purpose of their trips was an exchange of material goods, but the result was also an exchange and eventual blending of populations, cultures, languages, and ideas.

As the 1800s progressed, the northern boundary of the Hispanic frontier was steadily invaded by an influx of Anglo-Americans from the East until the entire area was eventually taken over by the United States by treaty with Mexico in 1848. This conquest from the East, however, could not, and did not, erase the cultural foundations that had been laid by the influence of Spanish (and later Mexican) rule that had lasted for the previous 250 years.

As the Americans pushed into the Southwest they found that they were not settling virgin wilderness, such as occurred during exploration of the Rocky Mountains and the Northwest, but eventually realized that they were encroaching on an established culture and way of life that had existed in the Southwest for centuries. The issue, then, became not one of exploration, but of how to assimilate the prevailing native Indian and Hispanic cultures into the Anglo-American way of life and blend the two together. In many ways this was a difficult task and was not completely successful.

In the second half of the nineteenth century the influence of Spanish culture was far more widespread in the southwestern United States than many Americans realized. Vast landholdings were based on Spanish land grants, the cattle industry originated with European stock brought to the Americas by the Spanish, the low, rambling thick-walled adobe houses of Spanish architecture filled the towns, and Spanish cooking was absorbed into mainstream Western cuisine.

American English has borrowed more words from Spanish than from any other modern language, particularly those terms involved with horsemanship. Stampede, rodeo, lariat, buckaroo, amigo, gringo, and bronco are examples of this. Barbecue, chocolate, tornado, and marijuana had their origins in Spanish words. Other Spanish terms adopted into American English included common features of the Southwestern landscape, such as arroyo, canyon, and mesa. Siesta, fiesta, and adios were popular Spanish language transplants. The names of Arizona, California, Colorado, Montana, Nevada, New Mexico, and Texas were derived from Spanish words. Spanish names, such as the Rio Grande and the Brazos, Pecos and Sacramento rivers, were readily adopted (note that the Rio Grande should be referred to without the redundant word "river" after it).

This Spanish influence has survived and lingered, and is prominent still in the Southwest of the United States, particularly in northern New Mexico, southern Arizona, southern Colorado, western Texas, and the mission areas of California. Visitors to these parts of the Southwest today are often surprised to find that many of the customs and culture, and even the architecture, are very different than those of traditional middle–America. This book will explore the origins of this culture and discuss how the arrival of the Spanish conquistadors of several hundred years ago influenced, and still influence, what may be seen today in the Southwest.

For simplicity in this book, I will employ the convention of using the names of modern states and cities without constantly adding the modifier "modern day," so that places described in the text are easy for the reader to identify and locate. The text, however, should be read with the understanding that these none of these American political boundaries and towns existed hundreds of years ago.

It is difficult in a book such as this to find a neutral name for the Native American Indian tribes that the Spanish encountered on the North American continent. They were first called "Indians" in error by Columbus, as he thought he had reached the East Indies. These native people were later called "American Indians" to differentiate them from the people of India. It is difficult in this instance to use this name because the area was owned by Spain and called New Spain, thus creating confusion in the terminology for the inhabitants. As an additional issue, these native peoples were not indigenous to North America, but migrated across the Bering Land Bridge from Asia. Though the name "Indian" may not seem appropriate to some people in today's social climate, the name is nevertheless part of the historical record for this particular period. I have, therefore, chosen to stay with Columbus' choice and the commonly accepted generic terminology of "Indian." As author David King has commented, "most of the people in question still call themselves *Indians*—or by their specific tribe name," so I have chosen to do the same.[3] I also use this name as a term to generically distinguish Native Americans from non–Indians. It must be remembered, however, that within this very general designation are a wide variety of distinct cultural and political groupings.

Viewed from a distance of almost 500 years with sometimes inadequate or missing documentation, some of the events, people, numbers and even dates in this story of Spanish colonization are still murky and are the subject of debate and speculation among historians. I have endeavored to find a consensus among experts in telling this story, but must take responsibility for accounts that differ from other sources.

Chronology

1492	Christopher Columbus lands in the New World
1521	Hernán Cortés completes the conquest of Mexico
1536	Cabeza de Vaca returns to Mexico from the Southwest with tales of cities of gold
1540	Coronado travels north from Mexico to hunt for gold; he is the first white man to visit the pueblos of New Mexico and claims the Southwest for Spain
1542	Portuguese navigator Juan Rodríguez Cabrillo lands at San Diego
1565	St. Augustine, Florida, the oldest town in the continental United States
1598	Juan de Oñate leads the first colonizing expedition to northern New Mexico
1610	Pedro de Peralta establishes Santa Fe as the capital of New Mexico
1680	The Pueblo Revolt drives the Spanish out of New Mexico back to Mexico
1682	First Spanish settlement established in Texas
1692	The Spanish re-conquer New Mexico
1706	Juan de Ulibarri claims Colorado for Spain
1762	France transfers the Louisiana Territory to Spain
1767	The Jesuits are expelled from the New World
1769	The first Spanish mission in California is founded in San Diego
1775	Monterey is declared the Spanish capital of California
1776	Spanish priests Dominguez and Escalante try to find a safe route to the California missions
1803	The Louisiana Purchase adds a vast area of land to the United States
1806	Lt. Zebulon Pike sets out to explore the headwaters of the Arkansas River
1821	First Americans settle in Texas; William Becknell pioneers the Santa Fe Trail; Mexico achieves Independence from Spain
1829	The first trade caravan from New Mexico to Los Angeles opens the Old Spanish Trail
1834	Bent's Fort completed as a trading center on the border between Mexico and the United States
1836	The Alamo falls to Mexican troops; Texas claims independence from Spain
1845	Texas admitted to the Union
1846	Start of the war between the United States and Mexico; Kearny takes over New Mexico; the American flag is raised over California
1847	War with Mexico ends; American Governor William Bent is killed in the Taos Pueblo Revolt
1848	Treaty of Guadalupe Hidalgo with Mexico adds more than a half-million square miles of territory in the West to the United States

1849	The Old Spanish Trail fades away as other forms of transportation develop; discovery of gold brings a flood of Anglo miners and settlers to California
1853	Gadsden Purchase adds further territory to Arizona and New Mexico, and sets modern boundaries
1861	Start of the American Civil War pits the Union against the Confederacy; New Mexico organized as a territory
1863	Arizona Territory separated from New Mexico Territory
1865	End of the American Civil War; cowboys in Texas start gathering up cattle that multiplied in the brush country of Texas and drive them to railheads in Kansas
1880	Arrival of the railroad in Santa Fe ends transportation over the Santa Fe Trail
1912	New Mexico achieves formal statehood in 1912 as the forty-seventh state; Arizona gains statehood.

CHAPTER ONE

The Beginning

The story of the Spanish in the American Southwest started with a significant event that took place in Europe in 1492. In that year Granada, the last stronghold of the Moors in Iberia, fell to the Christians.[1] This left King Ferdinand II of Spain free to turn his attentions from war at home to exploration to the west, across the Atlantic Ocean. The result was that Genoese sailor Christopher Columbus, sponsored by Queen Isabella of Castile, left Spain on August 3 and navigated his way across the Atlantic Ocean. He entered the Caribbean Sea and landed in the West Indies on the island of Hispaniola, called Española by Columbus. The modern island is now divided between Haiti and the Dominican Republic.

Columbus had intended to travel around the world, searching for a convenient trade route from Europe to China, Japan, and India—the Indies as they were then collectively known. The accepted thinking of the time was that the distance between Europe and Asia would be shorter sailing to the west than to the east. This concept was, of course, wrong and instead Columbus stumbled onto the West Indies and made land in the Americas. Thinking that he had arrived in India, Columbus called the people he encountered Indians.[2]

This discovery of the New World was only the beginning and the Spanish soon overran the Caribbean. During the early 1500s they rapidly settled Puerto Rico, Jamaica, Cuba, and other islands of the West Indies. From these islands it was an easy step for Spanish explorers to sail to North and South America. Over the following 350 years the Spanish explored and colonized these new continents, and exploited the native people they encountered. The explorers were driven by dreams of power and prestige, and conversion of the heathens they found there. The Spanish believed in their culture, their God, their church, and their superiority. What they did affected the course of history in North America.

One of the earliest of the Spanish explorers was Juan Ponce de León. In 1513 he led an expedition northwest from Puerto Rico to find the mythical "Fountain of Youth" of Spanish tradition, a legendary spring that was said to restore the prime of life and lost vitality to men who drank from it. At least that was the legend. The first story that claimed the Fountain of Youth was the reason for his trip actually did not surface until about twenty years after he had discovered Florida. Like many other legends, the best story was the one that survived. Perhaps the more important attractions for his trip to Florida were the gold and potential slaves that were rumored to be plentiful there.

Ponce de León sighted land on April 2, and named it *La Florida* ("The Flowery Land") after the luxuriant vegetation he found. The outcome of the trip was that he explored much of the east coast of Florida. In 1521 he returned to found a colony, but in the process was wounded by local Indians and died after his return to Cuba. One eventual legacy of his early explorations was the oldest known town in the continental United States, *San Agustín* (St. Augustine), which was founded in 1565 by Pedro Menéndez de Avilés.

Another exploration milestone during 1513 occurred when Vasco Núñez de Balboa led a expedition to the Pacific shores of California.

The Search for Treasure

As well as trying to find a direct passage to the Indies, Spanish explorers sailed to the New World looking for wealth to exploit. Their hope was to find rich gold and silver strikes, and a large compliant native population to work them into productive mines. This lust for gold and exploitable indigenous Indians led to terrible abuses in the Caribbean. Spanish fighting men pillaged, burned, killed men, raped women, plundered villages, and enslaved the local Indians in their search for gold. The prevailing attitude was summed up by Columbus when he wrote in his diary, "The best thing in the world is gold, it can even send souls to heaven."[3]

From their foothold on the islands of the Caribbean, Spanish explorers flocked to the North American mainland in search of more prizes to conquer, drawn by vague legends of endless supplies of gold and other great riches. One of the stories that helped to drive exploration of the New World was a persistent myth of a race of Amazon warrior women who fought with weapons made from pure gold. Their ruler was rumored to be a queen named Califia, for whom the Californias were eventually named.[4] A description of these female Amazon warriors appeared in a novel titled *Las Sergas de Esplandián* ("The Exploits of Esplandian") published in Seville around 1510. The story was about a knight who gathered a crusading army from various nations to defend Constantinople against an attack by the King of Persia. Among the warriors was a group of black female soldiers who were courageous and strong and who came from a race of people without men. These women's armor and weapons were made of gold because the island they lived on had no other metals.

In another version of the same apocryphal story, Spanish explorers in South America were supposedly attacked with bows and arrows by a group of naked women called *Amazonas*, who were tall and white-skinned, and were said to come from a village populated only by women. To fulfill their need to reproduce, they were impregnated occasionally by men from a neighboring kingdom. If the resulting child was male, he would be killed, but if the baby was female, she was trained for war. One supposedly knowledgeable observer commented that the women whom the explorers encountered could not be real Amazons because they had two breasts. Supposedly true Amazons had only a left breast, as possessing a right one interfered with shooting a bow and arrow.[5] Joining in the controversy, another "expert," who claimed to be just as knowledgeable, was of the opinion that these women could shoot perfectly well even with two breasts. Though the Spanish never found these remarkable women, when they discovered a large river during their explorations in South America they named it the Amazon.[6]

The most powerful of the myths of golden riches that attracted Spanish explorers to the New World was that of the Seven Cities of Antilia. Even before Columbus sailed across the Atlantic Ocean there was a persistent myth that stretched back to medieval times that somewhere to the west of Spain, across what was then called the Sea of Darkness, were seven cities rumored to be overflowing with riches. Several wishful mapmakers even located the mythical island on contemporary maps. The legend said that seven Catholic bishops and their followers sailed from Portugal in 714 to escape persecution and death as the Moors swept into Iberia. The group sailed westwards and were said to have landed on an unknown island whose streams were overflowing with gold. They used this riches to build seven cities, one for each bishop, with streets paved with gold, houses made of silver, and buildings studded with precious jewels. The island was called Antilia, which was the reason the Spanish eventually called a group of islands in the West Indies the Antilles, even though no gold was found there.

The Conquistadors

After the war with the Moors came to an end, Spain was left with many fighting men who had no immediate prospects of employment in their profession. The New World, on the other hand, was rumored to offer many opportunities for young, trained, fighting men. Particularly for those who would be inspired by the possibility of finding gold while they were doing God's work of conversion of the natives of the Americas.

Though the Spanish were the first Europeans to colonize North America, the Spanish crown did not have enough resources to support extensive exploration. In a shrewd business move, the king granted private contracts or licenses to wealthy Spanish nobles to explore new territory, to conquer and enslave the native people as required, and to generate income from any exploitable resources they happened to find. In return, the Crown was to receive 20 percent of the value of all the gold, silver, and jewels that the explorers found. In this way Spain did not risk any money in exploration that generated no revenue, but stood to profit if anything worthwhile was discovered.[7] As a result, expedition leaders, known as *conquistadors*, who wanted to claim the lands they explored were quick to report that they were rich in precious metals and contained compliant native people.

The Spanish believed that God's purpose for them was to conquer those they considered to be unenlightened heathens and unbelievers. Accordingly, they brought their Christian religion with them to the New World to save the souls of the natives and thus allow them to go to heaven. In return for their efforts in doing this, the conquistadors believed that they were rightfully due the rewards of whatever wealth they could take for themselves. Thus Spanish conquests were made in the name of God, Spain, and gold, though not necessarily in that order. One less-understanding Indian chief called them "holy bandits."[8] In modern times they would simply be called looters.

To the Spanish way of thinking, gold was the ultimate exploitable resource, though silver was considered to be a good second. Gold and silver not only had intrinsic value, but they were the best form of riches because they could be easily transported. Both were compact and were not perishable like crops and grain, or too bulky for easy shipment like woolen clothing and blankets.

The would-be conquerors of the New World were predominantly young fighting men, in their twenties and thirties, looking for adventure. Though most were of aristocratic birth from noble families, they were also mostly poor and were hoping to find their own wealth and power from the conquest of lands in the New World. Most of the men were mercenaries who had lived by their swords during the Spanish war against the Moors, with their skills gained from fighting the invading "infidels" from Africa. Once the Moors were beaten back, these men had no opponents to fight and needed new lands to conquer.

Though many historians refer to these early explorers as mounted warriors, giving the impression that they were similar to an organized cavalry, these early fighting men were not cavalry or infantry in the military sense. They were armed entrepreneurs hoping for profit and gain when they found the riches alleged to be in the Americas. They were not part of a specific army, but were young men looking for wealth and status. Original Spanish documents did not refer to these men as soldiers, but described them as either men on foot or men on horseback.[9] Their leaders did not have military ranks as would be found in regular armies, but had the title of "captain," as one who commanded a group of men.[10] The recruits were not specifically paid, but stood to gain a share of the profit of whatever they found.

Restall succinctly described the typical conquistador as "…a young man in his late twenties, semi-literate, from southwestern Spain, trained in a particular trade or profession, seeking opportunity through patronage networks based on family and home-town ties. Armed as well as he could afford, and with some experience already of exploration and conquest in the Americas, he would be ready to invest what he had and risk his life if absolutely necessary in order to be a member of the first company to conquer somewhere wealthy and well populated."[11] As manual labor was considered to be beneath the dignity of the Spanish aristocracy, the "well populated" part was necessary to provide slaves to perform free labor. The Spanish plan was to conquer, convert, exploit and then incorporate the natives into Spanish culture. They would conquer the provinces and enslave the native people to do useful work, and hopefully convert them to Catholicism, though the young fortune-seekers did not consider this last task to be essential.

Cortés and the Aztecs

Rumors of gold and other riches in the New World were persistent, and indeed some minor amount of the metal had been found in the riverbeds of Haiti. This occurred as placer gold, however, and the finds were soon exhausted.[12]

After an expedition to Mexico in 1517, Francisco Hernandez de Cordova brought news to the governor of Cuba, Diego Velásquez, that vast riches of gold and silver had been found on the mainland. The next year, the governor sent an expedition headed by his nephew, Juan de Grijalva, to confirm the news. After several months of trading with friendly Indians, Grijalva returned with enough gold and silver objects to stimulate further Spanish interest. Accordingly, the governor sent Hernán Cortés (also commonly spelled Cortez) to Mexico as captain-general of a major expedition with the goal of appropriating any gold and other riches he could find.

Cortés, an educated man who wrote poetry and could read Latin, was the first of the Spanish conquistadors to invade the Americas. He set sail from Cuba in 1519 for Vera Cruz with 400 fighting men, eleven ships, and a hundred sailors. He landed on the Yucatán Peninsula on the east side of the mainland of Mexico. According to Bryson, the Mexican

Before penetrating the interior of Mexico, both Juan de Grijalva in 1518 and Hernán Cortés in 1519 sailed to the Yucatán Peninsula in search of gold and other riches. There they encountered the Mayan people, who lived in an advanced civilization similar to the Aztecs. These are the ruins of Tulum, which once housed 1,000 to 1,500 people, on the coast of Yucatan.

state of Yucatán received its name because that was the response given by the natives to the first conquistadors who ended up on their shores. When the Spanish tried to communicate with them, the natives replied with "*yucatán?*" which in their native language meant "What?" or "What are you saying?"[13] The name, however, stuck.

Cortés intended from the beginning to conquer Mexico, so he immediately set plans in motion. He and his men rapidly defeated the Indians in the coastal area and then advanced westwards until he came into contact with the Aztecs. The Aztec people lived in several city-states dominated by the inhabitants of a town named Tenochtitlán, which was built on an island on the west side of Lake Texcoco in the central highlands. The architecture of the city was characterized by stepped pyramids and stone temples. Rock causeways throughout the city crossed a series of canals that were fed directly from the lake.

Tenochtitlán has variously been translated as "the place of the prickly pear cactus" or "the place of the cactus in the rock." The Aztecs also used the name *Mexico* for their capital to encompass the surrounding lands. *Mexico* means "the town in the middle of the lake of the moon." The two names were used separately or together as *Mexico-Tenochtitlán*. In turn, the Aztecs called themselves *Aztecs*, *Mexica*, or *Tenochca* after their homeland.

The legend of the founding of Tenochtitlán was that the gods told the Aztec people to build a city on an island in a lake where they saw an eagle on a cactus eating a serpent.

Today the center of the Mexican flag recalls the legend with an emblem that shows an eagle sitting on a prickly pear cactus on a rock above a lake, holding a snake in its beak with one talon.[14]

When the Spanish first arrived in Tenochtitlán, the ruler of the Aztec Empire, Montezuma, welcomed the bearded strangers and offered Cortés gifts of gold, silver, and precious jewels.[15] Montezuma, whose name meant "Angry Young Lord," was the chief spokesman for the Aztecs and a general of the army who led his troops into battle in person.

Montezuma believed that Cortés was the Aztec god Quetzalcoatl, who had returned to them from the east out of the sunrise to reclaim his kingdom, and indeed Cortés and his men had sailed to Mexico from Cuba in the east, as predicted by the ancient prophecy. Quetzalcoatl was coincidentally thought to be white-skinned and bearded. As an additional sign of respect and welcome, Montezuma offered Cortés chocolate, a food much revered by Aztec royalty.

Among the other gifts Montezuma gave Cortés were jewelry containing turquoise, a gemstone much prized by the Aztecs both for its beauty and its mystical properties. The Aztec god Quetzalcoatl was commonly depicted as being adorned with turquoise, including turquoise earrings. Cortés and the Spanish felt that this jewelry, beautiful though it appeared, was inferior to gold. To the Spanish, however, these gifts, which included a priceless ceremonial shield and mask encrusted with turquoise, confirmed the rumors of riches in the New World and further inflamed the Spanish lust for what they really wanted, which was gold. Cortés once said, "We Spaniards suffer from a disease of the heart, the specific remedy for which is gold."[16]

The Aztecs lived in a cruel society. Montezuma was also the chief priest of the Aztecs and presided over gruesome rituals that involved human victims. The priests plunged an obsidian knife deep into the chests of live sacrificial victims and pulled out their still-beating hearts.[17] The priests then smeared their idols with the victim's blood as a sacrifice, and ate the arms and legs.[18] The remaining parts of the body might be flayed and the skin worn by the priests as a ghoulish type of outer garment.

Blood was considered to be the ultimate offering to the Aztec gods.[19] Priests slashed their own bodies and ears with knives, and pierced their flesh with cactus thorns to draw blood for sacrifice. Franciscan friars in the 1560s noted that one of the most sacred forms of bloodletting mutilation practiced by the Maya of Yucatán, similar to the Aztecs, was to make a hole in their penis and pass thread through the hole to draw blood as part of their sacrificial offerings.[20] Other soft body parts, such as the ear or tongue, were also similarly pierced. Spanish priests, of course, condemned the practice.

Spanish Armament

The Spanish goal was to take over the Aztec empire. To achieve this they had five military advantages: horses; dogs used in combat; firearms; pikes, swords, and crossbows; and superior tactical fighting skills.[21] The Spanish lances, rifles, and crossbows could kill from a greater distance than any of the Indian weapons.

Men on foot were typically armed with lances or pikes. These were spears with a twelve- to fifteen-foot wooden shaft with a steel point ten to twelve inches long attached to the end. They were also armed with halberds, which were a combination of lance, hook and battle-ax. The design was a long, spear-like weapon that had a hook on the end for pulling an enemy to the ground from his horse and a heavy axe blade that could be used to cut through his armor. These long weapons gave the Spanish a distinct advantage against the shorter clubs and axes used by the natives. These weapons were also deadly against mounted opponents.

Spanish fighting men on horseback carried a tough leather shield (*adarga*) fashioned from at least three layers of cowhide for warding off deadly Indian arrows. The *adarga* was held on the left arm by two straps of leather fastened to the back.

Soldiers wore three-quarter-length sleeveless jackets of leather (*cuera*) that came down to their knees to protect the torso. This protective clothing, which had been copied directly from the Moorish soldiers of the old country, were stout enough to deflect an Indian arrow. The *cuera* consisted of up to eight layers of deerskin or bull-hide sewn together and could weight up to eighteen pounds. Because these jackets were so heavy, they were typically worn only during times of danger. This gave the soldiers the nickname of *soldados de cueras*, or "soldiers of leather jackets." Their outfit was completed by a broad-brimmed hat, cotton leggings and a leather bag slung over the shoulder to carry various supplies.

The most useful weapon for the Spanish was the sword (*espada*), which was used for slashing and piercing. Some of the men were armed with swords made in Toledo. These superb weapons, considered to be the best swords in Europe in the 1500s and 1600s, were three feet long, had a double edge that was extremely sharp, and narrowed down to a lethal point at the business end.

In addition to these weapons, thirty-two of Cortés' men were armed with crossbows, a deadly archery weapon that consisted of a fighting bow mounted horizontally on a shoulder stock like a rifle. The bowstring was drawn back by a winding mechanism, then released with a trigger pulled by the finger. This design made the crossbow a far more powerful and deadly weapon than the longbow. Crossbows fired a missile called a "bolt" or "quarrel," which was a short, heavy arrow with a thick head equipped with a steel point and barbs that could penetrate light armor. The arrow was often smeared with poison for greater killing power. Whether poisoned or not, the heavy arrow created painful wounds that frequently became infected. In a form of medieval version of the arms race, the crossbow was considered to be such a superior weapon that it was not supposed to be used against fellow Christians. Its use was, however, considered to be acceptable against heathen Indians.[22]

Horses and Dogs

Another significant Spanish military advantage was the support of horses and dogs. Horses, which were a vital part of Spanish soldiering, were superior in battles against men on foot on open ground. Large dogs, such as greyhounds and mastiffs, were trained as attack animals for hunting and combat, mostly at close quarters. They went into battle with collars decorated with long, lethal metal spikes to further wound whomever they attacked.

The horse turned out to be an important weapon in Cortés' overthrow of the Indians. There were no horses in Mexico until Cortés brought the first with him in 1519. As the Aztecs had never seen horses before, a further advantage for the Spanish was that they were frightened by these apparitions. To add to the Aztec's confusion, their superstitious nature convinced them that a horse and its rider were a single supernatural being with two heads. When the Spaniards realized that the Indians were afraid of horses they realized that they could retain a measure of their dominance if they could keep horses from the Indians.[23]

Though the Aztecs had never seen horses before, they had seen deer, so many believed that horses were an unusual type of deer.[24] Others thought they were big dogs. Some even believed that horses ate human flesh.[25]

Spanish horsemen wore steel helmets, polished steel breastplates, and steel arm protection. Their mounts were similarly armored. Horses were equipped with shields of wood and leather across their flanks, and masks of steel to protect their faces. Both men and riders were an impressive sight as their armor clanked as they rode and gleamed brilliantly in the sun.

Firearms

One of the primary tools of conquest used by Spanish conquistadors was firearms. Cortés brought with him thirteen musketeers, the name given to men armed with rifles. These early firearms incorporated a firing mechanism that gave them the name of matchlock. "Matchlock" was the generic name for either a fifteen- to twenty-pound musket or the lighter eight to ten pound arquebus, also called a harquebus or hackbut. These muskets were so large and heavy that they were typically placed on a forked pole jammed into the ground when they were aimed and fired. The name "lock" in matchlock (and the later flintlock) came about because the delicate and complicated firing mechanisms used in early guns were made originally by locksmiths.

Both musket and arquebus consisted basically of an iron tube mounted on a wooden stock, which resulted in a primitive type of smooth-bore rifle.[26] The firing mechanism contained gunpowder that was lit by a slow burning match, hence the name matchlock. To load either type of gun, the shooter poured black powder down the barrel and forced a lead bullet down on top of it.[27] He then forced a wad of cotton down onto the bullet to hold it in place. When the trigger was pulled, the glowing match, which looked like a long cord or wick, dropped into a pan of gunpowder (the primer) that forced a flash of fire into the chamber of the gun. This ignited the main charge of powder in the chamber and fired the lead ball out of the barrel. Depending on the caliber of the gun, which was essentially the diameter of the inside of the barrel, this lead bullet varied from 0.66 to 0.80 inches in diameter.

Both types of gun fired only a single shot before reloading was necessary. Both were considered unreliable as any wind tended to blow out the match and any rain dampened the powder and extinguished the match. Musketeers often fired their single shot then used the weapon as a club.[28] Another disadvantage was that after repeated firing these guns tended to overheat. This could result in the barrel clogging after repeated firing and explosion of the breech, producing unfortunate consequences for the gunner and anyone standing close to him.

The use of any firearms was problematic in a tropical climate as the gunpowder frequently became damp and often misfired. These guns were also subject to premature or accidental discharge. When the gun worked properly, however, the sound of the explosion, the belch of fire coming out of the end of the barrel, and the dense jet of gray smoke that accompanied it were enough to scare the daylights out of the Indians. In a similar manner, the Indians were terrified of the noise made by the several small cannons that Cortés brought with him.

A few years after the conquest of Mexico by Cortés a significant advance in firearms reliability took place in 1525 with the development of the flintlock. In this newer version of the musket, the match of the matchlock was replaced by a flint that struck a steel plate and sprayed sparks into the priming powder. Another development was a single-shot pistol version of the flintlock, which was easier to aim and fire, though it was large and unwieldy in comparison to today's handguns. A more significant disadvantage was that the rifle and the pistol fired only a single shot each before having to be reloaded. Thus even a soldier with both a pistol and a rifle had to choose his targets carefully as his combined weapons were only capable of two shots.

There were two further disadvantages to the flintlock that were common to all firearms of the period. One was that the gun was prone to misfires due to unreliability of the sparking mechanism. The other was that there was a delay between pulling the trigger and the bullet leaving the barrel, due to the time it took for the flint to fall and ignite the powder. This lessened the accuracy of the gun when firing at rapidly-moving men as the target might have moved by the time the bullet arrived.

Conquest by Disease

When the Spanish arrived in the New World, they unwittingly brought with them another aspect of Western civilization that was more deadly than their swords and firearms in decimating the native population. They carrried with them smallpox, measles, typhus, tuberculosis, chicken pox, influenza, typhoid, cholera, and other common European diseases against which the native population had no immunity. As the Aztecs had no natural defenses, these unknown and unseen killers caused them to sicken and die in large numbers. The diseases were soon rampant among the Indians, wiping out whole villages and decimating entire tribes. Further havoc was wrought by malaria and yellow fever that had accompanied the Spanish from Africa.

During the Spanish conquest, deaths from a combination of war, forced labor, and disease virtually wiped out the Aztecs. When Cortés arrived in 1519, the population of the Aztec capital city and the surrounding region was estimated to be nearly two million. By 1570, the original population had been reduced to only 300,000.[29] The entire population of Mexico declined from an estimated more than eighteen million in 1520 to less than two million in 1650. By the time Jesuit missionaries arrived in the late 1600s, the native population had been further reduced to about 50,000. By the time the Jesuits left seventy years later, the figure was only 10,000. By the early 1800s almost all the native Indians were gone.[30] This was the greatest population loss in human history.[31]

The Fall of the Aztecs

In spite of the superiority of Spanish weapons and various diseases, Cortés didn't have enough fighting men for a direct take over of the Aztec kingdom. His plan, therefore, was to gain control of the empire by working his way into Montezuma's confidence. Even though Montezuma did not totally trust Cortés, he hesitated to resist because of his continued belief that the Spanish might indeed be gods. So he did not take any action against them. After several months of procrastination on both sides, Cortés seized Montezuma and held him captive, hoping in this way to move the takeover along faster and quickly gain control of the Aztec kingdom.

Meanwhile a second Spanish expedition, motivated by political infighting in the government, landed on the Mexican coast, intending to seize power from Cortés. In order to head off confiscation of his prize of Mexico-Tenochtitlán, Cortés immediately set out to confront these newcomers. In his absence he left Pedro de Alvarado in charge.

After Cortés' departure, Alvarado became worried that an Aztec attack was pending, so he planned a preemptive strike. During a religious harvest celebration, Alvarado and his troops attacked a group of Aztecs, slaughtering several hundred of them with swords during the festivities. This was the final straw for the Aztecs. They could take no more oppression and fought back, in the process surrounding the Spaniards.

As soon as he received news of this rebellion, Cortés marched back to assist the trapped men. The result was several weeks of intermittent siege and fighting. Montezuma tried to bring an end to the fighting, but was injured in the head by a rock thrown at him when he tried to speak to his people on behalf of Cortés. He died three days later.[32]

The next day, the remaining Spaniards tried to force their way out of Tenochtitlán by bridging the network of canals scattered throughout the city. The plan failed and the Spanish tried to escape by swimming. With poetic justice, many of them drowned in the lake and the city's canals, weighted down by the looted gold that they were carrying and by their heavy suits of metal armor. The abortive retreat on June 30, 1519, was subsequently named *La Noche Triste* ("The Sorrowful Night").

Cortés, along with the men who escaped, retreated to the east of Tenochtitlán to the small city-state of Tlaxcala, where the Indians were friendly to the Spanish. During the rest of 1520, Cortés slowly regrouped his army, partially augmented by reinforcements from the coast and partly by making alliances with small kingdoms that felt oppressed by the Aztecs.

By 1521, Cortés was ready and the Spanish returned to Tenochtitlán in full force accompanied by various allies, particularly the Tlaxcalans (whose numbers are estimated to have been anywhere from six thousand to several hundred thousand), who wanted to be free from Aztec rule. Meanwhile, the city of Tenochtitlán had been struck by an epidemic of smallpox that had been brought by the Spanish invaders. The disease killed thousands and has been estimated to have reduced the population by half.[33] This made it easier for the combined force to destroy the capital city and kill thousands of the remaining Aztecs.

During the preliminary fighting Cortés realized that the Aztecs would never surrender, so he made the decision to destroy the city. His men looted, burned, and pulled down most of the houses. He was finally forced to level them, as the mud walls of the buildings did not burn well. Tenochtitlán, the former proud Aztec capital, lay buried under thirty feet of rubble and human bodies. Cortés had now completely conquered North America's richest empire.

Cortés forced the surviving Aztecs to build a new Spanish city on the ruins of Tenochtitlán. It was called Temixtlan by the Spanish until 1524, then it gradually became referred to as Mexico City after the *Mexica* people.[34] By the 1570s, Mexico City had a population of 15,000.[35] Aztec relics are still buried under the modern city.[36]

The remaining Aztecs were assimilated into the new Spanish Empire, which was run on the labor of Indian slaves. Cortés also forced the remaining natives to work in the gold and silver mines that had been discovered to the north. Though the Caribbean Islands had yielded a modest amount of gold, it was nothing compared to the amount that resulted from the conquest of the Aztecs. Gold, silver, and precious stones flowed back to Spain and helped to make it the greatest empire and military machine in the world at the time. These riches also helped to emphasize the potential for more gold in the New World and were the stimulus for further exploration. The conquistadors hoped that the rest of the Americas would yield the same sort of riches.

Cortés felt that the Mexican coastline reminded him so much of his Spanish homeland that he named the new territory *Nueva España*, or "New Spain." He was appointed governor, captain-general, and chief justice by King Charles of Spain. In his quest for domination, Cortés tried to convert the remaining Aztec to Christianity. His men destroyed idols, burned temples, and killed or imprisoned native priests. Those who did not accept conversion were put to the sword. To further spread the message of the Catholic Church, Cortés brought Franciscan priests who were specially trained to teach and preach about Christianity.

Though the price in human lives had been steep, the conquest of the Aztecs by Cortés and the establishment of New Spain was the beginning of Spanish settlement in Mexico. To aid in settlement, Cortés imported cattle, pigs, goats, sheep, and chickens. He planted European crops, such as wheat, sugar cane, grapes, and peach, almond, and olive trees. People of the Old and New Worlds blended in New Spain. The Spanish conquerors commonly married converted Indian women, thus producing a large population of "mestizos," the descendants of mixed Spanish and Indian blood. But Cortés didn't want bachelors in his new empire, he wanted settlement. He decreed that every new settler had to bring his own wife or send back to Spain at his own expense for a woman to marry.[37]

One problem in this new world was a lack of sufficient labor. Spanish gentlemen did not lower themselves to manual labor but used others to do this work. To solve the shortage of labor, Cortés instituted the traditional Spanish *encomienda* system. *Encomienda* in Spanish meant "to give in trust." It was a medieval term that referred to a grant by the governor of the labor and tribute of a certain number of natives living in a specific place. It was used in the re-conquest of Spain from the Moors and in the Caribbean conquest. The first *encomienda* was granted in New Spain in 1522.

In accordance with this system, the captains who fought with Cortés, and other later Spanish settlers, received extensive grants of land to encourage them to stay in New Spain. Settlers received not only the land, but the workers to go with it, as Cortés gave entire villages of hundreds of native people captured in battle to his men to work the land. In essence these Indians were slaves and their owners could control and punish them however they saw fit. A common punishment was to cut off a foot or a leg.

It is important to keep a balanced perspective on what the Spanish did as they tried to colonize the New World. While the treatment of the Indians of Central America, and later New Mexico, may seem unnecessarily harsh and cruel by today's standards, such behavior was acceptable to western European nations of the 1500s and 1600s whose behavior even to each other in the known civilized world was harsh and cruel.

This magnificent, though idealized picture by an unknown artist is titled *Entrance of Cortés into Mexico*. It shows the two cultures embracing each other with open arms, while Aztec nobles and Spanish conquistadors look on, and beautiful native women lounge around. Unfortunately this friendship was not to be and the Spanish rapidly destroyed the Aztec empire (Library of Congress).

Continued Spanish hopes for more gold and silver led to further expeditions to seek other lands as rich as New Spain. In 1532 Francisco Pizarro set sail to locate the source of gold contained in the legend of El Dorado. Supposedly El Dorado, the Gilded King, was covered with sacred oil and then sprinkled with gold dust every morning in lieu of clothing. Every evening he washed his body clean in a lake and the gilding process was repeated the next morning. The Spanish reasoned that if they could find this lake, they would presumably find years of accumulation of gold dust from generations of kings, as well as the supply of gold dust that was used to provide this metallic clothing.[38] Though the Spanish spent years looking for this legendary source of treasure they never found it. The name El Dorado eventually became the representation of all mythical sources of treasure, whether it was a lake, a king, a country or a buried mine of Spanish treasure. Though Pizarro did not find the Gilded King, in the process of searching he conquered the Inca Empire in Peru and added a fortune in gold to Spain's already vast store of riches.

Perversely, in the end, all the gold and silver that was shipped back to Spain from Mexico proved to be a burden rather than a blessing. The flood of precious metal from the New World caused inflation in Europe. This, coupled with continued massive military spending, put Spain into major debt and eventually caused the country to lose its prominent status as a world power.[39]

The Continued Search for Gold

The Spanish conquerors of the New World had been successful in their search for riches as they conquered the Aztecs in Mexico and the Incas in Peru. Stories of endless gold, freely available land, and plenty of natives to exploit in the Americas rapidly made their way back to Spain. The prospects of fame and further fortunes to be made in the New World induced many Spaniards to cross the ocean to join in the conquest. Having found the bountiful riches of Central America, the Spanish believed that they would find similar riches, including the fabled Seven Cities, if they continued further north. Adventurers used Mexico as a base to go in all directions, hoping to find similar "Mexicos" with equivalent riches for the taking. Luis Marín, for example, explored Oaxaca in 1521 and Pedro Alvarez explored Guatemala in 1523.

The whispered stories of riches spread rapidly and grew in the telling. One of these stories had some basis in fact. Around 1527, an Indian servant named Tejo told Nuño de Guzmán, governor of the province of Pánuco, that when he was a child he had traveled with his father to trade at large towns somewhere in the north. At that time it was not unusual for enterprising businessmen from Mexico to take macaw feathers, copper bells, and exotic seashells for long distances to trade with Indians who lived in the north. Among Tejo's memories were seven large cities and that his father had been paid in gold and silver for tropical bird feathers. He also remembered craftsmen in these cities who worked with gold and silver. Tejo thought that the cities were forty days' travel north across the barren desert lands.

This story sparked Guzmán's interest. In response, in 1530 he formed an expedition of 500 Spaniards and several thousand friendly Indians, and started north from New Spain to find what he assumed were the Seven Cities of Antilia.[40] Guzmán was a harsh taskmaster. Along the way he captured and enslaved at least 10,000 Indians. Those who resisted him were crucified or hanged. When one Spaniard cursed him, he had the man nailed to a post by his tongue.[41] Though Guzmán did not find the seven fabled cities, he was able to explore and seize new territory along the northwest coast of Mexico, in the process establishing the Spanish settlement of Culiacán in 1531, almost a hundred years before the founding of Boston in 1630.

Northward Again to Florida

Meanwhile, Spanish conquistadors continued to sail north from islands in the Caribbean to the United States. One of the best-known explorers of the Southeast was Hernando de Soto, who left Cuba in 1539 with seven ships to explore the coast of Florida. De Soto had previously served with Pizarro in Peru against the Incas and had returned a rich man. He had a royal commission to conquer, pacify, and settle any land he explored, but in reality he was primarily interested only in further riches, preferably gold. He traveled as far as Arkansas and Oklahoma before heading back east again. He discovered the Mississippi River, but died of a fever on its banks in 1542. He was buried in a hollowed-out log in the river to prevent desecration of his grave by local Indians.

The Indians of the Southeast became caught up in a crossfire of colonization efforts by Spain, France, and Britain and the desire of these nations to commandeer as much land as possible to plant crops. Explorers established missions to convert Indians to Christianity, schools to educate them and their children, and an agricultural system that required Indian labor.[42] But the Spanish brought with them the sword as well as the cross. Local Indians often greeted the conquistadors with friendship, but were rewarded with slavery and plunder of their villages. In retaliation, mission Indians rebelled and killed the monks who manned the religious outposts.[43]

Franciscan missionaries, hungry for lost souls to save, first arrived in Florida in 1593. They founded missions where Indians were gathered together and taught Christianity, along with the agricultural arts. By 1674 two chains of missions ministered to 26,000 Indians. One was on the Atlantic Coast, north from St. Augustine to Santa Catalina in Georgia. The other stretched from Gainesville through the interior, northwest to the Florida-Georgia border.[44]

Florida would never be colonized to the extent that the Southwest was and it would never be tied to the other provinces further west. In fact, Spanish Florida could not have survived except for annual royal subsidies from Spain. It was merely a defense outpost of the Spanish West Indies and was used as a buffer against any potential attack against the rich Spanish holdings of the Caribbean. It remained so until colonizers moving south from the Carolinas and Georgia ended Spanish missionary attempts.

One earlier expedition to Florida, however, turned out to have great significance for Spanish exploration. In 1528, an expedition of 600 men under Pánfilo de Narváez, governor of Cuba, sailed north to explore and colonize Florida. Narváez landed most of the party on the coast of Florida near Apalachicola to explore while his ships sailed on to investigate the rest of the coast. Unfortunately the ships lost track of the group on land. After a cursory search they presumed the men dead, abandoned them, and sailed back to Cuba.

The marooned expedition was involved in a disastrous battle with Indians, but some of the explorers escaped. They tried to sail home in makeshift boats they had built, but a storm washed them ashore near Galveston, Texas, where they were captured by the local natives. Most of the men eventually either died of thirst and starvation, drowned when primitive boats they made sank, or were killed in Indian attacks. The final group of four survivors consisted of Álvar Núñez Cabeza de Vaca, second in command to Narváez, along with Andrés de Dorantes and Alonso de Castillo Maldonado, two Spaniards from the aristocracy, and a dark-skinned Moorish slave from Morocco who belonged to Dorantes. The slave's name has been variously rendered as Estéban, Estevan, Estebanico, or Estevánico, and in English, "Stephen" or "Black Stephen," because of his skin color.[45]

Over the next eight years the little group of four journeyed on foot through the Southwest, moving slowly westward from tribe to tribe, posing as powerful medicine men so that they would not be harmed. They traveled across Texas towards the Rio Grande valley and northern Mexico, going as far as southern Arizona before turning further south, hoping to somehow encounter other Spanish settlers. Near the Rio Grande they stayed for a while with a group of Indians who traded arrow points for macaw feathers and plumes acquired in Mexico. These Indians told them that to the north were people who lived in large houses and among whom gold and silver was commonplace.

In 1536, after eight years of wandering, Vaca and the other three managed to reach Cullacán on the Pacific Coast and there met Nuño de Guzmán in the town he had founded.

The four brought with them the stories of the people they had seen during their lengthy journey. They told of people who lived in large communal houses, and who raised maize, squash, and beans. Some of the Indians the group encountered were dressed in leather from shaggy humpbacked cows (buffalo). Of more interest to Guzmán was that Cabeza de Vaca said he had seen gold, iron, copper, and other metals, as well as emeralds, turquoise, and pearls.

The Indians Vaca had encountered in Texas had told the same stories of wealth as the conquered natives of northern Mexico, that even greater riches could be found in cities in a region to the north. The Indians conceded that these might be the Seven Cities of Antilia. They said that in these cities the doors of houses were studded with jewels, and the streets were lined with the shops of goldsmiths. All this talk of gold immediately revived the myth of the Seven Cities of Gold.

The conquistadors, always on the lookout for treasure, pricked up their ears.

The Search for the Seven Cities

After these reports were received of remote cities that were as rich in gold as the cities of the Incas, the Viceroy of New Spain, Antonio de Mendoza, received permission for a preliminary exploratory expedition to search the lands to the north and hopefully finally find the Seven Cities of Cibola, as they were now called, after a native name for buffalo.

Many of the Native American buildings found in New Mexico and Arizona were thought at one time to have been built by the Aztecs. That is why this five-story building high in the cliffs of central Arizona was named Montezuma Castle. This lofty cliff dwelling was actually built by the Sinagua culture.

The Spanish hoped to duplicate their capture of vast stores of riches from Mexico and Peru in these northern lands.

In 1539 Mendoza sent a group north under the command of Franciscan friar Marcos de Niza. Niza was called Marcos of Nice, as that was where he had been born. Marcos had some experience in exploration as he been the chief chaplain under Pizarro during the conquest of Peru from 1531 to 1533. The Moorish slave Estéban was added to the expedition as a guide, both because he had been on the original Cabeza de Vaca expedition and he could communicate with the Indians in their own language.[46] Accompanying them were two other Franciscans and some friendly Indians. Marcos carried gold, silver, pearls, and precious gemstones as samples to show to any Indians they met to see if they recognized them.

The small expedition proceeded up the west coast of Mexico on the coastal plain between the Gulf of California and the mountains, then north through southern Arizona to just east of the Arizona–New Mexico border. Estéban and several companions, acting as scouts, forged ahead of the main party and found themselves at the Zuni village of Háwikuh, which was located fifteen miles south of the present Zuni Pueblo.[47] For his grand entry into the village Estéban decorated himself with animal pelts and large pieces of turquoise, and added bells and parrot feathers to his wrists and ankles. He apparently tried to make himself appear like a god to impress the Indians. From the Zuni point of view, warriors at the pueblo saw this giant black apparition approaching their village. He carried large crosses that they considered to be prayer sticks and also carried a gourd rattle that they recognized as belonging to another, hostile, tribe. They didn't know what to make of this dark-skinned phantom and his horse. They weren't even sure if he was part of the horse or not. They thought that perhaps he was a sorcerer.

A Zuni spokesman ordered him to go away and told him not to enter the village. But Estéban persisted. His manner turned sinister. He demanded food, gifts, and shelter, and threatened the Indians by saying he was leading white men even more powerful than he was. He demanded turquoise and women, then threatened the Zunis with a terrible fate if they did not comply. In response to this black devil they thought was a witch and a spy, they shot him full of arrows, and cut his body into pieces.[48]

Fray Marcos, who was lagging behind, encountered Estéban's companions fleeing back. They told him that Estéban had been killed and they were only just able to escape with their lives. Marcos proceeded anyway, but with caution, and on June 5 reported seeing a huge beautiful city in the distance.

Marcos decided not to enter the city, but turned back towards Mexico. By the time he reached Mexico City his stories had become exaggerated. Showing great optimism, he described what he saw by saying "the settlement is larger than the City of Mexico.... It appears to me that this land is the best and largest of all those that have been discovered."[49] His listeners heard his stories and added their own imagined details until eager audiences thought that Marcos had seen walled cities where the inhabitants wore huge belts of pure gold.

There were several possible explanations for what Marcos thought he saw. One possibility is that he saw the pueblo of Háwikuh glowing in the golden color of the rays of the setting sun and was convinced that he had found the fabled Seven Cities of Gold. Another possibility might be related to the way that the Zuni plastered their houses with mud and straw when they built them. If the sun was low in the sky they may have glistened with a golden hue and, viewed from a distance, Marcos may have thought this was a reflection from golden walls. Whatever the cause, the stories became embellished and grew more magnificent with each telling. As a result, Spanish explorers now entered into competition to lead expeditions north to relieve the Indians of their riches.

Coronado Marches North

Encouraged by Marcos' reports, Viceroy Mendoza followed up with a full-blown expedition that consisted of 230 horsemen in armor, 62 armed men on foot, and 800 friendly Tlaxcalan Indians from Mexico. The responsibility for organizing the expedition fell to twenty-eight-year-old Francisco Vásquez de Coronado, who had arrived in Mexico in 1535 and was currently the governor of the province of New Galica.[50] Marcos and five other friars accompanied the expedition to meet any religious needs. It was a colorful procession. The mounted men wore metal armor. Their horses had colored blankets, leather armor, and trappings mounted with silver. The foot soldiers were armed with swords and crossbows.

The expedition set off with high hopes on February 23, 1540, from Compostela, the capital of the province of New Galica.[51] The column was at least two miles long. The armed men took along 559 horses and 1,500 head of sheep, cattle, and pigs to be used as food.[52]

The expedition traveled north into unknown and strange lands, then turned east towards western New Mexico and the Zuni pueblo of Háwikuh, which was the largest of the villages that formed the Zuni nation. When Coronado arrived where Marcos guided him, he did not find the rich cities they sought, but only a few poor Zuni pueblos built out of adobe. These Indians were not goldsmiths, but poor farmers who worked hard to raise corn and squash.

The collection of Zuni pueblos were originally thought to be the mythical Seven Cities, but Marcos had been wrong even in that. Archeological evidence has shown that there were actually only six pueblos: Kiakima, Matsaki, Halona, Kwakina, Kechipauan, and Háwikuh.[53]

The Zuni were apparently warned of Coronado's arrival ahead of time, because when the expedition reached Háwikuh they found only men. The women and children had been sent to the summit of nearby Corn Mountain, away from potential danger.[54]

The remaining Zuni men resisted Coronado's entry into Háwikuh by drawing a line of sacred cornmeal on the ground and telling them not to cross it. Even if the Spanish could have understood the language, they would not have understood the symbolism and would have probably ignored it anyway. When the Spanish crossed the cornmeal line the Zuni responded with thrown rocks and arrows. Coronado later reported that the Zuni fought using hammer-like clubs, bows and arrows, and protected themselves with shields made from coiled basketry coated with pitch for strength. In spite of this, their primitive weapons were soon overcome. The soldiers replied with musket fire and swords and won the battle. The defeated Zuni offered Coronado turquoise, which they considered valuable for jewelry and for its magical properties, but the Spanish were not interested. They still wanted gold.

After this fiasco, Coronado sent Marcos back to Mexico with a letter discrediting him and stating that he had lied about almost everything.[55] Ever hopeful, though, Coronado considered what else he might find next in this strange country. There were no reliable maps of the area and the few maps that had been drawn from memory often contained false or imaginary details. Among the many misconceptions about the country beyond New Spain, one was that it was possible to travel north and eventually reach China.[56] Likewise, California was thought to be an island and was shown as such on maps.

Still hoping to find enough riches to make the expedition worthwhile, Coronado sent Pedro de Tovar with seventeen horsemen from the Zuni pueblos to explore further west. Tovar found only several Hopi villages in northeast Arizona that appeared even cruder than the Zuni ones. The first Hopi pueblo he came to was Awatovi, which stood on Antelope Mesa south of Keams Canyon in Arizona. Here Tovar met with resistance. He attacked after the Indians refused to pledge allegiance to God and Spain. After he easily overcame them the Spanish did not have trouble at the others.

Another group of men under García López de Cárdenas traveled even further west and became the first Europeans to see the Grand Canyon from a vantage point on the rim

The first Europeans to see the Grand Canyon were Spanish explorers led by García López de Cárdenas, who had a view from the rim near today's Moran Point. They did not realize how deep the canyon was and how wide the river really was. They vastly underestimated the distance and steepness of the terrain down to the bottom of the canyon and thought that the Colorado River, in the center, was only six feet or so across.

near today's Moran Point. Cárdenas and his men tried for several days to find a way down to the Colorado River. From the rim of the canyon they had erroneously estimated the river far below to only be six feet or so across and did not realize how deep the canyon was and how wide the river really was.

Coronado sent another scouting party under Pedro de Alvarado to explore the region along the Rio Grande from Albuquerque north to Taos, then south almost to the border of Mexico. At Pecos Pueblo, north of Santa Fe, Alvarado asked his Indian guide to show him the strange humped cattle (buffalo) that Cabeza de Vaca had reported seeing on the plains to the east. The guide offered two recent Indian captives from the Plains to show him. Alvarado thought that one of them looked like a Turk, so he used that name for the man. Turk was a Pawnee Indian who had been captured from the Plains. The other was named Ysopete, who came from the supposed land of Quivira to the northeast. Turk offered to lead the Spanish to Quivira, which he said contained so much wealth that the Spanish would have to use many wagons to haul it all away. Turk led his captors to believe that Quivira was in a land of wonders. He talked of a river six miles wide, fish bigger than horses, and ships covered with gold.

Meanwhile, Coronado with his 300 remaining soldiers and 800 Indian allies spent the winter of 1540–1541 camped several miles to the west of the pueblo of Kuaua ("Evergreen" in Tiwa) at Bernalillo, north of present-day Albuquerque.[57] When Alvarado's group joined Coronado's main army in winter camp, Turk told Coronado that in Quivira, far to the northeast, he would find all the gold and silver he wanted. Turk said he would take Coronado there in exchange for his freedom.

As a result, Coronado left his winter quarters on April 23, 1541, with the Turk, and took his men across northern Texas, headed towards central Kansas.[58] Indians they met along the way directed them to different places, but always further on east. One group of nomadic Plains Indians told them that the Seven Cities were to the north, others said to the southeast. Some said multistory cities, others said grass lodges. On June 29, 1541, Coronado reached the Arkansas River in central Kansas, somewhere near Lyons. Here he found the Indian village of Quivira, and found only Wichita Indians. The huts in their villages were made of straw, not gold.[59]

Finding nothing of value, Coronado finally became suspicious and questioned the Turk closely. The man admitted he had lied and confessed that the people of Pecos Pueblo (then called Cicuyé) had persuaded him to mislead the Spanish and take them far out onto the plains where they thought that Coronado's expedition would run out of food. When the horses were worn out and starving, and the expedition was forced to be on foot, the Indians planned to kill them easily. When several of the Spanish soldiers found out that they had been misled about the riches, they were so furious that they garroted the Turk by putting a rope around his neck and tightening it until he strangled to death.[60] After a month in Kansas, Coronado led his men back towards New Mexico in the spring of 1542. He might have explored further, but he fell from his mount while horse racing and was trampled by another, in the process sustaining serious head injuries.

Viceroy Mendoza was unhappy with Coronado for not finding the anticipated riches. So were the men who went with him, as they had expected a share of the loot. Coronado was removed as governor of his province and called back to Mexico City for an investigation, during which he was subjected to severe criticism for not finding the Seven Cities, as well as for alleged cruelty against the Indians. He was exonerated of the charges, but never fully recovered from his earlier horseback injuries. Coronado died in Mexico City on September 22, 1554.[61]

Coronado's expedition was a failure as far as finding gold. The Hopi pueblos had no more gold than did the Zuni. His explorations, however, gathered valuable information about the Southwest. Another legacy was that he called the land *San Felipe del Nuevo México* after King Philip of Spain. This became shortened to *Nuevo México*, or New Mexico.[62]

Chapter Two

Anasazi Descendants

After Coronado's fruitless search for the Cities of Gold, the Spanish temporarily gave up their search in the Southwest for the elusive wealth they had anticipated. For the next forty or so years, there was no real contact between New Spain and the Southwest, and the advance of the Spanish from Mexico essentially stopped at the country's northern border.

When the Spanish started expanding northwards from Mexico again in the 1580s, exploring and colonizing, they ran into the same groups of native people living in small villages of connected apartment buildings that the original conquistadors had encountered. The explorers called these communities *pueblos*, which meant "town" or "village" in Spanish. The clash between the meeting of these two cultures, the Spanish and the Pueblo Indians, was the basis for the next several centuries of conflict. To understand the reasons for this discord it is necessary to understand who these native people were and where they came from.

Pueblo Indians had lived in the Southwest for more than eleven thousand years. At the time of the Spanish arrival they lived in a series of villages, or *pueblos*, in the northern Rio Grande valley in central and western New Mexico, and in northeast Arizona. Some pueblos, such as Zuni and Acoma, probably founded in the late 1200s, were already more than 300 years old. Various groups had distinct native languages and dialects, and different customs. Though the tribes and their pueblos were independent autonomous villages, they were united by a shared cultural background and system of values. Their common religious beliefs had arisen from their agricultural lifestyle, which required fertility of the ground and rain to successfully raise crops. A prevalent concept was the Earth as Mother and the Sky as Father.

The ancestors of the Pueblo Indians who lived in northern New Mexico were given the name *Anasazi*, which was derived from an old Navajo Indian word meaning "Ancient Ones."[1] Other interpretations of the name are the Hopi name of *Hisatsinom*, or "People of Long Ago," or the Zuni *Enote:que*, meaning "Our Ancestors." Their culture influenced prehistoric Indian civilization in the Southwest.

The Anasazi lived on the Colorado Plateau in the Four Corners area, where southwest Colorado, southeast Utah, northeast Arizona, and northwest New Mexico meet at a single point.[2] The region was bounded by the Rocky Mountains on the north and the east, the Great Basin on the west, and the Sonoran Desert on the south. The Great Basin, which was centered in Nevada and included parts of California, Utah, and Oregon, was an area characterized by high desert. Most of the vegetation of the Colorado Plateau consisted of piñon-juniper woodlands, ponderosa pines, sagebrush, cedar trees, and various species of cactus. The terrain varied between high, arid mesas and deep canyons. The Anasazi and their descendents inhabited this area, mostly in the drainages of the San Juan and Little Colorado Rivers, from about 700 B.C.E. until the arrival of the Spanish.[3]

The Anasazi were, in turn, descended from older Indian groupings and may have been a combination of Shoshonean from the Great Basin, Tanoans from the Western Plains, and Keres from the mountains.[4] None of these Indian groups was indigenous to North America. The ancestors of all the natives of the Western Hemisphere before the arrival of Columbus migrated across the Bering Land Bridge from Siberia between about 25,000 and 11,000 B.C.E. This bridge was created when water from the oceans was trapped in glaciers of the Ice Age. This action lowered the level of the sea in the area of the Bering Strait, resulting in the emergence of a strip of dry land between Siberia and Alaska.

The migration of these people was not a single event, but was a gradual process of multiple crossings of the land bridge over many years. One reason for the crossings may have been that these native people hunted game animals and followed them across the dry land to the North American continent.

The migrants moved eastwards across Canada and down into North America, then slowly moved further south into Central and South America. Later, as the icy climate moderated and warmed, the glaciers receded and melted, the level of the oceans rose again, the land bridge submerged, and these ancestral native people were trapped in the New World.

The Evolving Anasazi

After many of the sources of large game animals in North America disappeared around 8000 B.C.E., the Indians evolved into a hunter-gatherer type of existence, catching small animals and collecting wild plants for their seeds, berries, and nuts.

Agriculture from prehistoric Mesoamerica gradually diffused northwards from central Mexico.[5] The diffusion was slow and took hundreds of years to work its way up to the Southwest. Around 2000 B.C.E. these Indians started to grow corn that had been domesticated by their cousins in Mexico, along with other plants, such as squash, beans, gourds, and melons.[6] Some of the earliest examples of corn from Mesoamerica have been found in dry caves in the Tehuacan Valley of central Mexico.[7] Indian corn was very small compared to today's familiar version, but it was extremely hardy. The plant matured quickly and was not harmed by the temperature extremes of the arid climate found in the Southwest.

Two earlier Indian cultures may have helped the spread of crops from Mexico to the north. One of these was the Mogollon people, who started a sedentary form of living in pithouses around the central Arizona–New Mexico border, then gradually spread north into the Four Corners area, probably assimilating into the Hopi and the Zuni. They may have influenced the explosion of Anasazi culture around 900 C.E.

A similar role may have performed by the Hohokam people of central and southern Arizona, who flourished between about 650 and 1450 C.E. before being assimilated into the Tohono O'odham ("The Desert People") culture of southern Arizona. These people were formerly known as the Papago, named "bean eaters" by the Spanish. After the number of large wild animals declined, beans became an important source of food, though the natives continued to hunt deer, rabbits, squirrels, and turkeys. Turkeys were first domesticated for their feathers, then were used as a food source. Another important food source

Indian corn was small and hardy, not like the large, fat, juicy ears of corn grown today. This typical cob found in an Anasazi granary is less than three inches long. On the positive side, this small type of corn matured quickly and was very hardy, making it ideal for the alternately hot and cold, dry climate of the Four Corners area. These tiny corn cobs, hundreds of years old, have been dried out and preserved by the extremely low humidity of the remote canyons of the Southwest.

for these people was mice, which were the commonest of the small mammals on the Colorado Plateau.

About 500 C.E. the Anasazi became sedentary instead of nomadic and relied more on agricultural crops as a food source than hunting. The climate of the Four Corners area was semiarid with scant rainfall and little other reliable moisture. As a result, most settlements and villages tended to be clustered around rivers, streams, natural springs, and other reliable supplies of water. But even then water had to be carried by hand to the fields from these water sources.

In a climate that received only six to twelve inches of rain a year or less, Anasazi crops required dryland farming techniques. Rainwater was collected, channeled, and used as much as possible. When the infrequent rains came, rainwater percolated through the porous sandstone that underlay the area and emerged as springs where it met a layer of impervious shale. Typically this occurred at the head of a canyon. To retain as much of the rain as possible, the Anasazi built low stone walls and check-dams on the cliff tops above the springs to hold the rainwater from running off. Here it would pool and soak into the rock, and percolate down to feed the underground springs. The Anasazi also diverted rainwater

Corn was ground into flour and added to stews or baked into large, flat wafers and eaten like bread. Kernels of corn were ground by hand by Anasazi women between two rocks, a *mano* and a *metate*. The *mano* (the smaller rock on the top) was rubbed back and forth over the *metate* with the corn between. Unfortunately this method left so much grit in the flour that teeth were rapidly worn away.

directly into their fields. In many instances, crops were grown on the tops of the mesas that were prevalent in the area, using small ditches and dams for irrigation.

Water was not the only problem to be overcome by farmers on the high, dry Colorado Plateau. If the crops were planted too early in the spring, they froze in the high altitude climate. If they were planted too late, they might not sprout and grow. In addition, crops required on-going attention and Anasazi farmers had to constantly drive off squirrels, rabbits, deer, birds, and other animals who ate them.

The Anasazi way of life as a farmer and hunter-gatherer was a full-time and precarious task. Food and water, and wood for building, heating, and cooking had to be carried for long distances, often up difficult cliff faces in the canyons of the Colorado Plateau. Judging by the small size of the rooms in the villages, they were probably used only for shelter from cold and bad weather, and most of the Indians' time was spent outside. Tasks such as grinding corn were done outside and so was cooking, which was performed over an open fire.

Anasazi men performed the heavy work required for farming, and hunted deer and other wild game using bows, arrows, and spears. Early hunting was performed with spears that were made more effective by an auxiliary spear-throwing device called an atlatl. This consisted of a wooden stick, about two feet long, that was held alongside the spear with the butt of the spear placed in a hole or cup at the end of the atlatl. The spear was thrown forward with an overhand motion while the thrower held onto the handgrip of the atlatl. This device effectively added the length of the atlatl to that of the arm, thus allowing a throw that was three or four times more powerful. At short ranges, its use for hunting was accurate and deadly. The atlatl was the only Indian weapon that the Spanish were afraid of, because with its use a spear could under the right conditions penetrate their armor. Ferguson and Rohn have commented that a spear thrown from the hand had a maximum range of about 75 feet, whereas with an atlatl the throw could be as much as 300 feet.[8] Somewhere between 500 and 700 C.E. bows and arrows became popular for hunting.[9]

Before the arrival of the Spanish, the Indians had no metal objects. Tools and weapons for farming and hunting were made from stone, wood, or bone. Rocks of various sizes were combined with wooden handles to make axes and hammers. Other small stones were used for arrow heads, spear points, and cutting implements. Bones were used for needles and scrapers.

While the men hunted, the women gathered wild berries, nuts, fruits, and other similar items for daily food and to store for winter.[10] Women ground corn by hand in shallow stone basins fashioned into the top of a piece of sandstone rock called a *metate*, using a corresponding hand grinding stone called a *mano* for pulverizing the kernels. The resulting corn meal was added to stews or cooked into large, flat wafers and eaten like bread.

The Cultural Centers

Three distinct Anasazi cultural centers evolved over a period of time: Mesa Verde in southwest Colorado, Chaco Canyon in northwest New Mexico, and Kayenta in northeast Arizona.

Mesa Verde

Early Spanish explorers were the ones who saw the looming flat-topped appearance of the high plateau of Mesa Verde and gave it the name that means "green table."

There are 3,900 known Anasazi sites and 600 cliff dwellings in today's Mesa Verde National Park.[11] Before 1250 C.E. the Anasazi typically lived in small independent villages. After about 1250 they gathered in much larger villages with multistoried buildings that contained up to 2,000 rooms. Mesa Verde is a good example of this progression of Anasazi cultures.

The early Anasazi were classified as the Basket Maker culture, because of the excellent woven baskets they made. These early inhabitants, who lived on Mesa Verde from about 700 B.C.E. to about 450 C.E., lived in pithouses that ranged in size from eight to twenty-five feet in diameter and were partially buried below ground level. The part of the house above the ground was constructed from logs that were tilted inwards to support a smaller flat roof, so that the completed structure took the shape of a truncated earthen pyramid. The outer logs were covered with small branches and the entire frame covered with mud to provide a waterproof dwelling. Entry was through a hole in the flat roof that also served as a vent to allow smoke from the fire pit inside to escape. Most pithouses were probably shared by several families.

The early inhabitants of Mesa Verde lived in scattered settlements. However, after a decade of severe drought between 1090 and 1100, many of them relocated to the northern end of the mesa where rainfall was more prevalent.

Around 1200 the Anasazi of Mesa Verde started to move from pithouses to complex pueblos, or communal houses, built under cliff overhangs.[12] This gave them their alternate name of Cliff Dwellers. Family groups started to congregate in larger and larger pueblos that contained fewer windows, and doors located at ground level instead of in the roof. These pueblos were often three or four stories high. The large pueblos were built from shaped stones using surprisingly sophisticated masonry techniques. The upper floors were supported by log beams, which were in turn covered by small poles, then covered by twigs and a layer of mud. The new style of building became very elaborate. Cliff Palace, which is the largest individual cliff dwelling in Mesa Verde, had 220 rooms and 23 kivas.[13]

Archeologists felt that this change from isolated pithouses to large, complex multi-family dwellings implied some form of defense. Building the pueblos on the top of cliffs and in inaccessible sheltered overhangs in cliff faces may have indicated a fear of attack,

Richard Wetherill and his cousin Charlie Mason, searching for lost cattle, chanced upon this huge stone structure built by the Anasazi, tucked safely under a cliff overhang on Mesa Verde. They gave the name Cliff Palace to this silent abandoned ruin that had more than 200 rooms.

whether any potential danger of invasion was real or imagined. Though these new locations in cliff alcoves provided better protection against attack, they were at the same time colder, damper, and harder to access. However, the location of these pueblo-style buildings on shelves under cliffs served to preserve them well and many of these impressive structures are visible today in Mesa Verde National Park.

After the Anasazi departed, the vacant stone buildings stood silent for hundreds of years until the large structure named Cliff Palace was accidentally discovered in December of 1888 by Richard Wetherill and his cousin Charles Mason from a ranching family in the Mancos Valley. What they saw was not really a palace, but was a huge Anasazi pueblo made up of more than 200 rooms. The two continued exploring and over the next few days found Spruce Tree House and Square Tower House in nearby canyons. Wetherill family records indicate that Alfred, Richard's brother, had seen the ruin of Cliff Palace about a year before, but had not taken the time to investigate, so he received no credit for the discovery.

Over next few years Wetherill and his four brothers explored the mesas of southwest Colorado, northern New Mexico, and northern Arizona, finding more and more abandoned Anasazi buildings. They collected many artifacts that went to museums in the United States and Europe. The Wetherills were subjected to harsh criticism at the time for breaking into Anasazi ruins and collecting artifacts, and for vandalism for putting their names on many of the ruins. Pot hunting, however, was not considered illegal at the time and was widely practiced, and collectors routinely left their names or initials on buildings to document that they had been there. Most of the pots and other artifacts collected by the Wetherills ended up in museums and private collections all over the world.

Chaco Canyon

By 1000 C.E. the Anasazi had constructed elaborate settlements in the San Juan River basin of northern New Mexico and at Chaco Canyon. The settlement at Chaco Canyon consisted of twelve major pueblos and 400 groups of houses spread out in the valley of Chaco Wash and on the surrounding mesa tops. By 1100 the Chaco Canyon complex was home to an estimated 7,000 people.[14] By this time construction techniques had advanced from mud pithouses to stone masonry and the Anasazi who settled in Chaco Canyon created elaborate stone pueblos. These pueblo houses were rarely a single structure, but were found in clusters of dwellings. In the first stages of building, large rocks were laid loosely in place and smaller rocks were used as a type of mortar to fill the gaps. Later techniques placed the larger rocks in more precise patterns and used a lesser amount of mortar.

The walled structure of Pueblo Bonito ("Beautiful Village"), spread out over more than three acres of ground and containing 600 rooms, was the largest community in the Southwest. Four and five stories high in places, it was built in a D-shape surrounding a central plaza. Scientists have estimated that its permanent population was perhaps only 50 to 100 people, but that it could house up to 1,000 people.[15] Pueblo Bonito was a significant public building. It is thought to have been used as housing by Anasazi from other communities coming together at Chaco Canyon for trading and ceremonial activities. The site was a major center for storage and astronomical studies, and was used primarily as a hospitality and communications center. Among other items found during modern excavations were a large number of jars containing chocolate from Mexico.

Pueblo Bonito was first described by Lt. James Simpson of the U.S. Army in 1849. The first excavations were performed by Richard Wetherill, who moved there from Mesa Verde in 1896. After heated criticism about his collection practices, Wetherill turned to ranching and opened a trading post. He met his end at Chaco Canyon when he was shot and killed by Navajo worker Chis-Chilling Begay on June 22, 1910, over some unfounded accusations surrounding Wetherill's practices at his trading post. He was buried beside the canyon cliffs.

The inhabitants of Chaco Canyon had direct connections with Mesoamerica. Traders came north from Mexico to barter copper bells (the only metal items known to the Anasazi), conch-shell trumpets, wooden flutes, and other items from along the Mexican coast for turquoise, slaves, peyote, and salt with the Anasazi of New Mexico and Arizona, and the Hohokam in Arizona.[16] Other important trade items were macaws and macaw feathers, and shells from the Pacific Coast and the Gulf of California.[17] Shell jewelry appears to also have been traded with the Hohokam. Seashells were strung onto cords to make necklaces. The Anasazi were expert jewelers. They made turquoise necklaces with beads and fashioned pendants of birds and animals out of stone and shell. Other jewelry included frog-shaped pendants, which have been found at various Anasazi sites. Frogs were considered important for the Pueblo people as they were messengers of water and rain.

The skeletons of three scarlet macaws found at Pueblo del Arroyo in Chaco Canyon was one indication of the southern trade connection, as these large parrots were not native to the Southwest. The bright red, yellow, and blue feathers of the scarlet macaw (*Ara macao*) were used for religious ceremonies, in ritual offerings, and as a part of Anasazi religious clothing and regalia. Curiously, only the remains of adult birds have been found, which suggests that these birds were not bred by the Anasazi, but were captured in the jungles of eastern Mexico and traded as immature birds, then raised in captivity at Chaco.[18] In addition, none of the bird remains are older than three years, which may indicate that they did not survive well in the harsh winters of the New Mexico desert.

Turquoise, obsidian, and petrified wood were also traded. One important trade item at Chaco was turquoise mined from the Cerrillos Hills region of New Mexico, south of Santa Fe, at the time one of the most extensive turquoise mining sites on the North American continent. One mine was called Mount Chalchihuitl, which was an ancient Mexican name for turquoise. The Cerillos area was a major source of turquoise for the Anasazi, much of which was traded with the Aztecs and in Central America where there were no turquoise mines. The Indians considered turquoise valuable for jewelry and trade, but it was not considered by the Spanish to be of any real value.[19] The techniques of making pottery, or at least the concepts, also came north from Mexico, and the Anasazi were well-known for their elaborate pottery. Pots were constructed from ropes of clay that were built up in layers to form jars, pitchers, and mugs.

Kayenta

The third important Anasazi cultural center was in the Kayenta region of northern Arizona. The Anasazi farmed the canyons and mesas of the Kayenta region for hundreds of years prior to their disappearance in the 1300s, possibly as far back as 1000 B.C.E.[20] The Kayenta region, which consisted primarily of the Anasazi communities of Keet Seel, Betatakin and Canyon de Chelly, were the last to be abandoned.[21]

Betatakin and Keet Seel were late pueblo cliff dwellings built into cave-like overhangs in Tsegi Canyon. The canyon below was lush and well-watered, including waterfalls, with stands of oak, fir, and aspen trees. Summers were very hot and dry in this part of Arizona, but the combination of the canyon and overhang, and the water below, kept the temperatures reasonably pleasant. Additional structures were granaries, storerooms, and kivas. The construction of these pueblos, however, was not as sophisticated as those in Chaco Canyon. The walls were thinner and the mortar used was essentially mud. As at other Anasazi sites, these cliff dwellers farmed corn, beans, and squash, and raised turkeys.

Canyon de Chelly, the third large population center in the Kayenta region, was the home of another group of Anasazi farmers who grew corn, squash, and beans. The name Canyon de Chelly (pronounced "de shay") comes from the Navajo word *tseqi*, which means "rock canyon."[22] The four major population sites in the canyon were Antelope House, White House, Big Cave, and Mummy Cave. Anasazi farmed the canyon floor and surrounding mesa tops, then abandoned the area after severe droughts in the 1200s. Shortly after this, Hopi farmers moved in and used the canyon on a seasonal basis. They were followed in the 1700s by a group of Navajo escaping from Spanish reprisals for persistent attacks on the villages along the Rio Grande to the east. The Navajo originally migrated down from Canada to the Colorado Plateau around 1400, along with the Apache, and became semi-nomadic hunter-gatherers. After contact with the Spanish and the pueblo people, they eventually became sedentary farmers.

The Navajo in Canyon de Chelly were never conquered by the Spanish, though the two cultures did skirmish and were in competition for land. Though the Spanish believed that no Indians could threaten them, they never subdued the Navajo, Apache, or Comanche. The Navajo did, however, leave vivid records of observing the Spanish. Pictographs on the walls of Canyon del Muerto ("Canyon of the Dead") in Canyon de Chelly showed the arrival of Spanish horsemen with lances and uniforms marching in to punish rebel tribesmen.[23] Inside Canyon del Muerto, Massacre Cave was appropriately named after 115 Navajo were trapped and killed there in the winter of 1805 by a Spanish expedition led by Antonio Narbona. The Indians had taken shelter on a ledge in a cave above the canyon floor when shots fired by the soldiers from the rim above ricocheted around in the small space and killed them all.

The Great Migration

In the late 1200s the Anasazi started to leave the three major population centers of Mesa Verde, Chaco Canyon, and Kayenta in what has been called the Great Migration. By 1300 most of the large pueblos became silent and abandoned as their inhabitants left to assimilate into other cultures. The Great Migration was unusual in that all the pueblo Anasazi left within a relatively short period of time. During other historical migrations, some people usually remained and the transition was slow. This was not the case for the Anasazi.

Before the Great Migration, Anasazi occupied the Northern San Juan area, north of the San Juan River, that included Aztec Ruins, Chimney Rock, and Hovenweep around the Four Corners region. They also occupied an area from Pagosa Springs, Colorado, south into northwestern New Mexico to the Abajo Mountains and Comb Ridge in southeast Utah, that included Grand Gulch and Cedar Mesa. Another grouping was in the Chaco Basin of New Mexico, which included Chaco Canyon. They were also located in the Kayenta region of northeast Arizona, which included the pueblos at Betatakin, Keet Seel, and Canyon de Chelly. Finally, they lived in the Little Colorado–Zuni River valleys of northern Arizona, which included the pueblos at El Morro (Atsinna), Zuni, and Hopi.

Two additional smaller population centers were located at Taos and along the Chama River from Chama to Espanola, both in New Mexico. After the Great Migration, the inhabitants of these two regions moved down into the Rio Grande valley from Taos to Socorro, New Mexico, into the Zuni River valley of west-central New Mexico, and to the four Hopi Mesas near Keams Canyon, Arizona.

The causes of the Great Migration are still obscure. One reason for the rapid departure may have been the severe and prolonged drought that was experienced over the entire Colorado Plateau between 1276 and 1299. As a result, the Anasazi could not farm successfully and the game animals they hunted moved away to other areas in search of water. The drought probably produced a severe drop in the water table and may have caused the trees used for construction and firewood to die off.

Another contributing factor to the departure may have been that the Anasazi's method of agriculture made continued farming difficult or impossible. Irrigation of the same fields year after year may have leached many of the natural minerals out of the soil. This practice would have increased the alkali content of the ground and made it poor for growing corn, unlike today's farming methods that replenish the soil with essential nutrients.

Another possibility is that the Anasazi way of life came under pressure from periodic attacks by warlike wandering Shoshonean raiders.[24] There is some scientific evidence of scalping and cannibalism, but whether this was due to external warfare or starvation is not clear. Support for outside attack theories is found in the radical shift the Anasazi made from living in unprotected pithouses to living in spaces that were brought inside the outer walls of the fortress-like structures of pueblos and cliff-dwellings. There are not, however, significant traces of nomadic Indians in the area at that time, so evidence for this cause is unclear. It is clear, however, that over time the pueblos developed and were adapted more and more for defense, with walls that grew thicker and taller. More stone towers were built, possibly for defense or to serve as lookouts, or as a combination of both.

Though there is a strong probability that drought was a major factor in the Anasazi departure, a causal link has not been conclusively proven either. The Anasazi had survived previous droughts before (including a severe one that lasted from 1130 to 1180) and might have been able to survive the one of the 1280s and 1290s. However, when combined with outside attacks or internal violence, and other factors, such as soil erosion, crop failure, and tribal feuds, the drought might have been the final straw.

Precisely why the Anasazi left is still a subject of debate and speculation among experts, but where they went is not. When the Anasazi abandoned their pueblos and cliff-dwellings, they spread out and dispersed. The living descendents of most of the Anasazi are the modern-day Pueblo Indians of the Rio Grande valley from Taos Pueblo to Isleta Pueblo south of Albuquerque. Others went to the upper and middle regions of the Rio Grande and joined or formed the present-day Acoma, Laguna, Hopi, and Zuni pueblos. Yet others joined the Hohokam people of Arizona to create the Sinagua and Salado cultures. The

Anasazi of Hovenweep, on the Colorado-Utah border, left for the Upper Rio Grande valley and the San Juan valley.[25]

The Anasazi from Aztec, New Mexico, left the region around 1300 and either migrated to the southeast to join existing pueblo communities along the Rio Grande, traveled west to join the Hopi in Arizona, or went south to the Zuni area. Similar to the Anasazi cliff dwellings, Hopi villages were built on defensible mesas. Like other pueblo dwellers, the Hopi did their farming on the flat lands below the mesas where springs and runoff from rain would irrigate the crops. The Zuni appeared along the Zuni and Little Colorado Rivers from east of Zuni to Cameron, Arizona. Though Coronado never found the fabled Seven Cities of Gold, the name Cibola was nonetheless attached to the region.

One fact consistent with the theory of the assimilation of the Anasazi into other cultures was that the population along the Rio Grande suddenly increased around 1300, just at the time the Great Migration was taking place. Another confirmation is that the community of Oraibi on Hopi Third Mesa dates from the early 1300s and is the oldest continuously occupied town in the United States.[26]

The Rio Grande valley made sense for human development as it was the largest river and watersource in New Mexico. It had the best agricultural lands due to periodic flooding, along with large areas of wetland and wildlife attracted by the forage and water. The Spanish called it the Río Bravo, as well as El Río Grande del Norte, or the Big River to the North.

Building with Adobe

One of the materials used by the prehistoric Indians for building pueblos, and later by the Spanish, was adobe brick. The name "adobe" comes from an Arabic word that simply means "sun-dried brick." Adobe was a mixture of adobe clay, sand, charcoal and water, using grass, straw, or sheep's wool as a binder. This compound was formed into wet round balls and piled up in layers to build walls. More of the material was plastered over the walls to fill the gaps between the balls. This technique of using round balls was called the "ball" or "puddled adobe" technique. The Indians did not have mortar made with lime, but instead concocted a mixture of ashes, coals, and adobe that did just as good a job. The technique used to make the mortar was to light a fire of twigs and grass and, when it had burned down to the coals, to add in clay and water, and stir the mixture up.

After the Spanish arrived, they taught the Indians to form the raw adobe mixture into rectangular bricks. Adobe clay was mixed with water to form a thick paste, then put into crude wooden molds and allowed to dry in the sun. The molded bricks were ten by twelve or fourteen inches (or any convenient size), about four to six inches thick, and weighed forty to fifty pounds each. After the bricks were dried, they were laid in rows then sealed together with a mortar of the same adobe material. After the mortar dried, an exterior coat of a paste of the same adobe clay was applied to produce a smooth surface. The bricks were also called "Spanish 'dobe."

The Indians quickly realized that molding bricks was a better building technique than puddled adobe because the rectangular shape allowed the bricks to be stacked on top of one another more evenly than the round balls. They immediately adopted their use. Because the building material was essentially mud, the pueblos had to be re-plastered every few years to offset erosion by wind and weather.

Women were the primary builders and were the ones who maintained the adobe structures. They made the adobe bricks and built the walls, as the men felt that making bricks was women's work. After the Spanish arrived the women continued to be the builders. Mission churches, *conventos* (the friar's living quarters), and other buildings were primarily the work of women under the direction of the friars.

The roofs of adobe buildings were flat, constructed by laying large poles across the tops of the walls. Smaller poles and twigs were laid across these large poles, then the entire upper side was coated with adobe.

As pueblo construction became more sophisticated, the builders turned from adobe mud bricks to masonry. As techniques advanced, the building blocks became more even and precisely-fitted. The mortar between the bricks advanced from a simple mud to a mixture of ashes and adobe, but less was required as the blocks fitted together better with smaller gaps between them. Other techniques were developed over time, such as using larger stones intermingled with smaller ones and making the corners of buildings more sturdy with interlocking stones. Walls became thicker, with interleaved stones, which allowed the rooms to be stacked up to three or four stories high. Doorways became more sophisticated, with raised sills to keep out drafts of cold air along the ground.

Another type of building was the *jacal* structure, which was basically a wattle-and-daub construction. The walls were made of logs dug into the ground, placed upright in a trench next to each. The ground was tamped into place on either side of the logs and the poles were interwoven with branches. Then the wall was completely plastered inside and out with adobe, hiding the poles and branches, and making a solid wall. The roof was laid across the walls and covered with adobe or earth. The Indians also built *ramadas*, a shelter that consisted of four upright poles supporting a simple flat, branch-covered roof to provide shade.

The Anasazi Way of Life

The Anasazi were matrilineal and traced their ancestry through their mothers, so women had an important influence on their society. For example, the family home was owned by the wife and important decisions were made by her family. Boys were taught the skills they needed as an adult by her male relatives. When a man married, he moved into his wife's house and, if the marriage was not successful, the wife could simply evict him by placing his belongings outside the front door if she desired.

Anasazi life was generally one of organization and cooperation, both of which traits were essential to maintain life in the pueblos and the success of communal farming. However, living in small rooms in pueblos meant that these people lived in crowded and unsanitary conditions. A lack of health care led to a high incidence of disease and a high mortality rate among children. The life expectancy of an Anasazi man or woman was probably only somewhere in their early twenties and it was unusual for them to live into their forties.

Their diet of maize, which was high in carbohydrates and low on protein, resulted in malnutrition. This diet deficiency resulted in various intestinal disorders, many of which were fatal. Unfortunately, also, the use of sandstone rocks for grinding their corn resulted in a large amount of grit in the corn meal. These sand particles in turn rapidly wore the enamel off the Indians' teeth and resulted in severe dental problems, most of which resulted in a loss of teeth.

Other common afflictions included osteoporosis due to dietary deficiencies, respiratory infections due to constant smoke from fires in the rooms, and a common occurrence of parasites, such as lice and pinworms. For the men, degenerative arthritis resulted in bad backs from lifting rocks and other heavy objects. For the women, elbows and knees ached from constantly kneeling and grinding corn.

The plaza of the pueblo was the focal point of many of the daily activities. There were often pens for turkeys raised for food and feathers. Domesticated dogs, kept as both pets and beasts of burden, ran loose around the buildings (they might also be eaten if times were hard). Women ground corn and cooked tortillas. Men used looms for weaving and women made pottery. The constant erosion of the adobe brick made repair and re-plastering of the buildings an endless job.

The Kiva

The center of religious life for the Pueblo Indians was the kiva, which was a round, stone-walled, underground ceremonial and meeting chamber. Each pueblo was divided into several religious kiva societies and every male Pueblo Indian was a member of one of the societies. The kiva symbolized the World Below, from which the spirits that were thought to inhabit all living and inanimate things emerged.

The name kiva came from the Hopi Indians. When the Spanish first encountered the Pueblo Indians, previous experience in Spain caused them to liken the Indians and their ways to the Moors. Interestingly they even initially referred to Indian kivas as "mosques."[27]

Most kivas were built underground in the central plaza of a pueblo and were entered from above by a ladder placed through a hole in the roof. One disadvantage to the kiva was that its underground nature was a liability in case of an invasion of the pueblo. Men who were inside during an attack could only climb up the ladder and out of the hole in the roof one at a time, thus leaving them vulnerable to assault by anyone standing by the top of the ladder.

The kiva played a special part in the religious lives of Pueblo people as the performance of sacred ceremonies and rituals was necessary to ensure plentiful rain, abundant crops, and good hunting. Though the Pueblo religion was centered on the kiva, religious activities also took place outside in the courtyard of the pueblo, where dances and other ceremonies were held.

Though the kiva was used for sacred rituals, it also served as a type of clubhouse for male members of the community. It was a masculine refuge where women were forbidden by tradition. Each kiva was owned by a single group. As a pueblo village might have several such groups, several kivas were usually found in larger communities.

The structure of the kiva evolved from changes in construction techniques used by the early Anasazi and was derived from their original underground pithouses. By 700 C.E. the holes the Anasazi dug for their early pithouses had become deeper and by 800 their

The inside of a kiva at Pecos Pueblo. The entrance is from above via the ladder. In front of the ladder is the fireplace with a deflector built around it to prevent drafts from the air inlet (behind the ladder) from blowing out the fire. These kivas were used by the men of the community for religious and recreational purposes.

houses had migrated almost completely below ground level. These underground chambers eventually became the kiva. The internal supports for the chamber added four to six sturdy posts which were strong enough to support the roof. The roof itself evolved into large logs laid in a circular fashion to form a wooden platform that was then covered with dirt. Stone masonry was used to line the interior walls, and to construct a bench that was two or three feet high and a foot deep inside the outer wall. Some kivas had plastered and whitewashed walls on the inside with elaborate murals of religious motifs. When dwelling spaces were brought above ground to form the pueblos, the kivas were the remnants that stayed underground.

Most kivas contained a firepit with a shaft up the outside wall for ventilation and to bring fresh air to the fire. A low stone slab was placed in front of the air inlet to disperse the draft.

An important feature in a kiva was a *sipapu*, a small, stone-lined hole in the floor. The name came from the Hopi word *sipap*. This opening symbolized the original point of emergence of the Anasazi people from the underworld, and was a point of access to the spirits in the World Below. Its underground location in the kiva was a symbolic placement between the underworld where the people originated and the world above where they currently lived.

Pueblo Bonito, one of the major pueblo buildings in Chaco Canyon. Two large kivas in the foreground dominate the plaza with the ruins of apartment-type houses behind. This one huge D-shaped pueblo may have housed as many as a thousand Indians in 600 rooms. Thirty-seven kivas have been excavated at this one site.

Kivas were built in various sizes and had differing designs. For example, not every kiva had a *sipapu*. Not all kivas were round, some were square. The pueblo of Atsinna, which was built around 1275, is interesting archeologically as it contains both round and rectangular kivas. Atsinna is one of two fortified pueblos built by the Anasazi on top of El Morro, the massive sandstone mesa 200 feet high that formed a striking landmark in north-central New Mexico. Here the inhabitants carried on dry-land farming, as well as hunting small game, gathering seeds and berries, and trading. Atsinna consisted of about 1,000 rooms surrounding a square plaza. The period of peak occupation of Atsinna was between 1275 and 1300. The pueblo was essentially abandoned around 1350, though it continued to be occupied until around 1400.

Kivas were typically located in the plazas and lower rooms, but not all kivas were located underground. Most kivas were less than twenty-five feet across, though a few pueblo communities contained huge kivas, called Great Kivas, some of which were forty to sixty feet in diameter.

Kivas reached their largest size in Chaco Canyon with the Great Kivas at Pueblo Bonito and Chetro Ketl, which were six to eight feet deep and up to sixty feet across. The largest was Casa Rinconada, a circular underground chamber that was sixty three feet in diameter.

Great Kivas such as these were probably used for group ceremonies that included the entire community.

Today the Great Kiva at Aztec National Monument, fifty-five miles northwest of Chaco Canyon, is the only reconstructed Great Kiva in the southwest. Forty-one feet in diameter inside, it was fully restored in 1934 by archeologist Earl Morris. The rest of the visible ruins were also impressive, with 405 rooms and 28 additional kivas.

The Katsina Belief

A major part of the later cultural clash between the Pueblo Indians and the Spanish was rooted in the differing religious beliefs of the two societies.

To the traveler of the Southwest today, the name *kachina*, or *katsina*, evokes a vision of the brightly-painted, elaborately-costumed wooden dolls decorated with feathers that are sold in tourist shops.[28] These dolls, however, particularly those originating in Hopi villages, were rooted in and symbolized a complex series of religious beliefs.

Katsinas were supernatural beings associated with the Pueblo Indians' origin myth that taught and guided their ancestors. In a simplistic sense, katsinas were collective ancestral figures who periodically visited the Pueblo Indians and acted as messengers between the people and their gods. Katsinas were rainmakers, coming to the villages each year as clouds. They were an integral part of ceremonies to attract the rains of spring weather, and as such controlled the fertility of the fields and crops.

Katsinas lived in a given pueblo from December to June, and then left for the other months. Among the Hopi, the belief was that shortly after the summer solstice the katsinas returned to the underworld by means of a ladder at the top of the San Francisco Peaks, which lay just north of Flagstaff, Arizona. If the people's prayers and dances produced the desired result, the katsinas regularly emerged from the mountaintops as clouds and brought rain to the crops of the pueblos.

According to ancient beliefs, when the ancestral Pueblo Indians migrated out of the *sipapu* from below the earth's surface, katsinas accompanied them from the spirit world to guide them.[29] When the katsinas departed again for the World Below, they left behind their images in a series of masks, which were stored in secret niches inside kivas. The katsinas were given tangible visible form during katsina dances in which male participants dressed in costumes and wore the masks. The dances were performed to ensure the coming of needed rain, which provided food and prosperity.

By using the katsina masks and following the proper rituals, Pueblo Indians could evoke the power of these supernatural beings. When a dancer put on a katsina mask, he was thought to receive its spirit. During the ritual ceremonies the masked dancers impersonated the katsinas and asked through prayer for the blessing of abundant rains and good crops. By using these masks and the proper rituals the people could bring the rain and thus produce successful crops. As their feet pounded on the Mother-Earth the dancers felt that this would waken the katsinas underground who would come to the surface to bring them prosperity and happiness.[30] Some of the bigger kivas contained large structures inside on the floor that may have been used during these ceremonies. Called vaults, these were rectangular hollow structures with masonry walls six to eight feet long, four or five feet wide, and several feet deep. Covered with wooden planks, poles, and willow matting, they formed giant foot drums that could be heard up to a mile away when pounded by the feet of participants dancing on top of them.

The origin of the katsina belief is unclear, but it appears to have reached the Pueblo Indians a little after 1300. The religion may have started to come north somewhere between 1150 to 1200 from the Casas Grandes culture of northern Sonora in Mexico. Evidence of the katsinas has been found in the Southwest that dates back to 1325.[31] The rise of the katsina religion around this time and the shift in living quarters to large pueblos are somehow tied together, but experts are divided in their opinions as to why and how.

By the time of the Spanish conquest of the Southwest, the katsina religion was widespread. The Spanish conquistadors described religious dances with participants depicted as masked beings which were almost certainly part of katsina ceremonies. Petroglyphs found in Cow Canyon near the Lowry Ruins on the Colorado-Utah border show katsinas. Confirming the importance of the fertility aspects of the katsinas, many of rock-art panels in Anasazi country depict males with large organs and similar sexual themes.[32] Other Anasazi rock-art panels show animals resembling deer, elk, bison, and bighorn sheep. Experts have theorized that these ancient rock-art panels may have served as hunting shrines or may have been used by religious leaders during rituals to achieve a successful hunt.

The importance and organization of the masked katsinas varied from pueblo to pueblo. At the pueblos of Hopi and Zuni they were very important. At Taos and Picuris they were virtually nonexistent.[33] Katsinas even had different names at different pueblos. At Zuni they were called *kokko*.

From the point of view of the Pueblo Indians of the 1540s, when the Spanish first arrived, the natives thought they were unusual katsinas approaching from far away. These strange katsinas (the Spanish) were accompanied by fire and noise (gunfire), they could hurl stones through the air (cannonballs), and were associated with the cries of strange, unknown birds (trumpets). These gods appeared to be a part of ferocious monsters (they rode horses), but had feathers on top of their heads (plumes on their helmets). Like gods, they shone with the brilliance of the sun (the reflections of the sun off their polished armor). The Indians of the Zuni pueblo later remembered that they wore coats of iron, war bonnets of metal, and carried short canes that spat fire and made a thunderous noise (muskets).

The Indian beliefs and the desire of the Spanish missionaries to stamp out the katsina religion set the stage for eventual conflict when the Spanish returned with phase two of their conquest plans, which was primarily conversion to Catholicism and assimilation of the natives into Spanish culture.

The Plains Indians

Though the major clash of the Spanish in the Southwest was with the Indians of the pueblos, another group of tribes that interacted strongly with the Spanish were the nomadic Indians that inhabited the plains east of New Mexico. The Plains Indians had a major impact on Spanish colonization in New Mexico and Texas, as will be discussed later, because a major element of the Apache Indian culture and economy was raiding Spanish settlements.[34] The name Apache most likely came from a Zuni word *apachu* that meant "enemy." The Apache did some farming, but preferred hunting, gathering, and raiding others.

The Pueblo Indians had earlier described the *Querechos*, the nomadic hunters of the eastern plains, to Coronado. The Spanish named one tribe *Apaches de Nabajo*. *Nabajo* is thought to be derived from Tewa words that meant "open spaces in which to plant crops."[35] The earliest mention of the Apaches appears in sixteenth century accounts by Spanish explorers.

The presence of the Plains Indians resulted in severe conflicts during the years of Spanish attempts at colonization. The Plains Indians used weapons that were primitive, but effective. One popular weapon was the war club, which consisted of a head of stone fastened onto a stick with a strip of sinew (the tendon from a buffalo softened in water). Among their defensive weapons were round shields made of dried elk or buffalo hide, particularly from the tough hide around the buffalo's neck. Shields were made from several layers of hide, hardened with glue made from the hooves.

The situation of the Plains Indians was not static. The Comanche did not arrive in the southwest until the early 1700s, after the arrival of the Spanish. The name for the Comanche came from the Ute word *kohmahts* or "those who are always against us." The Comanche moved around the Great Plains in the early 1700s, pushed the Jicarilla Apache into the mountains, and put pressure on the Mescalero Apaches to move. The Mescaleros of southern New Mexico were a nomadic people who gathered seeds, fruits and nuts. The Mescalero Apache received the name of "Mescal People" from their habit of eating mescal, a name which was applied to the agave cactus. They roasted the large bud that grew at the center of the plant when it flowered and stored it for later use as food. It was said to taste like a sweet potato with a smoky flavor.

The Cheyenne, another nomadic tribe from the Plains, arrived from northern Minnesota. They were forced out by tribes who were similarly uprooted and were moving west after being ousted from further east. As a result, the Cheyenne drifted south across the Great Plains. The Northern Cheyenne clustered around the North Platte River in Wyoming and Nebraska. The Southern Cheyenne clustered around the Arkansas River in Colorado. Their main hunting grounds were on the plains east of the Rocky Mountains.

Anthropologists believe that the ancestors of the Apache crossed the Bering Land Bridge about 4000 B.C.E. and gradually migrated down to the Great Plains, essentially as hunter-gatherers They moved further south to infiltrate New Mexico, Texas, and Mexico around 1100 as various bands occupied different areas. The Spanish found it difficult to confront and defeat the Apache as they operated in small bands that lived in no fixed location. After a surprise raid on a Spanish settlement, the warriors would split up, making it difficult for pursuing soldiers to fight them, let alone capture them. They were not a single nation, but loosely-knit group that owed allegiance more to family and clan than to any Apache leader. They would fight other tribes just as willingly as they would the Pueblo Indians or the Spanish.

CHAPTER THREE

Pushing North from New Spain

After Coronado's futile expedition looking for gold, the Spanish retreated to Mexico and had little contact with New Mexico for the next forty years or so. When the Spanish returned to New Mexico in the 1580s they came as missionaries.[1] Their belief was that they were the ones chosen to convert all the heathens of the New World to Christianity. Though a self-opinionated conceit, this drive forced the Spanish to explore some of the most fearsome country in the Southwest. Their goal was to mold the native people into sedentary farmers, make them Catholic converts, and form them into productive members of the Spanish Empire. These transformed citizens were supposed to live, dress, and talk in Spanish fashion, and adopt the lifestyle of civilized Spanish subjects. As Viceroy Antonio de Mendoza had earlier commanded fray Marcos de Niza in 1538, "Give the natives to understand that there is a God in heaven and the Emperor on the earth to command and govern it, to whom all have to be subjected and to serve."[2]

Slavery was an ancient concept for civilizing barbarians who refused to accept Christianity and rule by a civilized government. Through slavery, these infidels could be made to accept the blessings of civilization, wear civilized clothes, accept civilized ways, and made to see the rewards and redemption of a Christian life. The missionaries assumed that by forcing the Indians to accept the Christian religion, to share community property, and work for the good of all, that they would create paradise on earth for their converts.

In 1580 the desire for slaves to work the land of the New World for profit and souls to be saved by the Church generated further expeditions that headed north from Mexico. Between 1581 and 1593, five expeditions ventured north from Chihuahua to "pacify" the Pueblo world, but they achieved little in the way of results.[3] It was not until 1598 that a serious attempt was made to colonize New Mexico and establish a permanent settlement.

The Spanish returned not to start a new culture in the Southwest, but to transplant their existing one from Mexico, including the remnants of that brought to the New World from Spain. Their goal was not to annihilate the existing American Indians like the later Anglo colonists of the second half of the nineteenth century, but to assimilate them into Spanish culture. The conquerors originally intended to pursue peaceful conversion of the Indians while maintaining their rights and assuming a role of guardianship. The process of assimilation and conversion of the Indians into productive Spanish citizens was optimistically supposed to take ten years. Though some of the methods of the zealous Franciscans were misguided and harsh, their goals were lofty.

In 1581 fray Agustín Rodríguez left the Franciscan mission near the rich silver mines of Santa Bárbara in north-central Mexico with nine soldiers, two supporting friars, and sixteen Indians servants. Two of the soldiers had some previous mining experience and during the journey identified several mineral areas with silver in them, to which the Spanish later returned and mined. The military commander of the group was Francisco Sánchez Chamuscado. The expedition journeyed north along the Rio Grande intending to convert the heathens they had heard were in the pueblos of northern New Mexico. On the way, the expedition passed through the Cerrillos Hills, south of Santa Fe. Though the Cerrillos Hills contained some of the oldest and most substantial deposits of turquoise in North America, the Spanish did not value turquoise so they did not pursue any prospecting or mining.

After their arrival in New Mexico, one of the friars, Juan de Santa Maria, was so excited about the potential missionary situation that he started off alone back to Mexico to report progress. Conversion apparently had not gone as well as he had thought, and he was stalked and killed by Indians on the way. Not knowing this, the other two friars urged the soldiers to return home while they stayed to pursue their mission of conversion.

In 1582, concerned that nobody had heard from the friars, merchant Antonio de Espejo agreed to finance an expedition to follow them, ostensibly to assist fray Rodríguez, but in reality conveniently hoping to find gold and silver. After a search for the friars, Espejo found out that Rodríguez and his companion had been murdered soon after the soldiers left.

When Espejo returned to Mexico, he brought with him new fanciful stories about the riches of the area (though he had found primarily only copper). The Crown was more interested in the souls that could be saved than his supposed treasure and ordered the Viceroy to send an expedition north to colonize the upper Rio Grande valley and take possession of these rich lands for the Spanish Crown. By this time Spanish officials were calling the area *La Provincia de Nuevo Mexico* ("The Province of New Mexico").

The Viceroy was slow to respond, but eventually appointed forty-five-year-old Juan de Oñate as governor and sent him north to colonize New Mexico. Oñate had been born in the silver mining area of Zacatecas in northern Mexico and had previously served as a soldier fighting against belligerent Indians in the area. Oñate was part of the Mexican aristocracy and had a considerable private fortune. His wife was the great granddaughter of Montezuma and the granddaughter of Cortés.[4]

The Spanish Crown didn't provide Oñate with any financial support. The responsibility and cost of colonizing New Mexico were to be his alone, though the Crown did finance five missionaries to accompany him. Showing an obvious lack of knowledge of the geography of New Mexico, part of Oñate's instructions required him to survey New Mexico's coastline and harbors.[5]

The first order of business for taking possession of new lands such as these by Spain was a routine that had been followed in earlier conquests. The expedition leader read to the natives a legal document (*requerimiento*) that was a combination of a request for submission and conversion to Christianity, and a formal announcement of the acquisition of the territory. This bogus legal nonsense to validate the takeover of the native population was obviously ridiculous because in most cases the local Indians did not speak the Spanish language and had no idea what their conquerors were babbling on about. But they usually agreed anyway to be loyal subjects of the King of Spain.[6]

Part of the Spanish conquest procedure was to enlist native allies to fight with them, as Spanish expeditions often consisted of only a few hundred trained fighting men who were nearly always outnumbered by the Indians. It was almost always essential, then, to gain allies among the local natives. In spite of the deficiency, Spanish field cannons and harquebuses provided more than ample firepower to defeat most Indian resistance.

The second procedure to validate a takeover was to found a town. This was equated with bringing civilization to the natives. More than that, the intended result was to allow the formation of a legislative body that could pass laws. And even more important to the founders, these laws could be constructed to give the expedition leader a legal claim to local lands. Some cities were "founded" several times without any buildings being built, but the pretense gave a veneer of respectability to claims for the land and the success of the expedition.[7]

Oñate's Original Colony

Oñate finally started north from Zacatecas in January of 1598, accompanied by 500 colonists and 129 soldiers, along with assorted wives, children, servants, and Indian slaves. Most of the fighting men who accompanied Oñate were friendly Tlaxcalan Indians, mestizos, and other Indians from Mexico, as service to the crown gave them a privileged status. Women and children were included because Oñate knew that married men and families would succeed in colonizing the new province far better than single men.

Eight Franciscan friars and two lay brothers accompanied the expedition to act as missionaries to convert the heathen Indians to Christianity.[8] They had a large job ahead of them. Spanish records show that in 1598 there were 134 pueblos. Population estimates ranged from 16,000 to 248,000 natives, though with such a wide range of estimates, the extremes of these figures must be viewed as suspect.

Oñate's caravan of settlers included eighty-three supply carts drawn by oxen, and two luxury coaches drawn by mules. The carts were two-wheeled wooden carts or *carretas*, locally called "Chihuahua carts," drawn by three yoke (pairs) of oxen. By the end of the journey many of the carts had been abandoned and only sixty-one remained.

Everything to found a colony had to be brought north with the expedition, including clothing, kitchen supplies, furniture, seeds, and medical supplies. Tools brought for homesteading included plows and blacksmithing tools, along with guns, gunpowder, and three small cannons. The expedition also carried tools and supplies for mining and smelting in case the colonists found silver. One unusual item was 80,000 glass beads to trade to the Indians.[9] The expedition was accompanied by 7,000 head of livestock, including horses, donkeys, pigs, pack mules, cattle, extra oxen, sheep, and goats. The column moved about as fast as the slowest animals could travel, or only two or three miles a day.

The massive caravan of settlers and soldiers crossed the Rio Grande near El Paso, Texas. Here Oñate claimed New Mexico for Spain on April 15, 1598, in an expansive manner, "without excepting anything and without limitation, with the meadows, glens … towns, cities, villas, castles … the leaf on the mountain to the rock in the river."

Satisfied with this all-inclusive claim, the group moved north along the Rio Grande to its junction with the Rio Chama in the upper Río Grande valley of New Mexico. The confluence of the two rivers was near present-day Española, about twenty-five miles north of Santa Fe. The Spanish referred to this northern area of Mexico as "the great unknown north," as opposed to the Anglo viewpoint that this was "the West."

The journey north through the open wasteland from Mexico City was not easy and the distance of 750 miles took almost seven months. The crossing of the long, two-day stretch of waterless landscape in southern New Mexico that later became known as the *Jornada del Muerto* ("Journey of the Dead Man") was particularly difficult. The caravan finally arrived exhausted, hungry, and thirsty on the northern side of the desert at a friendly pueblo that gave them food and drink. As a result, Oñate named the pueblo *Socorro*, which was Spanish for "assistance" or "help." This pueblo thus became the first community in New Mexico to be named by the Spanish. A mission built there later was named *Nuestra Señora del Socorro*, or Our Lady of Help.

After reaching the upper Río Grande valley, Oñate decided to settle at an old abandoned pueblo named Ohke (also spelled O'ke, Ohkay, and Okeh), near what is now the Ohkay Owingeh Pueblo. Spanish law prohibited settling on Indian land currently in use, so the colony was established on the site of the empty pueblo. Oñate renamed the former pueblo *San Juan de los Caballeros* ("St. John of the Warrior Knights" in honor of John the Baptist), but it became more commonly known simply as San Juan Pueblo. This became the first Spanish settlement in New Mexico and the core of the early Spanish colonization of northern New Mexico. Today this area includes parts of Rio Arriba, Taos, Sandoval, and Santa Fe counties.

Unsatisfied with the location, or perhaps needing more space, in 1600 Oñate moved his settlement across the river from Ohke, to the west bank, to the 400-room partially-abandoned pueblo of Yúngé. The settlers moved into the pueblo, rebuilt it, constructed a church they named San Juan Bautista (St. John the Baptist), and called the settlement San Gabriel (sometimes also called San Gabriel del Yungue). This was the first permanent settlement and the first capital of Spain's province of New Mexico.[10] To put the event in perspective, this was nine years before a colony was founded at Jamestown.

New Mexico's initial settlers consisted mostly of Spanish from the upper classes who were eager to make a profit in the new land. Spanish gentlemen did not work. They felt that this was below their dignity. They expected the local Indians to perform the common labor required to run ranches, dig mines, and farm fields. As a result, Oñate brought with him the traditional Spanish *encomienda* system that granted settlers the rights to land they settled. The *encomiendas* were inheritable and the land could be claimed by the settlers' children and any other descendants. These recipients were called *encomenderos*, and were later required by Spanish law to maintain a house in Santa Fe. This was because many of the settlers were soldiers and part of their obligation was to provide military support for the capital in case of attack. Thirty-five of the original settlers were awarded *encomiendas*.[11] By the early 1600s, about sixty men held them.[12]

Accompanying the *encomienda* was the *repartimiento*, which was the right to use forced labor from the Indians on the land and to collect tribute from them, usually in the form of corn, animal hides, or blankets. The New Mexico Indians were required to give a bushel-and-a-half of maize plus a cotton blanket or deer hide each year in tribute. Though this may not sound like a lot, for a poor Indian family trying to scrape a living together under hard circumstances this could be an excessive amount, particularly in times of drought or other hardship. The theory was that Spanish citizens, mostly those of high-rank, were allowed to collect this tribute in return for providing protection, aid, and education to the natives, along with military support for the government whenever needed.

Some settlers held their *encomiendas* for providing armed escorts to Franciscan missionaries as they traveled around the region. Both the *encomienda* and the *repartimiento* had been declared illegal by the Spanish Crown, but they were practiced in New Mexico anyway.

Accompanying the settlers were professional fighting men and soldiers of fortune, all of whom were generally young but poor, but who became the dominant class because they subdued the Indians. In return, they were awarded grants of land that quickly gave them prestige. The new Spanish settlers were dependent on Indian slaves for labor to run their households. In return, the Indians were supposed to be paid a daily wage and fed, and the term of their labor limited. Abuse of the system was, of course, rampant. Even one of the governors, Bernardo de Menizábel was later charged in 1661 with the illegal use of native labor and withholding wages.[13]

Another illegal activity that was tacitly pursued was raids carried out against the nomadic Indian tribes who roamed the eastern edge of the pueblo world to provide a pool of fresh slaves. The self-serving reasoning given was that these expeditions were undertaken to protect the Pueblo Indians from the Apache. Conversely, however, they made the situation worse. The capture of Apache slaves resulted in Indian retributions in the form of raiding, attacking, and burning pueblos and Spanish settlements. In the best guerrilla fashion, these points of attack were, of course, the ones furthest from military protection.

A few of the male colonists brought their families, but others turned for female company to local Indian women and the slaves captured by the Apache. Most of the initial population increase in New Mexico was due to Spanish men marrying Indian women. As a result, the local population became a mixed lot due to interbreeding. Interestingly, though Spanish men married Indian women, Indian men did not marry Spanish women. The lack of Spanish women was the reason for the first practice, the excess availability of single Spanish men was the reason for the second.[14]

Intermarriages were common in colonial New Mexico in the 1700s and 1800s, resulting in people of mixed genetic backgrounds. The Spanish used different names to distinguish their heritage. A *mestizo* was a person of mixed Spanish and Indian ancestry. A *mulato* (*mulatto*) had mixed African and European ancestry. A *coyote*, also sometimes called a *sambohijo*, was one of mixed Indian and black ancestry in which the Indian side was dominant. A *genízaro* was a generic name for an Indian slave (typically ransomed by the Spanish government and given citizenship) who lived in a Spanish household.

The original friendliness between the Spanish and the Indians deteriorated very quickly as the Spanish commandeered local food and other supplies by force. This created a difficult situation for the native population as the Pueblo Indians were barely able to feed and clothe their own families before giving up a portion of their crops. From the Spanish viewpoint it was thought that exploiting the native people was the only way to get the work done and that this was a fair system.

Violence at Acoma

One of the significant battles opposing Spanish conquest occurred at Acoma Pueblo in December of 1598. Acoma was nicknamed the "sky city," because it was perched on a relatively-small, high mesa with limited access, 365 feet above the surrounding countryside.

From one standpoint, Acoma was not a practical location for the inhabitants, as it was far from the agricultural fields on the valley floor below and distant from sources of water.

Acoma was built around 900, which made it the oldest continuously-inhabited existing community in the United States. The pueblo was first described by one of Coronado's captains, Hernando de Alvarado.

The trouble started when Oñate's nephew Juan de Zaldívar and thirty-one soldiers stopped at Acoma for provisions and the Indians were reluctant to supply them. Reportedly a soldier named Martín de Vivero (or Ribero) acted on his own and seized two turkeys, which were sacred to the Indians. Some historical sources said he also violated an Indian woman. Whatever the cause, the Pueblo Indians attacked and killed Zaldívar and ten of his soldiers.[15]

In retaliation, Governor Oñate decided to take his vengeance against Acoma and hoped by this to stop any further Pueblo resistance. On January 21, 1599, Oñate sent seventy-two armed soldiers under Vicente de Zaldívar, Juan de Zaldívar's younger brother, to attack Acoma and carry out an appropriate punishment. While the main body of soldiers made a frontal attack from one side as a diversion, Zaldívar and twelve men climbed up the cliff

Acoma Pueblo sits high on an isolated mesa, 365 feet above the surrounding valley floor. Vicente de Zaldivar carried out reprisals for an earlier attack on the Spanish by scaling the almost-vertical cliffs and battling the rebels. The row of buildings at the top are individual houses. The large building in the foreground is the mission of San Estevan del Rey, built around 1629, with the church graveyard adjoining to the right (Library of Congress).

on the other side of the mesa. After they reached the top, they attacked the main group of defenders from the rear and killed between 600 and 800 Indians. They also took seventy to eighty men captive, along with 500 women and children.[16]

After extensive research, some historians feel that what actually happened may have been somewhat different. The official account of the battle says that Zaldívar climbed up the back of the mesa and caught the Indians in an attack from both sides. However, after the Acoma battle, Spanish captain Luis Gasco de Velasco gave a different account. He said that the Acoma Indians surrendered and offered the Spanish food, but Vicente de Zaldívar ordered them to be killed and their bodies thrown off the top of the cliffs.[17] The adobe houses and kivas were set on fire and many of the women and children who hid in them were burned alive.[18]

As an example to the other pueblos, Zaldívar took 600 of the Acoma Indian prisoners, mostly women and children, back to Santa Fe to stand trial. At their hearing in February of 1599, the Acoma residents were found guilty of murder and of not surrendering the provisions that the Spanish had demanded. In punishment, Oñate ordered that each of the men who looked to be aged twenty-five or older was to have a foot cut off and to serve twenty years as a slave. Males who appeared to be between the ages of twelve and twenty-four, and females over twelve were also to serve twenty years as slaves.[19] The younger children, those under twelve, were separated from their relatives. The boys were turned over to Vicente de Zaldívar and the girls were sent to Mexico City to be raised as Christians.[20] Two Hopi captives were to have their right hands cut off and be sent back to their people as a warning.[21]

This would seem to be a series of excessively harsh punishments, but as historian John Kessell has pointed out, "Dismemberment [was] a barbaric penalty routinely imposed by 'civilized' Europeans."[22] To the Spanish these were but routine punishments. Though severe, cutting off the foot was not quite as extreme as it sounds. In the Spanish Caribbean the common practice was to cut off only the front part of the foot so that the individual was still able to walk and function effectively as a slave.

Whether or not these mutilations were actually performed is controversial and historians are divided on the outcome.[23] Velasco noted without further details that twenty-four men had a foot cut off.[24] However, there were no further references in Spanish records to one-footed Acoma slaves, as would be expected after such wholesale punishment, thus some doubt has been raised as to whether the story was true.[25] None of the first three history books about Acoma Pueblo by Anglo-Americans (published in 1917, 1926, and 1932) describe the resolution of Oñate's sentence after the massacre. David Roberts, on the other hand, has theorized that the punishment was carried out, but was unrecorded because the memory of these events was too painful.[26]

To add another viewpoint, historians have commented that Pueblo Indians sentenced to death by the governor were often saved at the last minute by Franciscan priests pleading for mercy for the condemned. What happened in these cases was that the friars knelt at the feet of the local government official who had imposed the sentence and begged for mercy. In response, he routinely commuted the sentence. The hope was that in this way the friars would be perceived by the Indians as their saviors and they would come to love them, yet at the same time fearing the power of the government and the military.[27]

When the Acoma Pueblo rebelled, Oñate certainly suppressed it violently, but it is possible that the trial was mostly theatrics. The result, however, was what Oñate wanted. The fate of the Acoma rebels is unknown, but after the attack on Acoma, the last of the Pueblo resistance to the Spanish crumbled.

After 1629, the Indians of Acoma were put to work under fray Juan Ramírez building the mission church of San Estevan del Rey, one of the largest of its type in America.[28] The inside was 100 feet deep and 35 feet high, with pine pillars supporting the roof. The church was one of the few churches not burned in the later Pueblo Revolt of 1680, but it has been remodeled over the centuries.

Oñate's Other Exploits

During his tenure as governor, Oñate persisted in his dreams of conquest. In June of 1601 he led an expedition of seventy men several hundred miles north to the land that had become called Quivera, in what is now south-central Kansas, in search of riches. He was accompanied by eight wooden carts pulled by mules and oxen that carried his supplies. He found only the Wichita Indians who lived there in grass huts. The Quivera Indians told Oñate, as they commonly did the Spanish, that there were more Indians and gold, but always somewhere else to the north. Oñate's expedition continued east to the Great Plains, but did not find the riches with which he hoped to support his infant colony. After this fruitless search for gold, he gave up and went back to San Gabriel.[29]

Oñate left New Mexico with another expedition to the Gulf of California (called the "South Sea" by the Spaniards) with thirty men on October 7, 1604. He hoped to find a suitable port on the Pacific Coast that could be used to supply New Mexico from New Spain more easily by sea than via the laborious wagon route from Mexico City. The group crossed Arizona and followed the Colorado River. Indians that he met along the way tried to tell one of the accompanying missionaries by gesture, pantomime, and lines drawn in the sand about strange beings that lived along the Lower Colorado River and the Sea of Cortez. As the missionary Escobar understood the story, one tribe had ears so large that they dragged on the ground. Members of another had only one leg and foot. Others slept in trees, while still others slept under water. Some survived on only the smell of food as they had no digestive system or natural opening to expel food waste. One tribe was supposedly so virile that they wound their male organs four times around their waists. When copulating they had to perform with the man and woman far apart. Understandably, the Spanish never saw any of these oddities.

The expedition finally arrived at the head of the Gulf of California. Here on a beach, in a scene reminiscent of Don Quixote, Oñate took possession of the land in the following manner described by fray Alonso de Benavides, another of the Franciscan friars who accompanied the expedition. "Fully dressed and armed, with a shield on his arm and sword in hand, he gallantly waded into the water up to his waist, slashing the water with his sword and declaring, 'I take possession of this sea and harbor in the name of the king of Spain, our lord.'"[30] Oñate eventually realized that his route extended too far from New Mexico to be practical as a suitable port and abandoned any further pursuit of the idea.

Oñate stopped at El Morro (Spanish for "The Cliff") on the return trip from his expedition to the Gulf of California. At the base of the vertical rock was a natural basin of water that was named by the Spanish *El Estanque del Peñol* ("The Pool of the Great Rock"). El Morro had been visited for at least 700 years by Indian hunter-gatherers and itinerants who used the pool of water at the base. It was recommended as a water source by Diego Perez de Lujan in 1583. Travelers always stopped at El Morro as this was a reliable source of drinking water for the trip between the nearby Zuni and Acoma Pueblos.

Oñate, or one of his men, carved into the soft rock in Spanish, "Here passed the Adelantado Don Juan de Oñate, from the discovery of the Sea of the South, on the 16th of April, 1605."[31] *Adelantado* was an honorary title often applied to the conqueror of a new land. The "Sea of the South" or the "South Sea" was the Spanish name for the Sea of Cortez, known also as the Gulf of California.

El Morro was also known as Inscription Rock, because of the many travelers who carved records like these in the soft sandstone. Long before Spanish conquistadors and modern travelers carved their names and comments into El Morro, the Anasazi scratched figures of animals and symbols into its surface. These carvings can still be seen in the soft rock at El Morro National Monument, just south of Grants, New Mexico.

The carving by Oñate in 1605 was the oldest Spanish one and occurred fifteen years before the Pilgrims landed at Plymouth Rock. Later ones included inscriptions by American military expeditions sent to survey and explore the West after the Louisiana Purchase and travelers passing through the area.

The colonization of New Mexico turned out to be a difficult task for Oñate, and his settlers faced a series of challenges. For one thing, the climate was more varied than what they were used to in Mexico and winters in the high altitudes of northern New Mexico were colder than they are even now. Summers were warm, but provided only a very short growing season and the settlers did not like the extremes of heat and cold. One colonist was quoted as saying that the climate was eight months of winter and four months of hell.

To sustain the colony, the settlers needed land that was suitable for irrigation and a reliable water supply. As it unfortunately turned out, much of the land around the settlement was dry and barren, and the rains were only seasonal or intermittent, making farming difficult. Contrarily, these same rains could also be devastating, with an ability to flood the land with torrential downpours. Many of the original colonists grew to hate the New Mexico climate and many became disillusioned. Spanish settlers in New Mexico were faced with periodic droughts, epidemics of European diseases, attacks by nomadic Apaches, continuing conflicts between civil and religious leaders, and growing unrest among the Pueblo Indians. Then, on top of all this were minor irritations, such as the lice in their clothing, numerous field mice eating their crops, and plagues of bedbugs in their homes during the hot summer months. But Oñate was so committed to his project that he felt anyone wanting to leave the colony was a traitor.

As well as uncertain food supplies, the settlers had to contend with hostile Indians. The land that the Spanish were trying to colonize was inhabited by nomadic bands of marauding Indians who did not welcome the Spanish invaders as they tried to subjugate them and convert them to Christianity. As a result, the Spanish faced constant harassment. As long as colonists and soldiers stayed together in large groups, they were relatively safe. Single travelers, stragglers, or those who were lost on the trail were often attacked and killed by Indians.

It should be noted, however, that the Indians were just reacting to how they had been

This unusual watering hole in a dry land, at the base of the cliff at El Morro, was named *El Estanque del Peñol* (The Pool of the Great Rock) by the Spanish. This was used as a reliable source of water by Indians and other travelers crossing the arid plains of west-central New Mexico for hundreds of years.

treated. The Spanish had a reputation for dealing harshly with them, particularly during uprisings, believing (correctly) that such reprisals would create at least temporary submission. For example, when hostilities came to a head and Acoma Pueblo revolted, Oñate suppressed it with extreme violence. As another example of harsh treatment, the Spaniards burned Indians at the stake in what they considered to be just retribution for attacks on colonists and their settlements.[32]

In spite of Oñate's efforts, the Spanish Crown decided to replace him and he resigned as governor in 1607. He had spent most of his family money on his colonization effort, but had found no riches or anything else of significance in return. Oñate was recalled to Mexico City in 1608 to face charges of collecting excessive tribute, plundering the pueblos, and indiscriminately killing Indians. Other alleged excesses were the murder of deserters, robberies committed by his soldiers, living with native women, and the brutal treatment of the Indians at Acoma. He was charged with mismanaging the colony and abusing the native Indians. Though he was eventually exonerated, he was sentenced to permanent banishment from New Mexico.[33] He moved to Spain in 1621, became the king's chief mine inspector, and died in a mine shaft in 1626.[34]

After Oñate resigned, around 1607 and 1608, some of the dissatisfied colonists tried

El Morro was nicknamed Inscription Rock because of the many names carved by travelers into the soft sandstone walls near the pool. This writing notes the passage of a party of Spanish who traveled by in 1709.

to improve their situation by moving from San Gabriel. Led by interim governor Juan Martínez de Montoya, they started a second settlement twenty-one miles to the south at a site on the north bank of the Santa Fe River that they felt had better fields, good grazing land, and a conveniently-available supply of wood.[35] It was also a strategic site for trading with the Plains and Pueblo Indians. Archeological evidence has suggested that a new settlement was built at the site of an abandoned earlier pueblo named *Kuapoge* ("The Place of Shell Beads Near the Water").[36] The new location was accessible from the north by the Española Valley and from the south along the Santa Fe River (previously called Cichito Creek).

Oñate's permanent replacement was Pedro de Peralta, who arrived with eight Franciscans friars and a supply train of twenty wagons in 1610 (ten years before the Pilgrims arrived in New England). Acting under orders from the Crown to found a new capital, Peralta completed the move of the remaining colonists. The new settlement was named *La Villa de Santa Fe* ("The Royal City of the Holy Faith") or more simply Santa Fe. The only chartered municipality in New Mexico at the time, Santa Fe became the second oldest town in the continental United States after St. Augustine, Florida, which was settled in 1565. St. Augustine is the oldest continuously-occupied European community in the United States. As a fine distinction, Santa Fe is, however, the oldest continuously-occupied capital in the United States.[37]

The small settlement of Santa Fe was destined to become the chief trading center of Spain's northern province. In 1823 the local government adopted St. Francis as their patron saint and changed the name of the town to the wordier formal mouthful of *La Villa de Santa Fe de San Francisco de Assisi*, or "The Royal City of the Holy Faith of St. Francis of Assisi."[38]

The Franciscan Missionaries

Jesuits (The Society of Jesus) briefly worked on conversion of the natives in Florida from 1566 to 1572. In 1697 the Jesuit priests built a mission at Loreto, about two-thirds of the way down the Baja Peninsula on the Gulf of California side. They constructed a string of seventeen missions from the tip of the peninsula at Cabo San Lucas, up the coast towards California. The land was arid and the Jesuits found it a difficult task to maintain enough food to sustain the missions. Their work was concentrated mostly in Baja California, but they were active also in Mexico and founded missions in southern Arizona among the Pima Indians between 1700 and 1767.[39] In 1767 King Charles III of Spain ordered the Jesuits (also known as "Black Robes," because of the color of their robes) to be expelled from Spain and all Spanish colonies in North America. The French and Portuguese had already done the same. This was probably an excuse to remove for political reasons what Charles III considered to be a group that had become too powerful.[40] They were arrested, dispossessed, taken to Vera Cruz, and transported to prison in Spain.[41] After they left, the Franciscans took their place.

The Franciscans, a very active and influential order within the Catholic Church, were well-suited for this task as they had played a central role in conversion and mission work in the northern reaches of New Spain. But even before this, Cortés had brought twelve friars of the Order of St. Francis to the New World in 1524 to convert heathens to Christianity. The Franciscans were among the first missionaries to come to the New World, bringing with them wheat, grape cuttings, fruits, beans, and vegetables.

Franciscan priests had followed the conquistador gold-seekers to New Mexico to convert the natives, and were the most active of the religious groups that tried to convert the Pueblo Indians to Christianity. They had previously spread the Gospel as far as Asia and China, and were now anxious to tackle the New World. When Oñate arrived in 1598 there were only eight friars in all of New Mexico.[42] By 1619 there were twenty.[43]

The Franciscans, the Order of Friars Minor, the First Order of St. Francis, was formed in 1209 by Giovanni Francesco Bernardone, otherwise known to the English-speaking world as St. Francis of Assisi. Though born into a rich family in Assisi, Italy, he gave up his wealthy lifestyle and turned to living a humble and celibate life.

The order was famous for its holiness and simple living. The friars wore long tunics with hoods, made from coarse brown or gray cloth, similar to the Italian peasants of St. Francis' time. The robe was tied at the waist with a cord with three knots and topped by a cowl, a pointed hood to protect and shield the friar's shaven head. The robes the Franciscans originally wore in Europe were gray, but many in New Spain chose to wear blue to honor the Virgin Mary, whose primary color is blue.[44] This color gave them a later nickname among the Indians of "blue-robes." Brown robes persisted in Europe, much of the New World converted to blue, and gray was common in England.

Another distinguishing feature was the Franciscan's characteristic tonsure. The top of the head was shaved, leaving a circular fringe of hair below to represent Christ's crown of thorns.

The Franciscan friars took vows of chastity and poverty. Their intent was to work as ministers to the poor and to perform good deeds, so they were well-adapted to missionary work. Franciscan friars were bound by their vows to have no possessions or to own private or community property. They were supposed to walk barefoot and never ride a horse unless they were traveling far. Given the long distances between missions on the Southwestern frontier, however, they often found it appropriate to ride horses.

The Franciscans were particularly devoted to helping Indians. They taught them to farm, tend flocks, make soap, weave cloth, play musical instruments, and to read and write. The Franciscans had noted from their previous efforts in mission work that music was a powerful force in helping them and they continued the tradition of wind instruments, pipe organs, and chants in New Mexico. Music was also played for religious processions.

It was not an easy life for the Franciscans. The friars had to gather up the Indians and teach them about Christian life. They had to supervise the building of the mission church and support buildings, find water for crops, teach the Indians how to plant wheat and vegetables, and lay out and plant orchards and vineyards. The missions evolved as self-contained communities that contained quarters for both the Franciscans, the mission Indians, and traveling visitors, but also contained a school, workshops, storerooms, and gardens.

Conflict

As governor, Peralta exercised almost total control as the civil authority for the region. He functioned as the chief executive of the colony, and was the primary legislative, judicial, and military leader. The Franciscans, on the other hand, were the only Roman Catholic priests in New Mexico at the time, so they had complete control over any and all religious activities. As such, the Franciscans believed that they also had ultimate power over the people, which often caused conflicts between the governor and the chief priest. One of the tactics used by the priests was ecclesiastical resistance to civil control. Furthermore, as a punishment, they could threaten to withhold the sacraments of the church.

Fray Alonso Peinado, the head priest of the Franciscans in New Mexico, generally cooperated with Governor Peralta.[45] Conflict, however, immediately arose between Peralta and Peinado's successor, fray Isidro Ordóñez, who arrived in the summer of 1612. Ordóñez produced a letter of authority and used it to defy Peralta. Many historians, however, feel that the letter was probably forged. Ordóñez continually fought with the governor over who had the ultimate authority in the colony. Ordóñez wanted to control the settlement as he wanted, regardless of the governor, and the two were in constant conflict. Ordóñez ran rampant, bullying the townspeople and threatening them with excommunication if they did not comply with his wishes. Ordóñez finally excommunicated Peralta, posted a notice to that effect on the church door, and threw Peralta's chair from the church out into the street. Not to be outdone, Peralta had his men replace the chair in the back of the church by the baptismal font and sat there determinedly. The tension between the two continued and finally Ordóñez had Peralta arrested. The situation was only resolved by the arrival of a new governor. Peralta left in 1614 and became the governor of Acapulco. Ordóñez was replaced in 1616 and recalled to Mexico City for a disciplinary hearing.[46]

The Tribunal of the Holy Office of the Inquisition, more commonly known as the Spanish Inquisition, came to New Mexico in 1626. The Inquisition was established in 1478 by Ferdinand II of Aragon and Isabella I of Castile, and was intended to combat heresy and maintain Catholic orthodoxy in Spain. The wrong-doings investigated included heresy, blasphemy, witchcraft, bigamy, and sodomy (which was delicately termed "crimes against nature"). The extreme punishment for condemned heretics was to be tortured to produce a confession and then be burned at the stake. The office was eventually corrupted into a tool to persecute anyone in the name of Catholic orthodoxy. The first Spanish Grand Inquisitor, Tomás de Torquemada, a Dominican friar, is thought to have been responsible during the second half of the fifteenth century for the execution of an estimated 2,000 people that he deemed to be heretics.

In New Mexico, Indians were not subject to the Inquisition as they were considered to be mere beginners in matters of the Christian religion. Any breaches of the faith by the Indians were punished by the local missionaries. The Inquisition was instead directed against the settlers, and its work was largely independent of both religious and civil authorities.[47] The more serious charges investigated in New Mexico involved witchcraft and pacts with the Devil, but there were also frivolous accusations, such blasphemy, cases of suspected infidelity, and wives trying to win back their husband's affections by using Indian love potions. Investigators, in New Mexico at least, generally separated gossip from the more serious accusations. Though the Inquisition had little impact on most of the inhabitants of Santa Fe, it gave the ambitious Franciscans another potential tool to use against the colony's governors in their unending struggle for power.[48]

Eventually Franciscan zeal and their attempts to create a private domain independent of the civil government backfired, as two irreconcilable issues developed between the missionaries and the Indians that later led to unrest and revolt. The first was ongoing attempts to persecute and stamp out the native religion and convert the Pueblo Indians to Christianity when they did not want to be converted. The second was the attempt to transfer more and more of the Indian labor and wealth to the missions.

Disappointment

The Spanish Crown finally realized that New Mexico did not hold the riches that it had expected. The province had not provided much in the way of material returns for Spain and the isolated colony of Santa Fe in the backwaters of the Rio Grande valley did not have the strategic importance of California or Florida. Situated 1,600 miles from Mexico City, Santa Fe was isolated and hard to defend, and had poor communications with Mexico City because of the lack of regular supply caravans to and from the south.

The question was what to do with it. New Mexico was intended to be a mission province, supported by Spanish colonists and government officials. Part of the problem was that Oñate's colonists had expected to find plenty of gold and a horde of docile natives to act as free labor. In reality, they found neither. What was left was trade and woolen goods, both of which relied on exploitation of the Indian labor and the *encomiendas*.

In short, there was no wealth of any importance to exploit. No gold or silver had been found, the missionaries had not been particularly successful in converting the Indians, and the colonists were difficult to supply because of their distance from Mexico City. As early as 1608 New Mexico was not a profitable colony.

There was no real reason to subsidize New Mexico except the religious, so the final decision on whether or not to abandon New Mexico was to be based on the number of natives baptized. Estimates put the number of those converted to Christianity at only 400 to 600. Therefore, in 1608, a formal recommendation was made to abandon the province.

The Crown was on the verge of withdrawing all the colonists from New Mexico when the Franciscans sent a representative north to baptize as many Indians as possible to show some degree of missionary success.[49] At the last minute, fray Lázaro Ximénez suddenly stepped forward and said that 7,000 Indians had been baptized and could not be abandoned. This was probably an inflated, self-serving number, but then again, what to do?[50] One recommendation was to remove the Indians to New Spain in order to continue to minister to their religious needs. But after suitable deliberation, King Philip III rescinded the abandonment and ordered that New Mexico must be maintained.[51]

There were, however, two other subtler reasons for keeping Santa Fe and the surrounding area in Spanish hands. One reason was to hold onto the Spanish claim of the vast empty country that lay to the north of Mexico. The other was that part of the Franciscan's calling was to extend the true faith to all. As a result, New Mexico continued to be maintained as a Christian mission.

To rejuvenate the New Mexican economy the Spanish Crown had to splinter three powerful early colonial groups that had resisted authority. These were the Church, the Inquisition, and the civil government. The governors wanted the Franciscans removed so that they could have full power over the Indians, so they claimed that the friars had failed in their obligations. The friars, of course, contested these charges. Indeed, the Franciscans had expended large amounts of energy to minister to the Indians, to convert them and to instruct them, but could show little success in return. Though some of the friars were morally weak and dissolute, most were very conscientious in their duties. They counter-claimed that the governors were trying to get rid of the Indians' protectors (i.e., themselves) in order to exploit the natives and their labor.

The Importance of the Missions

After the decision was made to keep New Mexico as a province, missionary work continued to try to convert the native population to Christianity. In their calling to convert what they considered to be the heathen Indians, the Franciscans reached out to the pueblos of New Mexico to bring their gospel and beliefs to the native population. The friars instructed mission Indians in the basics of Catholic doctrine, though frequently the Indians only absorbed answers by rote and spouted back memorized versions of prayers and catechisms. They were also taught to sing Christian hymns and play musical instruments to accompany church services. They participated in Catholic Masses, often assisting as altar boys.

The interior of the Spanish missions contained high ceilings, an elaborate altar, and a large open space for worshippers. Typically no benches were installed and the audience either stood or knelt during the service, or brought their own chairs.

The mission services and churches were deliberately given an imposing air to impress the converts with the superiority of the Christian religion. Elaborate vestments, solemn music and singing, shining silver communion wine vessels and platters, and beautiful statues and paintings of sacred images made an impressive showing for the uneducated natives.

To some extent the missionaries concentrated harder on converting children than adults. They assumed correctly that the adults were typically more set in their ways and religious beliefs, whereas the children were more likely to accept new ideas and beliefs that could be instilled in them. They hoped that these children could also be used to influence their elders and, eventually, their own children. There were some attempts to teach the natives to speak and write Spanish, but how successful this was on a universal scale is debatable. Some natives learned to write and speak it fluently, others never did, and the majority probably only used it occasionally when there was a need to.

The goal of the missionaries was also to teach the Indians to tend the European animals they brought with them, such as cows, sheep, chickens, and pigs. Missionaries taught them how to raise European crops, such as wheat, watermelons, and fruit trees. When these crops started to be produced in excess, several of the missions turned into important trade centers where surplus crops were bartered.

Part of the rationale for converting the Indians was that by doing this the province would expand the number of laborers and taxpayers, which in turn was necessary to support distant Spain through trade revenues and taxes. Though the mission Indians did not directly pay taxes, they were expected to contribute labor to construct the churches and surrounding buildings, to perform daily work around the missions, and to raise mission crops and livestock.

Though New Mexico had not produced the gold and other riches that was hoped for, the colonists and missions were generally self-sufficient. The colonial economy was based on small-scale farming, and raising sheep and cattle introduced by the Spanish. Each friar brought with him ten heifers, ten sheep, and forty-eight chickens. Despite their vows of poverty, many of the friars eventually increased this modest start into rich flocks of sheep, herds of horses, and large collections of firearms, and had their own groups of Indian workers. By the 1600s, most missions had accumulated large herds of sheep.

There was a lack of trained workmen in New Mexico, so the Franciscans had to be capable of building their own churches by themselves. Part of the building and maintenance of the mission buildings required the converts to learn masonry and carpentry, and the use of tools, such as saws, chisels, and planes. A general lack of expertise meant that the mission buildings were often more functional than esthetic. The friars used whatever materials were available locally, such as rock, adobe clay, and wood. The walls of the churches were made very thick, usually with adobe brick, in order to hold up the heavy wooden crossbeams needed to support a simple, flat roof. Most New Mexico mission churches had a 200-pound bronze church bell made in Mexico, most of which came from the same mold.

Making the Indians construct the church buildings was an indignity for the men, as adobe construction was considered to be woman's work (yet interestingly weaving was considered to be an acceptable male pursuit). Continued indignities like this festered for years before finally erupting in massive revolt.

Founding a mission was not easy, as all the supplies had to be brought north from Mexico City. Each friar received two blankets, a hat, and two pairs of woolen stockings. Kitchen supplies included iron spoons, barrels for water, and all the utensils necessary for cooking. Miscellaneous clerical supplies included paper, pens, and ink made of tannic acid mixed with iron oxide. All the ecclesiastical supplies had to be brought also. This included altar cloths, tallow candles, missals, chalices, crucifixes, votive lamps, and olive oil for the lamps. All the supplies had to last for three years, which was the interval between supply trains. Each mission also had to make the allotted forty-five gallons of sacramental wine last for this same period. Medical supplies for the primitive remedies of the time included instruments such as lancets (fleams) for bleeding treatments, syringes for enemas, and scissors and knives for surgical operations. Musical instruments included trumpets and flutes. Supplies were primarily intended for the missions, but the missionaries also brought a few luxury goods, such as chocolate, sugar, knives, and other manufactured goods for trade.

The priests and friars lived in a building called a *convento*, located next to the mission church. These buildings in the cold climate of northern New Mexico winters were heated by corner fireplaces or braziers that used wood or burning charcoal.

Pecos

One of the most important centers for trade among the Indians was the Spanish mission at Pecos, which was the gateway to the Eastern Plains. Similar to other Anasazi sites, the village of Pecos started around 800 as a group of pithouses built as permanent homes when the Indians turned to farming for subsistence and the abundant natural resources of the area attracted native hunters and gatherers. The native population grew in the early 1100s when the Anasazi started to migrate from the arid areas and joined the existing groups in the Rio Grande valley. Between about 1100 and 1300, the Indians emerged from a pithouse way of life and Pecos grew into a series of small villages of rambling, connected one-story buildings. Around 1450 these small pueblos were gradually deserted as the people started to construct a huge, easily-defended, fortress-like structure, four and five stories high, that was large enough to house the entire 2,000 inhabitants of the villages. This fortress-like structure had 700 rooms arranged around a central courtyard with balconies connecting the upper rooms.

The reason for building this pueblo is not clear, but it was probably intended to provide better defense against the marauding tribes of Plains Indians who lived to the east. This pueblo was originally called Cicuyé by the Indians. The Pecos Pueblo was at the height of its development when the Spanish first saw and renamed it in 1540.

Pecos was located on the dividing line between the agricultural Pueblo Indians of the Rio Grande valley and the nomadic hunter-gatherers, mostly Apaches, from the Plains to the east. The pueblo, therefore, became an important trading center for the farmers and the nomadic hunting tribes. Ironically, Pueblo Indians could not communicate with nomadic Indians in their native tongues because the Apache and Navajo spoke Athabascan and the Utes spoke Shoshonean. Linguistic difficulties existed even among Pueblo Indians. Indians in the area north of Bernalillo and at Acoma spoke Keresan, south of Taos they spoke Tanoan, the Hopi spoke Shoshonean (though inconveniently a different dialect than the Utes), and the Zuni spoke Zunian.[52]

In spite of language barriers, a thriving business grew at Pecos that exported surplus crops and cloth, and imported buffalo hides, dried meat, flint tools, and human slaves. The Apache traded meat, buffalo hides, tallow, and salt, for cotton blankets, pottery, shells, surplus corn, turquoise, and other items produced by the pueblos. When the Spanish started to colonize New Mexico after 1598, they joined in the existing system at Pecos and traded agricultural products, such as surplus grain, fruit, and livestock, as well as some goods manufactured from metal, such as axes and spears.

In the 1620s Franciscan friar Andrés Juárez built a huge church at Pecos named the Mission de Nuestra Señora de los Angeles de Porcinucula. The building was completed and dedicated by 1625. At one time this was the largest structure in New Mexico and was a prominent reminder of Spanish rule. It was probably the most imposing of the New Mexico mission churches, with huge towers, buttresses, and pine-log ceiling beams. The walls, made of adobe brick covered with lime plaster, were eight to ten feet thick in places and forty feet high. It has been estimated that building the church and *convento* required 300,000 adobe bricks. Roof beams were huge wooden logs 150 feet long. The nave was 133 feet long and 41 feet wide. The adjoining *convento* contained the priest's quarters, workshops, corrals, stables, the kitchen, the kitchen gardens, and the priests' dining room.[53]

As newer settlements were established further to the east, the importance of Pecos as a trade center lessened. The original church was destroyed in the Pueblo Revolt of 1680 (described in Chapter Five), and the smaller church structure that is visible today was built on top of the ruined foundations in 1717, after the re-conquest of New Mexico by the Spanish. However, disease, continued raids by Apache and Comanche, and migration reduced the population. Repeated epidemics of smallpox, influenza, measles, and other diseases continued through the 1600s and 1700s. A smallpox epidemic killed many of the Indians in 1781, and by 1786 when peace was finally made with the Comanche, the population had dropped to 200. The Pecos mission was finally abandoned in 1838 when the last seventeen survivors left to join their kinsmen in Texas.

The prevalent scholarly thinking has been that diseases such as smallpox had not existed among the Indians before the arrival of the Europeans, leaving the natives with no immunity against them. It is now thought, however, that some of these diseases may have been present in the New World before the arrival of the Spanish. There is speculation that the communities existing in the Southwest before the Spanish arrival were so small and geographically scattered that infectious diseases were originally unable to spread widely among them and cause serious epidemics. After the Spanish arrived, the roaming conquistadors carried virulent diseases from tribe to tribe, thus infecting large numbers of Indians in a short period of time. Another factor in the spread of disease may have been that Spanish missionaries, in attempting to gather their converts into the missions, created a fertile breeding ground for disease among the closely-packed Indians that was not present before.

In an ironic twist of perspective, the fact that the missionaries were mostly immune to these European diseases helped to raise their stature among the Indians. The converts felt that the friars must be very powerful indeed to be able to withstand the mysterious illnesses that carried off so many of their fellow natives.[54]

The mission building at Quarai in the Salinas area of New Mexico is one of the most complete seventeenth-century Spanish missions existing today. The mission was built in 1626. Though a flourishing pueblo of a thousand rooms was located just west of the main church building, the mission was deserted by 1677.

The Salinas Missions

This group of three missions was located southeast of Albuquerque at the sites of three pueblos. Abó was a thriving community when the Spanish first saw it in 1581 and Oñate accepted its oath of allegiance to Spain in 1598. Between 1622 and 1627 fray Francisco Fonte, Abó's first priest, built a mission named San Gregorio de Abó at Salinas Pueblo, the oldest part of which dates from late 1200s. The original mission building at Abó was replaced by a larger church in 1651 after eleven years of construction by fray Francisco de Acevado. An organ was added around 1660. The second mission, Quarai, was built in 1626 under Father Juan Gutierrez de la Chica. The mission eventually became the home of 400 to 600 Indians. In 1629 Father Francisco Letrado built the third mission of Gran Quivera at the thriving pueblo of Las Humanas. Today these three mission churches of Abó, Quarai, and Gran Quivera are part of Salinas Pueblo Missions National Monument. They are three of the oldest and most intact seventeenth century Spanish missions existing in the United States.

Salinas meant "salt lakes." The Salinas pueblos and the later missions were important trade centers due to the abundance in nearby Estancia Basin of salt, an essential mineral for everyday diet and valuable as a food preservative. Salt was used as a trade item and was important for the processing of silver at the mines in northern Mexico. Oñate called salt one of the four riches of New Mexico. As at other missions, trade goods included flint from Texas, seashells from the Gulf of California, and scarlet macaws from Mexico. The Plains Indians brought hides and meat to trade for corn, salt, blankets, and pottery.

As at other missions, disease and starvation wiped out 450 Indians at Gran Quivera in 1668 and the mission was essentially abandoned by 1672. The Mission of San Gregorio de Abó was abandoned in 1675, until it was reoccupied by Spanish sheep ranchers around 1815. The mission at Quarai was deserted by 1677. By 1678 any remaining Indians in the Salinas area had disappeared to live at other pueblos along the Rio Grande and all three of the missions were deserted. The pueblo people never returned.

Taos

Taos Pueblo, about 75 miles north of Santa Fe, was an important trading center that held a large fair every fall.[55] Nomadic Indians from the east, the Comanche and Apache, along with Ute and Navajo, came to trade, bringing deer and buffalo skins, jerky, stolen livestock, slaves, and other plunder from their raids to trade for corn, food, horses, knives, and other manufactured hardware. Ute Indians from the north came to trade for horses, guns, tools, axes, and knives, as well as blankets, beads, and other trinkets. The participants of the fair included tribes who were normally hostile to the Spanish, but observed a temporary truce for trading. After the fair was over, any truce was abandoned and the participants went home to plot further depredations against the people they had been peacefully trading with a few days earlier.

Indians regularly brought enemy captives, mostly Indian women and children from other tribes, to trade, sell, or ransom. When the Spanish joined in the trading, they also traded slaves back and forth. By the 1600s Indians were delivering buffalo and deer hides to the Spanish and the Spanish took Indians in trade as slaves. Colonists used them as household servants, and young boys and girls brought large amounts of money in the mining districts of Mexico and central Mexico.

After Mexican Independence in 1821, and until the early 1840s, the village of Taos developed as the center of trade for beaver pelts. It became one of the important centers of the fur trade in the West as hardy French and Anglo-American mountain men swarmed over the high valleys of the upper Rio Grande to supply the hat-makers of the United States and Europe.[56] Similar trade fairs were held at Santa Fe, Chama, Santa Clara, Santa Cruz, and Abiqui.

CHAPTER FOUR

The City of the Holy Faith

By the mid-1600s the Spanish were firmly established in New Mexico, though their numbers were relatively small compared to the overall population. The number of Spanish in New Mexico in the 1600s was probably never more than about 3,000 while there were an estimated 50,000 Pueblo Indians in 50 villages.[1]

The central outpost for the Spanish in northern New Spain was the provincial capital at Santa Fe. This was the capital of the territory that is now New Mexico and Arizona, as well as parts of Colorado and Utah. In 1630 the Spanish population of Santa Fe was only about 250, with 700 Indian servants.[2] The intent of the Catholic missionaries and the wealthy Spanish settlers was to establish in New Mexico (specifically in Santa Fe) the aristocratic lifestyle that they had known in Spain and Mexico. To maintain their image they brought with them luxuries, such as olive oil, chocolate, wine, and musical instruments.

Since its founding, Santa Fe has been colonized by the Spanish, overrun by Pueblo Indians during the revolt of 1680, recaptured by the Spanish, owned by Mexico from 1821 to 1846, and finally taken over the Americans. In it heyday it was the central marketplace and thoroughfare for international trade in the Southwest.

As the center of Spanish government for New Mexico, Santa Fe was the location of the governor's residence and the military garrison (presidio). Most of the military were used to protect the Spanish settlements and the Pueblo Indians from nomadic raids by Plains Indians. To assist in this task, many men from the friendly pueblos were used as supplemental soldiers. There were not enough Spanish soldiers to dominate the pueblos and their inhabitants if they rebelled, so the governor relied on the missionaries to control the Pueblo Indians through religion and goodwill.

The power of the Spanish Crown in New Spain was exercised by three branches of government. The first was the office of the viceroy in Mexico City, which represented the King in Spain and was in charge of all civil and military matters. The second was the legal branch in the form of the district court of appeal, or the *audienca*. The third was the office of the bishop, which was responsible for the administration of the church and its priests. These three bureaucracies were intentionally set up to be relatively independent of each other in order to provide checks and balances on each group.

On the local level in Santa Fe was the governor, who was appointed by the viceroy in Mexico City. The governor was the head of the secular administration and was responsible for all government business, such as the collection of taxes, other than the religious affairs of the church. The governor was also in charge of the military, and was the head judicial officer for the province, administering justice in civil and criminal cases. Isolated as he was, over 1,600 miles north of Mexico City, the governor was essentially out of touch from the governing viceroy of New Spain and was forced by necessity to operate in an independent and autonomous fashion. News and even official documents moved very slowly. Letters and official communications were sent to and from Mexico City by supply caravans that took months to make the trip from Santa Fe to Mexico. The next wagon train might not arrive for another three years, thus it could be that long before the Governor received any reply to a request for instructions. So, though the governor technically answered to the viceroy, the practical result was that the lack of communication meant that the governor usually did what he wanted and often arbitrarily imposed his will as law.[3]

The governor's powers included the ability to assign *encomiendas* and to grant land to settlers, which was often done for personal profit. Land grants were made by the governor in the name of the king. Such grants were not supposed to encroach on the lands of the pueblos, but large ranches of up to several thousand acres (most often termed *estancias*) were common in New Mexico before the Pueblo Revolt of 1680.

The governor's authority was divided into six (later eight) administrative jurisdictions in New Mexico, each of which was presided over by a local *alcalde* or mayor, whose function was to act as the military commander for the district, the local justice of the peace, and the general supervisor of the settlers and Indians. These local officials commonly had no formal training in law or administration, but based their decisions on common sense and local practices. They often made decisions based simply on their own opinions, though their rulings could be appealed to the governor. Serious cases were referred to Mexico City. On the local level, as on the provincial level, the authority of these civil leaders overlapped that of the Franciscan missionaries, which often created conflicts.

Santa Fe was the furthest provincial outpost from Mexico City in the New World. Due to the difficulty in communicating requests and orders from the viceroy, New Mexico operated under a certain degree of anarchy. The governors set themselves up as absolute rulers with unlimited powers and Spanish laws were regularly ignored. On the ecclesiastical side, the friars freely punished the Indians, including the use of torture and execution, for what they considered to be heresy. Rape of Indian women was commonplace, even by priests sworn to celibacy. To make the situation worse, the secular authorities and the church struggled against each other for power, neither one answering to anybody. The friars believed that the primary purpose for colonization was to convert the Indians to Christianity and thus they felt that their projects should take priority. If they needed to, the Franciscans were determined to impress their will on others in New Mexico through censures, interdicts, excommunications, and threats of Inquisition proceedings.[4] At stake was control of the Pueblo Indians and the potential for wealth and power they represented.

The governor, on the other hand, felt that his position was the supreme authority. The main attraction for the settlers was the hope of making a profit and most of the colonial officials, including the governors, used their positions to add to their personal fortunes. For this reason the rights to use Indians labor on farms and make products through the *repartimiento* system were very important. This became the basis for a struggle between the Church and the secular government over which one had the right to the maximum amount of native labor.

The Plaza

The focal point of government and trade in Santa Fe was The Plaza, originally named *La Plaza Mayor*, which was a large open space in the center of town surrounded by the important buildings. Towns in the New World were intended to conform to a standard design planned by King Philip, so the Plaza was laid out in a manner similar to towns in Spain. The north side of the plaza was occupied by government buildings. At the east end stood a church with an attached building that housed the Franciscan friars. The other two sides of the plaza were lined by the one-story residences of prominent citizens. The open area in the center of the square was used as a market-place by vendors and traders and for social functions, and was where all the official, military, and religious events took place. The public stocks and flogging post were also located there.

The plaza that exists today in Santa Fe, about a city block in size, is thought to be only about half of its size when the town was first built. The plaza was originally about two city blocks long by a block wide, and extended as far as the present Cathedral Basilica of St. Francis of Assisi. Until the 1830s, the plaza was surrounded by an eight-foot-high wall for defense.

The original Palace of the Governors, which stood on the north side of the plaza, was completed 1612, which made it the oldest government building in continuous use in the country. The original building was larger than today, extending further north and to the west. The original Palace was the headquarters for the government of New Mexico, and was built as a fortress, complete with large square defensive towers on the front at each end. The building contained the governor's private apartments and his official reception rooms, along with supporting offices, the military barracks and arsenal, a prison (*calabozo*), stables, and the servant's quarters. The original Palace was built from adobe brick and had a floor made of adobe clay mixed with straw, animal blood, and wood ashes to bind the material together and give the surface a hard, shiny appearance. This mixture also made the floor waterproof.

The Palace of the Governors has had several names over the years, among them *El Palacio* and "the adobe palace." In Spanish records the building was known as *Casa Reales* (Royal Houses) or *El Palacio Real* (The Royal Palace). The old adobe building has undergone almost continual change, remodeling, and repair since it was first built. The name was changed to the Palace of the Governors after the building became the Museum of New Mexico in 1909. The building was restored between 1909 and 1912, with the new exterior reflecting Spanish architecture with the more informal style of the missions and pueblos.

Other important buildings near the plaza were churches. One is the Chapel of San Miguel, the oldest active church still in use in the United States. It was originally built in 1610 by fray Alonso de Benavides on the site of an Indian pueblo that may have been occupied as early as 1300. The original chapel was partially destroyed in the Pueblo Revolt of 1680. As a result, the remains were torn down and the present church was rebuilt in 1710 on the previous foundation, using an adobe design with extensive buttresses.

Across the alley from the chapel is a building reputed to be the oldest house in Santa Fe. This could be, as the oldest beams that make up the ceiling have been dated back to 1740. It was built by Tlaxcalan Indians who helped to build the Chapel of San Miguel across

Pictured here in 1873 is the Chapel of San Miguel in Santa Fe, the oldest active church still in use in the United States. Originally built in 1610 by fray Alonso de Benavides on the site of an Indian pueblo, the roof of the chapel was partially destroyed in the Pueblo Revolt of 1680. The remains were renovated and rebuilt in 1710 on the original foundation. Renovation and alterations have continued since then. The original adobe walls remain under the stucco exterior (Library of Congress).

the alley. The interior style of the house, with thick adobe walls, low ceilings, and a dirt floor, confirms its antiquity.

Close to the plaza was the Cathedral Basilica of St. Francis of Assisi. The first parish church (*la parroquia*) on this site was built in 1626 by fray Alonso de Benavides, but it was destroyed in the Pueblo Revolt of 1680. After the re-conquest of Santa Fe, another parish church was built on this location between 1714 and 1717. Construction of the present cathedral, under the guidance of Archbishop John Baptiste Lamy, the first bishop of Santa Fe, was started in 1869 and essentially completed by 1887.

The Town

Society in Santa Fe was divided into several social classes. At the top were the high government officials, such as the governor, who typically came from the upper classes of Spain, and the leaders of the church. These were the educated classes. In the middle were the moderately wealthy merchants, the landowners, and other military and secular officials who were lower in the official hierarchy. Most households had Indian slaves who were Apache, Navajo, or Ute. At the bottom of the class structure were the ordinary people who made up the ranks of farmers, stock herders, domestic servants, and common laborers.

The central place of business where vendors sold their wares was the plaza. Small wooden carts squealed their way around town, carrying a variety of goods for sale. Donkeys carried loads of firewood for cooking and heating in the winter. Women sold soap, cheese, chilis and various other foodstuffs. Firewood, beans, hay, goats, and sheep were bartered and sold.

Away from the central plaza, early Santa Fe was a haphazard collection of houses lining a series of narrow streets. Though planners in Mexico wanted Spanish towns to be built on an orderly grid system, this often did not happen on the frontier. In Santa Fe, the unpaved streets were dusty, with rocks and potholes producing an uneven surface for the wooden carts used to carry merchandise around the town. Like most other early Western towns, Santa Fe was not a particularly clean town. Even after settlement by the Americans, there were complaints from residents about animal excrement in the streets and dead dogs in the irrigation ditches. Piles of garbage from houses lined the streets.

Early Santa Fe was a primitive place, surrounded by stagnant pools of water. At the time of Santa Fe's settlement a series of swampy marshes (called *ciénegas* by the Spanish) were located north, east, and south of the plaza area. These swamps covered about thirty-five acres and contained several springs that kept them wet. Settlers tried to build their houses close to streams or springs such as these, as water for domestic use had to be carried to the houses in wooden buckets or pottery jars. Washing clothes took place outside in creeks.

The Santa Fe River running through town had a heavier flow than now.[5] Water was distributed via man-made ditches called *acequias*, which also formed a simple irrigation system.[6] The water was used to irrigate fruit trees and grazing lands. Santa Fe's primary water system on the south side of town was called the *acequia madre* ("mother ditch"), that had a generous flow of water with side ditches branching out from it. A similar ditch, called the *acequia de la muralla*, served the same purpose on the north side of the infant town. Landowners not lucky enough to live close to a ditch had to perform dry-land farming or carry heavy buckets of water suspended from yokes around their shoulders to their fields. Other *acequias* distributed water to other parts of town.

Early settlers copied the Indian pueblos and made their homes with adobe, as this was a convenient and cheap building material. Most of the homes of the town were low, rec-

Adobe bricks were made from a mixture of adobe clay, water, and a binder, in this case straw. The raw mixture was formed in crude wooden molds (left front) then turned out to dry in the sun. Though it was a cheap building material with good insulating properties, adobe brick tended to weather fast and had to be continually maintained.

tangular, narrow, one-story, one-room houses built from adobe brick. The thick adobe walls kept the houses warm in winter and cool in summer.

The flat roofs of the houses (*azotea*) were made from long wooden ceiling beams (*vigas*) fashioned from ponderosa pine, spruce, or aspen trees placed across the tops of the walls. On top of the *vigas* the builder place a layer of peeled saplings or branches (*latillas*) interlaced in a crisscrossed pattern, which were then covered with twigs, brush, and straw, then adobe or dirt. The roofs were slightly slanted so that rainwater drained into wooden troughs (*canales*) at the edges that carried it away. Wooden doors, often with ornate frames, completed the structure. Metal goods, such as hinges, locks, and latches, were rare. Instead of hinges, the wooden outer doors used round wooden pegs placed in sockets in the lintel and sill to allow them open and close. Windows might be left open to the outside in the summer and covered with shutters in winter. Any windows were small and sometimes used oiled cloth or thin layers of sheets of mica to let in a hazy light. Floors might simply be earth that was beaten flat.

After the first room was built, more long narrow rooms might be added at each end. Thus the house ended up in an L-shape or U-shape, or eventually totally enclosed a small private courtyard (*placita* or *plazuela*) in the middle, with doors and windows opening into it. The principal rooms were the bedroom, the living room, and the kitchen. Open patios or courtyards often had a single door opening onto the street through a large gate called *la puerta del zaguan* (the door of the vestibule).[7] The back of the building housed the kitchen (*cocina*), the provision store (*dispensa*), and the granary (*granero*).

Buildings were clustered into single-story compounds that housed multiple families. For protection, the houses were built around a common plaza that was used to plant gardens and orchards, with all windows facing into the interior of the plaza. The exterior walls of the compound might be solid, without windows, to provide for some defense against marauding Indians. For security in case of attack, the few doors that were built into the outer walls were only large enough to allow passage of a single person or animal at a time.

The interior walls of the houses were painted with a mixture of pulverized gypsum, wheat paste, and water, spread over the surface with a sheepskin. Cloth might be hung from the walls to prevent the white gypsum material from wiping off onto clothing. The adobe floor was tamped solid and soaked with animal blood to make the surface hard and give it a sheen and solid footing that was easy to clean. Woolen rugs might be thrown at random around the floors. A wooden painting or statue of a saint might bring good luck to the home from a hollow in the wall (*nicho*).

Families, except those of the highest government officials and the rich, had few possessions and little furniture. Books found around the home were mostly missals, bibles, and other religious material, though a few of the wealthier, educated residents might have books on science or novels such as *Don Quixote* by Cervantes.

Clothing and valuables were stored in a chest in the bedroom, where male and female visitors often had to share accommodations. Wealthier families might have built-in benches (*bancos*) or one or two wooden chairs, stools, tables, storage shelves, and perhaps a bed made by hand from simple planks. Poor families slept on the floor on mattresses (*colchones*) stuffed with straw, and during the day doubled them up and sat on them or on the bare floor to eat their meals at a low table. The family possessions, along with clothing, dishes, and food, might be stored in armoires (*armarios*), moveable cupboards (*trasteros*), or chests (*cajas*) scattered throughout the house.

The Spanish colonists quickly adapted to Indian foods. *Posole* (a stew or soup containing corn), tamales, and tortillas (a large, flat, unleavened wafer of corn eaten instead of bread) became common in the Hispanic diet. Meals were eaten around a common cooking pot, with each person using a tortilla as a type of spoon to scoop up chili stew or the beans that were a staple of their diet. Corn for the tortillas eaten with almost every meal was prepared with a grinding system such as the Anasazi used before them, consisting of a *mano* and a *metate*, then formed into very thin, flat wafers about eight inches in diameter. These were baked on a large flat griddle (*comal*) made of copper or iron, or on a flat stone. Strings of chilis, herbs, and gourds were hung from the *vigas* to dry. Baskets and clay pots used for cooking and eating were traded from local Indians.

Adobe fireplaces were used for indoor cooking and for heating the home, but not all rooms were heated. Some rooms were equipped with a corner fireplace with a hearth six or eight inches high. Fireplaces mostly burned wood, but occasionally charcoal. Much of the cooking, such as baking corn tortillas and chili peppers, was performed outdoors in an outdoor oven, called a *horno*. The *horno*, shaped like a beehive and made from adobe, was built in the common courtyard for communal use. The *horno* was introduced by the

Typical interior of a Spanish adobe house in New Mexico. Furniture consists of a simple combination couch and bed, a few chairs, some stools, and a rough table. A corner fireplace provides heat in winter. Religious icons on the left wall are reminders of the saints. The window on the right is covered by wooden shutters in the winter and left open in the summer. A woolen blanket covers a floor made of packed dirt mixed with ox-blood to harden it and give it a sheen.

Spanish and had been originally adopted by them from similar beehive ovens used by the Moors.

The colonists brought with them fruit trees, such as plums and peaches, and grape vines. Vegetables included onions, cabbage, carrots, and peas. Grains included wheat and barley. Cats were used to control undesired rats and mice in the grain storage bins. The origin of these cats in New Mexico is unclear, but they probably arrived with the Spanish.[8]

Livestock included turkeys, sheep, goats, pigs, and chickens. Sheep were prolific breeders and could have two breeding cycles a year, so their offspring became widespread in a short amount of time. Most of the flocks were owned by the missionaries.

Life in the new colony was hard and there were many threats to life from natural sources. Deaths could occur from disease, rattlesnake bites, bears, irritable cattle, hostile Indians, floods, river crossings, and unpredictable accidents. In 1805 the husband of Maria Sanchez, a soldier in Santa Fe, and the government mule he was riding on were both killed by a lightning bolt. Sadly she not only lost her husband, but the authorities made her pay for the mule.[9]

The infant town had no schools and no regular facilities for medical treatment. The practice of medicine at the time was still primitive and based on theories that dated back to Greek and Roman times. Materials used for treatments were based on common medical practices in Europe at the time, including the use of gunpowder, white lead, mercury, alum, arsenic, wine, and various powdered barks. The practice of bleeding as a cure was common, along with laxatives and purgatives presumed to flush any illness out of the patient's system.[10]

Given the lack of trained medical men, folk medicine was popular. Illness was often treated by various materials derived from plants and minerals from the surrounding countryside. Among the more bizarre treatments was one for disorders of the spleen, which consisted of administering to the patient his own urine mixed with honey. Urine was also used to treat gumboils, which were small abscesses of the gums. Fevers were treated with ground snake skin mixed with wine or soup. Patients with stomach problems were dosed for three consecutive mornings before breakfast with fresh horse manure mixed into wine, beer, or soup.[11] It was primitive medicine indeed.

Links to Mexico City

Barter with local Indians was limited to the amount of goods they could absorb, so an important source of trade for the infant colony was with Mexico. Mexican law made it illegal to trade with the United States, so the merchants in Chihuahua became rich by overpricing supplies. Unfortunately the trade monopoly held by the Chihuahua merchants meant that they bought New Mexico's surplus goods for low prices, and then in turn sold New Mexicans the goods they needed from Spain and Mexico for inflated prices. This led to a definite imbalance of trade and a lack of hard currency in the northern province.

There were two main methods of transportation of people and goods in New Mexico. The basic beast of burden was the mule and supplies were often packed on mule trains. The second method was to use a small two-wheeled wooden cart, called a *carreta*, that was drawn by pairs of oxen. This type of vehicle was common in Mexico in the 1530s and was what Oñate used when he came north in 1598. The *carreta* consisted of a wooden box about three or four feet wide, seven feet long, and four or five feet high that sat on a hand-hewn cottonwood or pine axle. At each end of the axle was a rimless wheel made from a round piece of wood either cut from a single slice of a large cottonwood tree or constructed from shaped sections of log held together with wooden pins that passed through the sections. The wheels were attached by wooden pins cut to go through holes in the outside ends of the axle. As the wooden wheels rode on the dry, wooden axles they rubbed and made an appalling blood-curdling screeching noise. One observer commented that it was "a siren song which wakened the dead for five miles or more." The noise also gave them the politer name of "singing carts." A lubricant, such as tallow, was sometimes used to try to quiet the howling noise, though this racket conveniently provided a warning to others that a wagon was approaching.

When the colonization of New Mexico started, the Franciscan friars operated freight caravans (*cuadrillas de carros*) of large wagons (*carros*) that traveled north from Mexico City to supply their missions with new clothing, sacramental wine, musical instruments, candles, altar pieces, cooking utensils, tools, and miscellaneous iron hardware, such as nails and hinges. During the 1600s these supply trains arrived only once every three years. Another important function of the wagon train was to carry Franciscans between missions. The Franciscan operated the supply route until about 1680.

The journey stretched from Mexico City to Santa Fe along a route named *El Camino Real de Tierra Adentro*, "The Royal Road of the Interior" or "The Inland Highway"[12] This route later became known as the *Camino Real del Norte* or "The Royal North Road."[13] The journey along *El Camino Real* was lengthy and took about six months to complete the more than 1,600 miles between the cities.

Supply caravans typically consisted of a column of thirty-two large, heavy wagons, each of which could carry up to two tons of freight. The wagons were equipped with four iron-rimmed wheels and were pulled by eight mules or oxen. The solid iron rims on wagon wheels were called "tires," notwithstanding their fundamental difference from the rubber tires inflated with air on modern automobiles.

The early *Camino Real* was long, rough, and unimproved. On a good day a caravan could travel perhaps ten miles. This was considered to be an acceptable distance due to the poor condition of the roads, the weight of the wagons, and the logistical complexity of organizing the wagon train and all its livestock. Each wagon was accompanied by two mule teams, and there were thirty-two extra mules to replace animals that died or became sick. This meant organizing a total of 544 mules for the entire wagon train, plus the beef cattle used to feed the drivers, the friars, and the other men. A caravan needed one driver for each wagon, or thirty-two men, plus various scouts, hunters, and cooks. The caravans also typically had a military escort of anywhere from twelve to twenty-five armed men with their captain, for defense against marauding Indians.[14]

To repair any breakdowns, each group of eight wagons carried 16 spare axles, 150 extra spokes, 24 spare iron tires for the wheels, and 500 pounds of tallow for lubricating the axles. They also carried other miscellaneous spare parts, such as bolts, washers, pins, and tools for repairs, such as hammers, axes, picks, and crowbars.

As trade increased, wagon trains from Mexico City came more often, but round trips typically still took about a year-and-a-half to complete. The trip from Mexico City to Santa Fe took six months, six months were spent unloading and distributing supplies, and six months were required for the return trip.

The supply trains were originally intended to supply the missions and carry Franciscans between them. However, because these supply caravans were the only regular link between Santa Fe and Mexico City, they soon added a variety of other cargo. Incoming wagons carried government officials, commercial merchandise, new settlers and their baggage, miscellaneous freight, and letters. Returning wagons carried goods for freight and commerce in Mexico City. The wagon trains usually arrived in the fall in time to pick up the year's harvest, including corn and wheat. Other items carried south were corn, salt, pine nuts, and cloth and blankets made by Indian labor.

As use of the road increased, it was widened for the use of ox-carts and mule trains and it became well-organized and maintained. The road was guarded by soldiers to ensure safe travel for traders and travelers.

Scattered every twenty miles or so along the road from northern Mexico to northern New Mexico were *ranchos*, *haciendas*, and simple campsites to serve as rest stops (*parajés*) during the trip.[15] Northbound wagon trains stopped to rest at Zacatecas, 400 miles north of Mexico City, and then again at Parral, after another 500 miles. The final leg of the journey north was another 700 miles along the Rio Grande to Santa Fe. Trade goods returned to Mexico included buffalo, deer, elk, and antelope hides. The missions shipped brandy produced from the fruit they grew and the wine they made. Other freight included piñon nuts from local trees, salt, candles, wool, woven goods such as blankets and clothing made in the colony, and any excess corn. Slaves, mostly women and children captured from the Apache, were also sent south to Mexico City. When they returned, the wagon trains from Mexico brought with them items that could not otherwise be obtained in New Mexico, such as sugar, chocolate, jewelry, liquor, gunpowder, and exotic items such as oysters, almonds, pepper, and raisins.

The position of governor carried with it only a very small salary of 2,000 pesos per year. As the governor was considered to be only a temporary resident of the province he was not allowed to hold an *encomienda*, but was expected to augment his income through whatever business dealings he could arrange. In this way the governor's office was often used to advance the current governor's own ends. Bernardo López de Mendizábel, for example, who was governor from 1659 to 1661, ran a retail shop in the Palace of the Governors. He also accumulated enough goods to form a caravan for export worth 12,000 pesos, six times his yearly salary. Trade items included 1,350 deerskins, 600 pairs of woolen stockings, 300 bushels of piñon nuts, salt, and various leather goods.[16] Even Governor Oñate started large-scale trading when he brought with him large quantities of trade goods, including glass beads, small bells, rings, earrings, needles, medals, mirrors, knives, toys, and buttons.

By the early 1700s, the annual supply caravans originated in Chihuahua, Mexico, which shortened the trip to about six weeks.

The Church

Spanish New Mexico was firmly anchored in the Catholic religion and Santa Fe was the religious center of the region. The church was a dominant and unifying force in the lives of the colonists, providing leadership and spiritual guidance. The church was not only the center of religious life, but was at the center of the social life of the villagers. The saints were commonly asked for help with everyday life. Examples were asking San Isidro, the patron saint of farmers, for help with crops; San Cristobal for a safe journey; San Antonio to find things lost around the house; and San Pasqual, the patron saint of cooks, for a good meal.

During the first forty years in New Mexico, the Franciscans built more than forty churches. Many of these were small local churches, built to serve small settlements. Some, however, such as the huge missions buildings at Gran Quivera, Quarai, Abó, Acoma, and Pecos were complex stone structures, surrounded by supporting outbuildings, such as the *convento* used to house the priests.

Spanish settlements commonly grew up around the missions, which resembled fortresses and were centers of farming, commerce, and education. In addition to being the center of religious life, the missions and later church buildings with their heavy doors and thick walls acted as places of safety during attack by marauding Indians.

Even small villages in New Mexico had a Catholic church, which often faced the village's plaza or the main road. For example, the town of Las Trampas (officially Santo Tomás Apostal del Río de Las Trampas, "Saint Thomas the Apostle of the River of Traps") was founded in 1751 and construction of the Catholic church, San José de Graciá de Las Trampas, was started in the early 1760s and completed in 1776. The town and its mission helped to serve as buffer against marauding Indians. The original town was built as a stronghold with adobe houses surrounding a square plaza that could protect the livestock in case of attack. Two narrow entrances to the plaza could be barricaded if necessary.

The church built at Abiquiu was Santa Tomás. The massive San Francisco de Asis ("St. Francis of Assisi") Church was built about four miles south of Taos in 1772 by Franciscan missionaries. San Felipe de Neri church was built on the plaza in Albuquerque, which was founded in 1706 around a plaza that was similar to Santa Fe. The church at Truchas (for *las truchas*, the trout in nearby mountain streams), named Nuestra Señora del Rosario, San Fernando y Santiago del Río de las Truchas, was founded in 1754.[17]

The church of El Santuario de Chimayó, often called the "Lourdes of America" was noted for its reputed healing powers for physical and mental ills. A little dry well (*pocito*) in a side room supplied holy dirt and the room was lined with crutches of those who had allegedly been healed. As many as 30,000 people, young and old, still come to the Santuario, many on foot, at Easter time when pilgrims can be seen walking along the highways, some carrying wooden crosses on their shoulders.[18] The name *Chimayó* came from a Tewa Indian word *tsimayo* that meant "good flaking stone."

Mission churches typically had no pews or benches inside. Indians and others who came to hear Mass had to stand or kneel. Seats were added later. Mass was recited in Latin, the same as churches in Europe at the time.

Wine

When the Franciscan missionaries arrived in the 1500s they brought wine with them. Wine for church purposes was originally brought by ship from Spain to Mexico in stone jugs, then was carried north to Santa Fe from Chihuahua in the mission wagon trains. Some wine was also grown around El Paso del Norte (near modern El Paso) along the Camino Real highway, just south of the Mexican border on the Rio Grande.

As colonization efforts increased in the 1600s the friars brought grapevines north from Mexico in order to make their own sacramental wine instead of relying on shipments from Mexico. Some of the oldest wineries in the United States were located in New Mexico. Franciscan friars planted some of the first vines near present-day Socorro in the Rio Grande valley in 1630. This was probably the first vineyard in the United States. In 1776 friar Francisco Domínguez noted that the Indians of the Isleta Pueblo, just south of Albuquerque, were growing grapes and drinking wine.

The wine produced for church masses was fermented by a wild yeast that occurred naturally on the skin of the grapes. Grapes of this variety, which still grow in New Mexico today, were known as "mission grapes." The grapes were crushed in the traditional European manner in large wooden vats by women who walked up and down on the ripe fruit with their bare feet. Fermentation was carried out in wooden kegs or large ceramic jugs. As small glass bottles were scarce at the time, wine was typically served from a *bota*, a traditional wine bag made from leather and lined with a goat's bladder. In more affluent households, the large glass jugs that were used for shipping olive oil from Spain were re-used for bulk storage of wine.

By the mid-nineteenth century, more wine was being produced in New Mexico than in California. By 1884, over 3,000 acres of grapes were providing about a million gallons of wine a year and New Mexico was the fifth largest producer of wine in the United States.

Religious Art

Hispanic artists called *santeros* (saint-makers) crafted sacred objects that reflected the strong faith of the people. The first generation of *santeros* who migrated northwards from the area of southern New Spain were active from about 1750 to 1800, with new concepts and techniques being introduced by New Mexican-born artists after about 1800. The *santero* art and traditions are fully active today.

Among the works these artisans created were religious images of saints called *santos*, which occupied altars, decorated churches, and were placed in niches (*nichos*) in homes. Most of the art was founded on traditional Christian images that had been brought north from Mexico, which in turn were based on Northern European religious art. Some of the art was used to decorate mission churches. The *santos* consisted of carved and painted wooden statues of the saints (*bultos*) and paintings of religious scenes (*retablos*). Retablos were two-dimensional images ordinarily painted with bright pigments on skin panels or pine boards coated with gesso. The images were not sacred, but the saints they represented were. These unique forms of religious folk art reached a peak in northern New Mexico in the late 1700s and lasted well into the last half of the 1800s. Among the important saints were San José (St. Joseph), San Francisco (St. Francis), San Felipe (St. Philip), and San Antonio (St. Anthony). Other important religious figures were the Virgin Mary and the Holy Child.

Santeros were generally limited to making wooden carvings from soft pine or cottonwood, as those were the only materials available locally to them. *Bultos* were typically carved from cottonwood. Paint did not stick to the newly-carved wood, so the images were coated with gesso (*yeso*) to prepare the surface and then painted with pigments made from home-made natural materials. The gesso was a mixture of crushed gypsum (chalk), water, and glue.

The *santero* made his own paints. The *bultos* were first coated with the gesso and then were painted with pigments from homemade natural materials. Black coloration was created from soot or charcoal from wood ashes. Blue pigments were extracted from the indigo plant and yellow from the chamisa plant. Browns were created from limonite (a yellowish-brown iron ore) and red from hematite (iron ore). After the paint was dry, the *santos* were covered with a protective coating of varnish made from wax, water, and pine sap.

Religious statues were often decorated with marbles for eyes and hair on their heads, and were dressed in cloth garments. A favorite subject of the *santeros* was Our Lady of Sorrows, a painted statue made primarily from pine.

Images of the Virgin Mary, in particular, became a focus for the religious beliefs in Spanish colonial life from the 1500s well into the 1900s. Paintings and statues depicted various events in her life and were displayed in churches and the homes of the upper classes. Missionaries used these images as both a focus for religious devotion and as a teaching tool for the uneducated and illiterate. Figures of the crucified Christ, for example, were an important theme in churches.[19] Altars frequently displayed life-sized effigies of Christ on the Cross and the Virgin Mary. Behind them, elaborately-carved altar screens (*reredos*) were found in many churches and chapels in New Mexico. One of the oldest in New Mexico, dating from 1798, is in the Chapel of San Miguel in Santa Fe.

Another common religious object was the *milagro* (miracle), a metal charm used as a personal amulet or given as an offering to a saint. *Milagros* were also left as offerings at churches or shrines to ask for help with a particular personal problem or to offer thanks for a prayer that was answered. They were small and flat, made typically from tin, metal, or even pure silver. They were made as a likeness of humans, animals, or an object related to the prayer being made. First introduced by Spanish missionaries, *milagros* continue as important religious tokens today.

Many *santos* were taken from northern New Mexico into southern Colorado as settlers moved there in the mid–1800s. The images the *santeros* made were not merely decorative. They were used in ceremonies celebrating birth, marriage, and death, and for agricultural festivals and daily religious worship. The *santos* were addressed with prayers in times of need, and might be offered food, clothing, or flowers to obtain intervention by the saints they represented. If the prayer was not answered, the *santo* might be turned temporarily to face the wall.

A popular subject for the *santeros* was the *carreta de la muerte* ("cart of death"), a replica of a two-wheeled *carreta* ranging from a small model to life-size. The cart contained an upright carved wooden skeleton of a woman dressed in long garments with a black shawl over her head and shoulders, armed with a bow and arrow. This was the allegorical Angel of Death (*La Doña Sebastiana*). The origin of the name is unclear, but may be somehow related to the killing of St. Sebastian with arrows. The skeleton figure usually held the bow in its hands with the bowstring pulled back and an arrow ready to be released, symbolizing death as omnipresent. Sometimes the figure held an axe. The face often had a blindfold over the eye sockets to symbolize the uncertainty of the time when death would strike.[20] The figure was a constant reminder that those on this earth should not be beguiled by human joys without due consideration of the next world.

Death was a constant reality for the colonists, often from disease, accidents, or raiding Indians. However, death and the dead were not treated as morbid subjects. The *Dia de los Muertos* ("Day of the Dead"), a tradition popularized in the late 1800s (though probably having its origins in an Aztec festival far earlier than Spanish colonization), was a private or family feast on November 2 each year that took place in the family home. It was not a morbid event and did not involves graves, but was a time of celebration when the departed souls were considered to return as spirits for a few brief hours to be with their living relatives at a family reunion.

The Penitentes

A darker side of religion in New Mexico and southern Colorado was provided by the Penitentes, a lay religious order. The Penitentes, known also as *Los Hermanos Penitentes* ("The Penitent Brothers") and *Los Hermanos de Jesús* ("The Brothers of Jesus"), were a religious sect that flourished in the remoter regions of northern New Mexico and southern Colorado, particularly during the 1800s. It is possible that the origin of the religious group that became known in America as the Penitentes was as an offshoot of the secular workers from the Third Order of St. Francis.[21] Others scholars, however, feel that the Penitentes were unrelated of the Orders of St. Francis.[22] Admittedly, though, St. Francis was a man who was considered to be an ideal penitent.

The First Order of St. Francis consisted of the Franciscan priests. The Second Order was composed of nuns. The Third Order were lay Franciscans whose members preferred the secular life and were not part of the clergy, but satisfied their religious desires by living holy lives and dedicating themselves to assisting Franciscan friars in the saving of souls. The name "Penitente" appears to be of Anglo-American origin and was not commonly used by Spanish Americans.[23]

The Penitentes believed that the way to be cleansed of earthly sin was through bodily punishment. They achieved this by flogging themselves, walking, standing, or lying on the thorns of the *cholla* cactus, placing sharp stones in their shoes, and being bound to wooden crosses in mock crucifixions.[24] The instruments for flogging were whips (*disciplinas*) made from the roots or spines of the yucca plant that was common to the region. Some scourges were made from chain-link or iron wire with protruding barbs, similar to barbed-wire. Some were made from leather with small pieces of glass or metal embedded in them to ensure that they cut into the skin when used.[25]

A few of the more fervent believers re-enacted the crucifixion, acting as a substitute Christ by being strapped to a wooden cross at Easter. One brother carried the cross while others beat him and themselves with yucca, chains, and other whips that left bloody wounds on their backs.[26] The rituals were accompanied by the singing of hymns (*alabados*).

The Penitente belief of the atonement for sin through personal suffering was influenced in the Southwest by the dark side of religion in Europe in the Middle Ages. The Penitentes were not a new brotherhood, but had existed in the 1400s and 1500s in Spain and Portugal, and had arrived with the conquistadors. Self-inflicted penance to gain purification by religious orders, and particularly the use of flagellation, was well-known in medieval Europe and had been used as far back as biblical times. By the 1100s and 1200s, the practice of self-flagellation had spread to almost every village in Europe. Organized societies of flagellants existed in Italy in the 1200s.[27] Self-inflicted whipping was practiced in Germany during the Black Plague of the 1300s, and then spread to Spain and Portugal, where it was used in festivals and by secretive brotherhoods.[28] By 1349 the practice became so widespread and violent that Pope Clement VI issued a papal edict to suppress it; however, the appeal to some of the participants was so great that the directive failed to stop the practice.

The Franciscans, the Dominicans, the Jesuits, and the Carmelites all practiced self-flagellation.[29] The Franciscan friars believed that holiness and humility were promoted through mortification of the flesh, thus the practice of self-flagellation appealed to them. This led to penance of fanatical proportions, particularly during Easter Holy Week when they re-enacted the suffering and crucifixion of Christ. During the Holy Week of 1598, Gaspar Perez de Villagrá, traveling with Juan de Oñate to found the northern province of New Mexico wrote, "The night was one of prayer and penance for all. The soldiers, with cruel scourges, beat their backs unmercifully until the camp ran crimson with their blood. The humble Franciscan friars, barefoot and clothed in cruel, thorny girdles, devoutly chanted their doleful hymns, praying forgiveness for their sins. Don Juan [de Oñate], unknown to anyone except me, went to a secluded spot where he cruelly scourged himself, mingling bitter tears with the blood which flowed from the many wounds."[30]

The emergence of the Penitentes in New Mexico may have been the result of a lack of formal visits by priests to serve the needs of devout Spanish-Americans in isolated rural and poor areas. In 1750, there were about 4,200 Spanish colonists in New Mexico, but only 25 resident priests. Under Spanish rule, therefore, settlers received only occasional visits from priests from the larger churches. When the Mexican government took control of New Mexico in 1821, it secularized the territory by expelling the Franciscan priests. Secularization was complete by 1840. Thus, though nearly all villages had their own Catholic church, there was no resident priest. In response, the richer colonists built small private family chapels on their own land to met their spiritual needs.

As the church system disintegrated, an inadequate number of priests was available to serve the common population and Catholic rituals fell into neglect. In response, men in the small villages of northern New Mexico organized into local groups to maintain Christian values and customs in the absence of any other religious leadership. The Penitentes strove for a higher understanding of God through prayer and penance, and sought the ideals of Christian morality and brotherly love, thus providing a religious focus for the villagers.[31]

Though the origin of the Penitentes in New Mexico will probably never be conclusively proven, there is some historical evidence that the Penitente organization may have had its formal beginnings in 1810 in Santa Cruz de la Cañada, an important religious center on the Santa Cruz land grant in north-central New Mexico near Chimayó. There may also have been a previous organization that practiced ceremonies that resembled Penitente rituals in the mid–1790s in Santa Cruz and Santa Fe.[32] According to fray Alonso de Benavides, there were Penitentes in Santa Cruz as early as 1634.

A more recent Franciscan, fray Angélico Chávez, writing about the Hispanic people of northern New Mexico, believed that the Penitentes emerged in the Santa Cruz region in the late 1700s due to migration of Penitente members from Mexico, whose origins can be traced back to Spanish roots.[33] The Penitentes are certainly recorded to have been in existence in New Mexico in 1818.[34] One creditable account was given by Josiah Gregg, an early Santa Fe trader, who later recorded his observations of frontier life in a popular book titled *Commerce of the Prairies* (1840).

The Penitentes were outlawed in Spain, Portugal, and New Spain in the 1700s. Taking their cue from their European forerunners, Penitente practices in New Mexico included self-flagellation, simulated crucifixions, prayers, and devotional exercises. Because of these extreme practices, the Catholic Church banned the Penitente brotherhood from its inception and ordered that it be suppressed, but circumstances in New Mexico were such that it flourished instead.

Though the Penitentes were best-known for their Holy Week rituals, they also furnished charitable services for their fellow villagers and rendered assistance to them whenever necessary. Isolated far from civil and religious leaders in small villages, they provided leadership, charity, and mutual aid. Their duties included Christian deeds, such as clothing, feeding, and providing food and firewood for the poor, tending crops and animals for disabled people, visiting and caring for the sick, comforting the sorrowing, conducting burial services for the dead, and organizing religious feasts.

In the 1800s, the Penitentes came into conflict with the Catholic Church, who tried to suppress the movement for what the Church saw as excessive zeal during their extreme rituals practiced during Holy Week. Bishop Zubíria from Durango, who visited Santa Cruz in 1833 was horrified at the excesses he saw there and claimed that it was the "devil's workshop."[35] In spite of their charitable side, condemnation of the Pentitentes occurred in the 1880s and 1890s when Anglo-Americans settled in New Mexico. As late as the 1880s the brotherhood was still so active that additional church bans were issued.[36] In 1899 the Penitentes were explicitly condemned and members excommunicated by the Archbishop of Santa Fe. Penitente practices were perceived as barbaric rituals and were condemned for this. Whether there was proof of this or not, or whether this view was based on legend and speculation has not been definitively proven.[37]

Popular books and magazines aroused an interest in the reading public when they reported melodramatic accounts of Penitente rituals, often unsubstantiated, in which participants staggered beneath huge crosses, whipped themselves during ceremonies, and stabbed themselves with thorns and cactus as they toiled to their place of crucifixion. One article in *Harper's* magazine in 1876 reported: "The cross is laid upon the ground and the bearer is so firmly bound to it by lengths of rawhide that the circulation of the blood is retarded, and a gradual discoloration of the body follows."[38] Resting places (*descansos*) were available along the way for the participating Penitentes to rest for a few moments during

The penitentes practiced their beliefs in secret in unobtrusive windowless meeting houses called *moradas*, where they could perform their rituals in private. Penitente *moradas* were typically found in isolated areas on the edges of small villages of northern New Mexico and southern Colorado, and could often be identified by tall wooden crosses located nearby.

their wearisome trek. The *carreta de la muerte* was commonly used in these outdoor Penitente processions. The wheels of the cart were usually locked in place to provide greater resistance, so it had to be dragged along by one or two Penitente brothers using a rough rope that cut severely into the flesh of their bare shoulders.

Because of these sensational accounts and the ensuing uproar they caused, the Penitentes disappeared from public view after the 1880s and practiced their beliefs in secret in unobtrusive meeting houses and lodges with small windows, called *moradas*, where they could practice their rituals in private. Participants concealed their identities with black hoods. Pressure, however, was still applied by the church and civil government to stop these practices.

The penitentes were most active in northern New Mexico and southern Colorado between about 1850 and 1890.[39] Their *moradas* were typically found in isolated areas on the edges of small villages and could often be identified by tall wooden crosses located nearby. By the late 1800s *moradas* were found in most villages in north-central New Mexico that lay east of the Sangre de Cristo Mountains.[40]

The Penitente *morada* was usually a long, flat-roofed, adobe-walled building containing a meeting room, a chapel (*oratorio*) with an altar and religious ornaments, and a third room for storing Penitente equipment and paraphernalia, such as crosses, masks the men wore, and the whips they used during self-flagellation. The *moradas* were built for prayers and penance, so were not elaborate inside, though figures of the crucified Christ formed a prominent theme of the decorations.

Southern Colorado and northern New Mexico still contain the ruins of former *moradas* that have been abandoned. In Colorado the majority were in Las Animas, Conejos, and Costilla counties, and in New Mexico in Taos, Rio Arriba, and San Miguel counties. Abandoned *moradas* can still be seen next to many of the old villages, such as San Francisco, San Luis, and Fowler in Colorado. A penitente *morada* was located in Los Pinos east of the bridge. A *morada*, now abandoned, stands on Eighth Street in San Luis. A reproduction of a *morada* can be visited among the buildings at *El Rancho de las Golondrinas*, south of Santa Fe.

The Penitentes were a powerful influence in rural northern New Mexico and southern Colorado until the 1920s. They filled a responsible role in rural communities by taking care of spiritual functions when no clergy available, caring for the sick, punishing miscreants if necessary, and administering charitable aspects of the villages as necessary. Membership dwindled severely by the 1940s as changing social conditions and government assistance programs lessened the need for their services.[41]

In 1947, the Catholic Church recognized the estimated 10,000 Penitentes in New Mexico and southern Colorado as a lay brotherhood, officially known as the *Hermanos de Nuestro Padre Jesús Nazareno*.[42] As part of this recognition, the Penitentes were ordered to stop their fanatical methods of penance, including self-flagellation and any activities related to crucifixion. Carlson, however, has claimed that as late as 1952 there were ninety active Penitente chapters in Rio Arriba and forty more in New Mexico.[43] Medical examiners at military induction centers have reportedly noted scars on the backs of Penitente brothers.[44] Though not visible, Warren claimed that Penitente chapters were still active as late as 1987.[45]

CHAPTER FIVE

A Clash of Beliefs

When the Spanish returned to New Mexico in the 1580s and 1590s they came as missionaries and then colonizers. Missionary activity in the Southwest by the Spanish, however, turned into a fierce struggle between two religious ideologies. On one side was the existing native religion and beliefs of the Pueblo Indians, and on the other was the Christian missionary zeal of the Franciscan friars. The Franciscans wielded the power to force their views on the Indians as the Spanish were backed by fighting men. There was no way that the natives could win a battle on equal terms against the skilled and disciplined Spanish troops.[1] Bows, arrows, and spears could not prevail over Spanish swords, rifles, chain mail, and cannons.

Another factor in the conflict was that secular colonial officials were continually at odds with the church over control of the labor and the souls of Indian converts, the most prevalent and richest resource that New Mexico had to offer. To fuel the struggle, secular officials sometimes quietly encouraged Indians to resist church control. In return, the Franciscans claimed that government officials were undermining their authority. One typical example occurred on a Sunday in the early 1660s at the Quarai mission during a sermon by Fray Nicholás de Freitas about the importance of obedience to God. Nicolás de Aguilar, the local government magistrate, suddenly interrupted him by shouting that the Indians owed their primary allegiance to the King of Spain and his government officials, not to God.

Resistance by local natives to Spanish rule stretched back to the early conquest by Columbus. Under the *encomienda*, the feudal system that allotted conquered natives to the Spanish as workers, the Indians were forced to dredge streams looking for gold, to work the fields for Spanish land owners, and to build towns for them. As part of their resistance, Indians even killed their families and committed suicide rather than submit to Spanish rule. Others resisted more actively and fought back. But, along the way, the Indians also learned much about Spanish tactics and strategy, and other techniques of warfare. Those who captured Spanish soldiers were merciless. To satisfy the apparent Spanish hunger for gold, some captured conquistadors had the molten metal poured down their throats.[2]

The Spanish explorers who colonized the Southwest in the early 1600s claimed the land and existing settlements for Spain, in the process enslaving as many of the Indian inhabitants as possible. The colonists were unaware of the diversity in cultures that existed between the two overall existing Indian groups, the sedentary Pueblos with their multi-story adobe towns and fixed farmlands, and the mobile nomadic and semi-nomadic groups of raiding Apache, Comanche, Ute, and Navajo. The Spanish assumed that the Pueblo Indians, because they lived in permanent locations, were more civilized than other Indians who lived a nomadic existence with no permanent "towns." The Spanish, however, did not understand that the pueblos were not the same as European villages, but were made up of groups of people living together in large buildings with their internal relationships defined by kin.[3]

Though the Franciscan friars attempted to expand their area of Indian conversion to the Plains tribes, the nomadic ways of these groups and their warlike tendencies made the task difficult. The Pueblo Indians were indeed more suited to become converts to the way of life around the missions than their nomadic cousins due to their sedentary existence, and were easier to convert and control as they lived in a fixed location.

By the time Oñate and his colonists arrived in New Mexico in 1598, the pueblo people already had a well-developed culture and agriculture, and were generally not aggressive. In fact, the tribal name Hopi means "peaceful ones." However, the arrival of the Spanish with their priests and soldiers overran and almost destroyed the existing culture. The colonists introduced forced labor for the men and sexually abused the women, treating both with contempt and hostility. They seized Indian corn as tribute and pastured their horses in the cornfields. The colonizers looked upon the Indians as being incapable of assimilating true civilization and as merely a pool of labor to be exploited in the interests of the more "advanced" Spanish civilization.

When missionaries arrived at the pueblos, further conflict was inevitable. Religious beliefs were at the center of Indian lives and they did not want to change their ways. The friars, on their side, felt that any means of saving the Indians from eternal damnation was acceptable, including floggings and hangings.

Along with basic instruction in Christianity, the Pueblo Indians who were forced under the mission umbrella were taught European farming, iron and leather working, carpentry, and methods of weaving with wool. The priests focused much of their attention on the children hoping that when they grew up they would already be converted.

The Clash of Beliefs

When the Spanish sought to alter and suppress native religious beliefs in favor of Christian conversion, problems arose immediately because the missionaries did not understand the existing Indian culture or religion, and attempted to suppress Indian religious practices as superstitions. Indian shamans, or medicine men, were considered by the Franciscans to be sorcerers and agents of the Devil. Those who dared resist or deny the Spanish religion were flogged, burned at the stake, garroted or made into slaves.

The issues surrounding the clash between the missionaries and the native Indian inhabitants of New Mexico cannot be understood in only Spanish terms or Indian terms, but it is necessary to consider both viewpoints. As author Carroll Riley has pointed out, "Religion—any religion—obtains its validity from internal acceptance and not from any external 'proof.'"[4]

Among other Indian habits, the Franciscans strongly opposed the katsina religion and its outward expression of native prayers and ceremonies. They were repelled because they felt the Pueblo fertility and weather-control ceremonies, along with what they felt were accompanying horrendous costumes, masks, and infernal singing that ended in orgies, were a form of Devil worship. Conversion for the masses, therefore, began with renouncing Satan, banishing his earthly assistants (i.e., the Indian medicine men), and forsaking all superstitious beliefs and idols. At one point the friars petitioned Governor Mendizábel to ban any native celebrations. Mendizábel, however, thought that the dances were simply pleasurable entertainment and saw no reason to prohibit them, thus infuriating the friars.

To the Pueblo Indians, however, these ceremonies and rituals were essential to ensure plentiful rain, abundant crops, and good hunting, particularly at the time of the terrible droughts of the late 1660s and early 1670s. The katsina ceremonies were also performed to keep the Pueblo world in balance and participants felt that without them the Pueblo people would suffer. For this reason it was difficult for the Franciscan fathers to stamp out the katsina ceremonies, and they continued to be practiced in secret. The prevailing opinion of the friars in New Mexico was summed up in 1660 by fray Nicolás de Freitas when he said, "It has been impossible to correct their concubinage, the abominable crime of idolatry, their accursed superstitions, idolatrous dances, and other faults."[5]

To emphasize the perceived superiority of the Catholic Church over the katsina religion, the friars often built their churches directly on top of existing pueblos and kivas. The

These ruins are at Wupatki in north-central Arizona, which was occupied by Sinagua Indians between about 1120 and 1210. In the background are the snow-capped San Francisco Peaks. The Hopi believed that the *katsinas* returned to the underworld by means of a ladder on top of the peaks, staying there until they emerged again in the spring to bring rain to the crops.

Spanish tried to eradicate the kiva because of its religious significance to the people. Missionaries supported by soldiers went into kivas and defiled and destroyed sacred artifacts, such as the katsina masks, fetishes, and prayer bundles, thus destroying a village's most important religious symbols. In 1661, for example, fray Alonso de Posada at Quarai outlawed the dances and burned all the masks and other katsina paraphernalia that he could lay his hands on.

The Spanish believed that the perceived superiority of their religion would eventually overcome the native beliefs. To help to convince the Indians, friars at the missions staged religious dramas which depicted the defeat of the Indian culture and the triumph of Christianity. The Franciscans tried to achieve total control of the Pueblo Indians. Converts were expected to kneel before the Franciscans and kiss their hands or feet. In return the priests offered salvation and a better way of life. How much of this the natives actually understood is doubtful. In one sense, the friars assumed the role of the native shaman and simply took the place of Indian rain-priests, hunt chiefs, and medicine men.[6] The Christian cross, for example, was perceived by the Indians as a type of prayer stick.[7] At first the medicine men were willing to accept the new Christian God and saints if that would help to create and maintain the harmony in the world that they sought. They hoped that acceptance of Christian beliefs would tie the Spanish and Indian cultures together. Soon, however, during the ensuing years of drought and disease, they felt that these new gods were not powerful enough to grant their requests for summer rains and productive harvests, so they turned away from them and went back to their traditional religious leaders and ceremonies. The religious leaders of the pueblos derisively called converts "wet-heads" from the practice of baptism.[8]

Drugs

Part of Indian ritual and religious ceremonies involved the use of drugs from various plants for spiritual purposes, a practice that the Franciscans perceived as diabolical. Various plants were used for their narcotic and hallucinatory properties.

One such drug commonly used was a hallucinogen that came from the datura plant, *Datura meteloides*, a desert-growing plant with large leaves and trumpet-shaped flowers that ranged in color from white to purple. This plant and others in the same botanical family are also variously known as Jimson weed, devil's weed, loco weed, hell's bells, thorn apple, and stinkweed. The plant was either squeezed into a liquid or dried and powdered. When ingested, the preparation produced hallucinations and bizarre behavior that were used to interpret religious visions. This drug was used by the Hopi, Zuni, Navajo, Apache, and Utes.

The use of the hallucinogen peyote by the Indians to produce euphoric visions during religious practices was documented by the Spanish as early as 1631.[9] Peyote occurred as a small, low-growing, spineless cactus with the scientific name of *Lophophora williamsii*. The top, or crown, which grew above ground, consisted of flattened spheres called buttons that were dried in the sun and then chewed to release an alkaloid called mescaline. This substance induced changes in consciousness and produced psychedelic effects. The Spanish priests called peyote buttons *raiz diabolica* (literally the "Devil's Root" in Spanish) as they did not like its use in native ceremonies.

Pueblo Sexuality

Another of the major clashes between the missionaries and the Indians concerned native sexuality, which the Franciscans sought to alter from what they saw as inappropriate behavior. For the Pueblo Indians, sex was a natural part of their way of life. Sexual intercourse was a symbol of cosmic harmony through the union of opposites, male-female and sky-earth.[10] The Pueblo Indians were open and uninhibited with their sexuality, whereas the Franciscans friars were celibate and the Indians felt that made them incomplete men.

As one example, many Indian men liked having sex with the woman on all fours using rear entry. The priests did not like this. They felt it violated nature by its bestial character and lowered the Indians to the level of animals.[11] The missionaries felt that what was known as the "missionary position," with the man on top and the woman underneath, was the only correct and proper way.[12] Similarly, intercourse with the woman on top was considered "contrary to the order of nature."[13] One rather personal question asked by priests of native converts in the confessional was "Have you had intercourse with someone contrary to the ordinary manner?"[14] Men and women who engaged in such "bestial" activities and violated the Franciscans' perceived Christian morality were publicly whipped to purge such behavior out of them.[15]

The Franciscans wanted the Indians to accept chastity before marriage, fidelity within it, lifelong monogamy, and modesty and shame in bodily matters. Another question asked in the confessional was, "Have you shown some part of your body to arouse in some person desires of lust or to excite them?"[16] The friars prohibited polygamy, concubines, and promiscuity. The Pueblo Indians, on the other hand, practiced serial monogamy, polygamy, bisexuality, and tolerated sexual variations.[17]

One social and sexual variation was the *berdache*, a man who played the cultural role of a woman in pueblo society. A *berdache*, also common among other American Indians tribes, was a biological male who dressed as a woman, adopted women's mannerisms and role in society, and submitted to sodomy. In the Indian world these men were accepted as followers of religious visions and were considered to have special cultural and religious powers. The Spanish, on the other hand, viewed them as male whores (*putos*) and sodomites (*sodomitas*).[18] The friars considered the practice to be despicable. Part of this practice may have drifted north from Central America, where Aztec priests were unmarried, but practiced sodomy.[19]

The Franciscan priests were in a difficult position regarding sex. In the Spanish world, the size of the male organ was equated with virility and masculinity, and a man who did not assert his sexuality was considered to be tame, submissive, and perhaps lacking in physical endowment. Priests were supposed to be aggressive, masculine authority figures, yet their vows of chastity reduced them to the position of being pure and sexually inactive, which the Indians did not understand.

The priests vowed celibacy, and sexual desire in friars was supposed to be sublimated through prayers, hymns, and sermons. However, many of them fornicated with local women with little discretion and kept the resulting children around them at their missions. Fray Nicolás Hidalgo at Taos Pueblo, for example, raped Indian women and fathered a number of illegitimate children.[20] Others practiced sexual variations, such as sodomy.

Another gender-based issue was that the Pueblo Indians were matrilineal at the time of the Spanish conquest. Women controlled much of Pueblo society and an individual's lineage was traced through his or her female ancestors. Women owned the houses and land, and gave their clan name to their children. The Spanish, who traced their ancestry through their fathers, did not understand or agree with this ancient Indian system and tried to convert the Pueblo Indians to patrilineal thinking. In some cases they succeeded, but the Pueblos that resisted Christianity, primarily the Hopi and Zuni, remained matrilineal.[21]

Abuse of the Indians

The Franciscans did not like the katsina ceremonies and, in retaliation for their practice by the Indians, tried to eliminate them through severe disciplinary actions. Whipping and hanging were common punishments. Retributions were often cruel and fueled by religious bigotry. One common punishment was flogging the offender to beat the "badness" out of him, even to the point of death. In 1655, when Hopi Indian Juan Cuna was caught practicing his own religion, fray Salvador de Guerra whipped him in public until he was covered in blood. He was taken inside the church and whipped again, then drenched in turpentine and set on fire. Even though Cuna died, Guerra continued to administer the same punishment to others. He was known to use his whipping and hot turpentine treatment on both boys and girls.[22] Governor Fernando de Argüello Carvajál had forty Indians whipped and imprisoned for "sedition." Another form of severe punishment was hanging these "devil-worshippers." Carvajál hanged twenty-nine leaders from the Jemez Pueblo for aiding the Apache and Navajo.[23]

Though whipping would seem like an excessive punishment for minor transgressions, at the time it was commonly administered by the Spanish as punishment for a multitude of infractions. The recipients ranged from schoolboys to soldiers. At the same time, eager for self-mortification, some of the Franciscans wore hair shirts containing bristle or metal wires on the inside and practiced self-flagellation, painful practices that the Indians did not understand. As friars routinely beat themselves with whips to the point of bleeding to atone for their sins, they assumed that this was also an appropriate punishment for the Indians. Some friars were even not averse to martyrdom, a circumstance that came sooner than some of them had thought, given the likelihood of Indian rebellions and attacks by raiders.

As milder forms of punishment, friars publicly humiliated native holy men and compelled them and the villagers to perform penance by working on irrigation ditches and fields. Another punishment technique was to humiliate the Indians in front of their children.

A person's head was considered to be the symbol of his personal honor. For example, the King's honor was symbolized by his crown, and that of the Pope and bishops through their miters. Similarly the tonsure of priests was a sign of their vows of chastity and purity. Knowing this, priests cut the hair or shaved the heads of recalcitrant mission Indians to punish them with an act that was considered to be a dreadful punishment and indignity. Some subjected to this punishment were so mortified that they ran away from the missions. Decapitation, or total loss of the head, was thought to be a particularly dishonorable punishment.

Other punishments handed out by some priests would today be considered to be sexual abuse. Loss of the penis (the virile member or *miembro*) was considered to be emasculation and abuse of this was used as a punishment. For example, when friar Baltasar Baca found Asensio, a Nambé Indian, stealing his watermelons in 1743, he grabbed him by the penis and twisted it until Asensio fainted from the pain.[24] Indians of the Taos Pueblo complained to the governor about the harsh treatment they received from fray Nicolás Hidalgo, who punished insolence in the natives by castration and sodomy.[25] In one instance, Pedro Acomilla of Taos Pueblo complained in court in 1638 that fray Nicolás Hidalgo had twisted his virile member so much that it literally broke off the end.[26] Hidalgo was also known for punishing rebellious Indians by grabbing them by their testicles and twisting them until the victims collapsed in pain. He was relieved of his duties in 1639.

Hidalgo's replacement, fray Pedro de Miranda, became angry at the Indians for their complaints. Finally they had enough and, on December 28, 1639, they rebelled and killed him and two soldiers. For good measure they then demolished the church and *convento*. This same scene was repeated at Jemez Pueblo a few days later and fray Diego de San Lucas was killed. Both pueblos rejected the Franciscans and killed the friars and their escorts. These rebellions shook the colony and brought down a storm of protest against the governor.

Contemporary court records describe sodomy as another of the punishments that some of the priests used. The offending Indian was made to assume a position on his hands and knees while the priest sodomized him. This was considered to be a humiliating and degrading punishment and was equated with submission and defeat.[27] In one instance, Francisco Quaelone and an Indian called "El Mulatto" were sodomized for insubordination, using this submissive posture that the Spanish regarded as a symbol of capitulation.[28]

Repressed sexuality among some priests led to instances of sodomy other than its use for punishment. In 1606 a Franciscan friar named Pedro tried to overwhelm Gaspar Reyes with food and wine with the intent of sodomizing him.[29] According to government records, in 1761 fray Francisco Pulido confessed his human frailty by admitting to investigators of the Inquisition that he had committed the sin of sodomy several times with an Indian servant.[30] Other complaints about sodomy from Indians are found in contemporary records from the 1600s. Indians continued to be punished in this way into the 1700s.[31]

A sexual double-standard existed also among Spanish men. Hispanic males judged masculinity by the number of female conquests a man made. The Franciscans preached monogamy to the Indians and expected it of them, while soldiers and some of the priests, in spite of the shortage of women in the provinces, were indulging in extramarital affairs, molesting their Indians servants, and having illegitimate children by both. Such hypocrisy must have been duly noted by the Pueblo Indians.

Pueblo Discontent

Conversion of the Pueblo Indians left them in a situation of mixed blessings. Among the advantages were new types of crops and farm animals, a safe place to live at the missions with sufficient food, and access to trade goods. On the other side of the coin, they were subject to strange new diseases, were forced to labor for the good of the missions, were subject to attempts to stamp out their native religious practices, and had many of their cultural ways destroyed because such practices did not suit their new Christian masters.

Resentment by pueblo residents that they had to give up their religion and, at the same time, donate a large part of their crops to the missions, led to the Indians trying to overthrow their conquerors in various rebellions. At Jemez Pueblo in 1623, Indians killed the friars, burned the church, and fled to the hills. Fray Pedro de Miranda was killed in fighting at Taos Pueblo in 1631. In 1632 Zunis killed friar Francisco de Letrado and friar Martín de Arvide, decapitated and scalped them, and cut off their hands and feet for trophies.[32]

The residents of Taos Pueblo rebelled again in 1639. Rebellions took place again at Jemez in 1644 and 1647. These frequent attempts to overthrow Spanish rule and drive them out were quickly and brutally suppressed by the Spanish and rebels were severely punished. Leaders were either summarily hanged or sold into slavery. As a result, opposition to the Spanish went underground. Forms of resistance became passive and were more subtle. The medicine men at Taos Pueblo, for example, added urine and mouse meat to the friar's corn tortillas.[33]

The Spanish managed to easily crush smaller uprisings because Pueblo resistance was not organized and the Spanish had superior fighting tactics. In another attempt at rebellion, Esteban Clemente, a Hispanicized Indian who was the local governor of the Salinas and Tano Pueblos, planned a revolt against the Spanish in 1670. His plan was to drive the Spaniards' horses away, which would leave them on foot, and then he and his men could kill them. The Spanish, however, learned of his plot and he was captured and hanged.[34]

Uprisings were triggered by Spanish demands and exploitation, years of drought and poor crops, disease, and increasing attacks by nomadic Apache Indians. Infectious European diseases that came with the Spanish could not be cured by them and continued to ravage the pueblos. For example, a smallpox epidemic in 1636 killed 20,000 Indians, reducing their numbers from 60,000 to 40,000. At least 3,000 Indians, or about 10 percent of the Pueblo population at the time, died in another smallpox epidemic in 1640. In 1769 San Ildefonso Pueblo declined from 500 inhabitants to only 200 after a smallpox epidemic.

By the mid–1600s, the Pueblo Indians had been trying to cope with an extended drought for some years, which led to crop failure and famine. Families were reduced to eating hides to exist. On top of this, they had to put up with attacks by nomadic tribes that were also faced with drought and began to raid pueblo granaries looking for food.

By the mid–1630s the Apache had obtained horses and became mounted nomads. Hungry Apaches and Navajos increased raids on settlements for food, in the process killing, looting, and stealing. There were not enough soldiers to stop them. By the mid–1640s many Indians felt that the God of the Franciscans was not as powerful as had been claimed, because he did not provide rain, health, prosperity, or peace. As a result, the Indians began to turn away from Catholicism and started to celebrate the katsina dances and rites again. The friars again determined that they should be punished as nonbelievers. A small pueblo uprising broke out in 1642, but was easily suppressed.

From 1660 to 1680 the friars made further active attempts to suppress the native religion. Starvation due to drought and poor crops, enslavement of the people, excessive demands for tribute, and repression of the native religion finally became too much for the Pueblo Indians. As a result, the continued oppression by the Spanish and attempts at suppression of the katsina rituals by Franciscan priests incited a major and unprecedented rebellion against Spanish rule in New Mexico in 1680.

The Pueblo Revolt of 1680

In spite of the efforts of Spanish missionaries, native religion did not go away. Indigenous rites and katsina dances merely appeared to go dormant because the rituals were practiced in secret. At first the katsina dances had been held openly in the village plazas, but Spanish oppression drove the performance of these ceremonies underground, out of public view. Many of the pueblos yielded nominally to avoid retaliation and brutal punishment, but continued incidents of oppression fueled Indian hate and led to the Pueblo Revolt of 1680. This rebellion and temporary overthrow of Spanish rule was the Indian's most successful and spectacular act of defiance against their oppressors. Though the Pueblo Revolt was directed against all Spaniards, vengeance was directed primarily at the missionaries.[35] During the revolt, the Indians destroyed most of the missions and returned to their traditional ways. From the Indian point of view the rebellion was successful as it drove the Spanish out of New Mexico for the next twelve years.

The causes of the revolt were many and complex, but the seeds of the rebellion had been sown many years before. The primary cause was the buildup of resentment in the Pueblo Indians against the Spanish colonial occupation that had taken complete control over their lives. The other significant cause was the continued attacks by the friars on the native ritual beliefs and on Indian spiritual leaders.

The immediate cause of the rebellion occurred in 1675 when Governor Antonio de Otermín's predecessor, Governor Juan Francisco Treviño, rounded up forty-seven Indian religious leaders from several pueblos and brought them to trial as sorcerers, charging them with witchcraft. As a punishment for continuing to practice idolatry and the katsina religion instead of Catholicism, these "sorcerers" were imprisoned in Santa Fe and the governor had them severely flogged. Treviño had three of them (one each at Nambé, San Felipe, and Jemez pueblos) hanged as examples. A fourth hanged himself in prison. The others were reluctantly released after a confrontation between armed Tewa Pueblo warriors and the governor in Santa Fe.[36]

One of the survivors of the incident was Popé (also spelled Popay), a Tewa medicine man from the San Juan Pueblo who had been whipped by the Spanish for refusing to adopt Christianity. Popé, whose name meant "ripe planting," went into hiding at Taos Pueblo and started to make plans to drive the Spanish from New Mexico. Popé preached that happiness and prosperity would not return until the Spanish had been driven out of New Mexico or killed.[37] He accordingly planned an uprising and became the leader of the Pueblo Revolt of 1680. Popé was a religious leader, not a warrior chief, so his role is thought to have been mostly to create organization, to plan strategy, and to provide support through prayer.[38] Popé was a good organizer and public speaker, and had the ability to inflame his fellow Indians with impassioned rhetoric. One of the incentives he promised his followers was that, "who shall kill a Spaniard will get an Indian woman for a wife, and he who kills four will get four women, and he who kills ten or more will have a like number of women."[39]

The rebellion was a complex logistical undertaking and took time to organize. The pueblo culture encouraged independence and the villages had no formal leaders or government, so those who agreed to the revolt had to be persuaded to act in unison. It was a difficult task to contact and enlist the aid of various pueblos, as some of the villages were separated by hundred of miles and the messengers had to travel on foot. To coordinate the attacks, Popé sent two runners from the Tesuque Pueblo to each of the participating pueblos with a knotted cord (called a *mecate de palmilla* in Spanish) that indicated the number of days before the rebellion was to start. Each pueblo was to untie a knot each day. When the last knot was untied, the attack was to begin.

The pueblos were divided in their acceptance of the Spanish. Some Indians were loyal to the Spanish government, which meant that Popé had to be careful that the news of the plot did not leak out to the wrong people who might warn of the impending attack. To keep the plot secret, Popé was even forced to kill his own son-in-law, who was sympathetic to the Spanish cause and opposed the revolt.[40] The leaders of the rebellion did not include the pueblos south of Isleta, because they were not sure of their loyalty.[41]

The pueblos of San Marcos, Taos, Pecos, and La Ciénega had leaders who were friendly to the Spanish. They opposed the revolt and informed Governor Otermín of the plot. Otermín captured the two runners and had them tortured until they told what the knotted cords meant. The plot was exposed; however, the information was garbled and Otermín was convinced that the revolt was supposed to take place on August 13 instead of the actual chosen date of August 11.[42] In any case, when Popé realized what had happened, he moved the date of the attack forward to August 10 in order to take the Spanish by surprise.

The Pueblo Revolt started in the Tesuque Pueblo. The first casualties were a Spanish civil official and a priest who were killed on August 10, 1680. Indians at Santa Clara Pueblo followed with attacks on local New Mexicans. The pueblos at Acoma, Hopi, and Zuni became involved. Governor Otermín was not able to assemble his *encomenderos* and their troops from their outlying ranches and farms in time to provide protection.

The rebelling Indians concentrated first on capturing Spanish horses and mules. They figured that without them the Spaniards could not stand up to mounted Indians. The original plan was to kill all the Spanish males; however, during the first days of the revolt, the Pueblo Indians killed indiscriminately. Within a few days, 401 Spanish men, women, children, and friars out of the 2,500 Spanish residents of New Mexico had been killed, including 21 priests whose mutilated bodies were left on their altars. Churches were ransacked and burned, and their holy furnishings desecrated. Entire families were killed in their homes and fields. Seventy people were killed in the Taos area alone. Thirty were killed at Tiwa.[43]

Pecos was one of the many villages involved in the revolt and the mission church at the pueblo was destroyed by Indians. The rebels heaped branches and brush inside and set fire to the roof and the wooden choir loft. After the roof burned, Tewa and Pecos Indians tore down the bricks that formed the walls until the front of the building collapsed. The Indians built a kiva in the ruins of the *convento*.

Indians involved in the revolt also ransacked and burned the chapel of San Miguel in Santa Fe. In a reflection of what had been done to them earlier, the rebels destroyed and ridiculed sacred Spanish religious symbols. Popé's followers broke and burned the images of Christ, the Virgin Mary and other saints, crosses, and everything related to Christianity.[44]

On August 14, Indians under Popé started a siege of Santa Fe. Otermín and the remain

Pecos Pueblo was a busy crossroads that was the site of trading between the pueblo Indians and those of the Plains. A huge church, at one time the largest structure in New Mexico, was built here in the 1620s. It has been estimated that the building required 300,000 bricks. The church roof was burned and the walls torn down during the Pueblo Revolt of 1680. This is the abandoned shell of the smaller church built on the ruins in 1717 after the Spanish re-took New Mexico.

ing colonists, whose numbers had grown to more than a thousand, barricaded themselves in the Palace of the Governors, placing cannons on the roof for protection. The colonists were besieged with intermittent fighting for five days by 2,000 Indians, some of whom were armed with captured Spanish weapons.[45] Fighting was fierce, but localized, as the rebels overran the houses in the plaza. Finally, they cut off the water supply for Santa Fe. Fearing the worst, Otermín rallied a group of remaining colonists and broke out on August 20 to perform a counterattack against the rebels. He and his men successfully killed 300 Indians and captured 47 others. These prisoners were interrogated, then summarily executed.[46]

On August 21, Otermín reluctantly decided to abandon Santa Fe. Surprisingly, the Indians stood by in silence and let them go. As the colonists retreated south from Santa Fe on a 300-mile journey south to El Paso, they saw burned buildings and piles of mutilated bodies. As the Spanish Catholic friars had shown no tolerance for religion other than their own, the Indians had vented special anger against all the symbols of Christianity, killing and mutilating Franciscan priests, and even covering the chalices with human excrement.[47] Christian crosses, along with images of Christ, the Virgin Mary, and the saints, were all destroyed. Churches were burned and torn down. The church bells were destroyed. At

Sandía Pueblo the mission's statues were covered with excrement. Two chalices were discarded in a basket of manure and the paint on the crucifix had been flayed off with a whip. Feces covered the holy communion table and the arms of a statue of St. Francis had been hacked off with an ax. Similar defilement occurred at other missions.[48]

The most hated symbol of all the Spanish occupation were the Franciscan priests. Twenty-one were killed and many were murdered with extra cruelty. Their bodies were stripped and in some cases were mutilated. The priests at Acoma, Jemez, and Zuni were tortured.[49] At Jemez, fray Juan de Jesús was stripped, tied to the back of a pig, and paraded around the town. Then he was forced to crawl on his hands and knees while warriors rode on his back before they killed him with a sword. All three friars, Francisco Antonio de Loranzana, Juan de Talaban, and José Montes de Oca, were killed at Santo Domingo. Their bodies were dragged into the church and were piled in front of the altar where they were allowed to rot to show the Indian hatred of the missionaries.[50] At Acoma, the Indians stripped fray Lucas Maldonado naked, paraded him through the street, whipping and stoning him, then finished him off with lance thrusts.[51] Two friars, Juan Bernal and Juan Domingo de Vera, were killed at Galisteo, and fray Fernando de Velasco at Pecos.

The retreating Spanish were confused by this show of Indian anger. They could not understand why the revolt had occurred in the first place, as they felt they had tried to offer the Indians only Christian love and redemption. Though the Spanish were horrified by what had happened and what they saw, in all fairness to the Indians, the friars had done the same to katsina masks, kivas, and other Indian religious articles during the conquest, and the Indians simply retaliated in the same way. A group of captured Indians confirmed this when they told Otermin that the Indians had resented Spanish rule because the priests destroyed their religious objects, prohibited their ceremonies, and punished their holy men.

Before 1680 there were 250 Franciscan missionaries in New Mexico. At the end of the revolt, the Indians had killed 21 missionaries and 380 Hispanic colonists.[52] The Indians had destroyed everything made by the Spanish. Kivas that had been filled in with sand by the Spanish missionaries were excavated and put into use again. The Indians were finally free after more than eighty years of oppression.

Otermín and the 1,946 colonists who escaped traveled south to safety to the village of El Paso del Norte and settled on the south side of the Rio Grande near the mission of Nuestra Señora de Guadalupe, which had been built as a way station between Chihuahua City and Santa Fe. Otermín remained the governor in exile until the time when the Spanish could take back New Mexico.

In November, 1881, Otermín, with 146 soldiers, 112 friendly Indians, and 28 servants marched back north in an attempt to take back what the Spanish had lost and wrest Santa Fe away from the Indians.[53] Obviously not understanding the causes of the rebellion, he repeated the very behavior that had precipitated the revolt in the first place. As he passed various pueblos he ransacked them, destroyed the kivas that had been rebuilt, and burned the paraphernalia of the katsina religion.

In defiance, the Indians regrouped and prepared to engage Otermín's meager Spanish forces. Faced with a serious fight, the approaching winter weather, and a lack of food for his horses, Otermín reconsidered his position and marched back to El Paso, leaving the re-conquest to others in the future.

Taking Back New Mexico

The Pueblo Revolt of 1680 was a stunning defeat for the Spanish. Nowhere else in the Spanish world had native people overthrown their authority and taken back a province. This affront to Spanish pride and honor had to be avenged. Another serious consideration was that the loss of New Mexico as a buffer left the northern provinces of New Spain vulnerable to attack by aggressive nomadic Indians.

Even with the Spanish gone, New Mexico lay uneasy. When the colonists and friars were driven away, Popé became the nominal ruler. Not everyone, however, agreed with his decisions. For example, Popé ordered the destruction of all traces of everything Spanish, and ordered his followers to bathe with yucca soap to wash away the perceived contamination of baptism. However, by then the culture of the Indians had changed and it was not possible to go completely back. The Indians had incorporated the use of horses, carts, iron tools, grain, sheep and other livestock, fruit trees, and other Spanish improvements into their lives. They did not want to give them up, which made it difficult to change their way of life. Another issue was that with the Spanish gone, they were now missing the protection that the Spanish had provided against raiding Apache and Navajo.

Between 1681 and 1691 an impasse existed between the Indians and the Spanish. Popé died in 1688, leaving behind a power struggle among the pueblos. The Spanish took advantage of this lack of unity to make a bid for a successful re-conquest. But even then it took four years, from 1692 and 1696, before the Spanish finally reclaimed New Mexico.

The man who finally re-conquered New Mexico came from Madrid and had the impressive name of Diego José de Vargas Zapata Luján Ponce de León y Contreras. Vargas paid the required contribution to the Crown and was appointed governor of New Mexico in 1691 for a five-year term. But before he could address the issue of re-conquest, he had to put down a rebellion in the area surrounding El Paso by Indians who were inspired to revolt against the Spanish like their brothers to the north. After accomplishing this task, Vargas was free to concentrate on recapturing New Mexico.

Vargas marched north from El Paso on September 13, 1692, with forty mounted soldiers, ten armed citizens, fifty Indians, and three Franciscan friars to recapture Santa Fe. He and his force stopped at El Morro to carve a message into the soft sandstone that read, "Here was the General Don Diego de Vargas who conquered for our Holy Faith, and for the Royal Crown, all of New Mexico, at his own expense, year of 1692."[54]

Vargas and his contingent marched towards Santa Fe. Though the popular accounts of the re-conquest say that it was peaceful, Vargas met pockets of fierce resistance at several pueblos that had to be overcome.[55] When Vargas reached Santa Fe, he found that the Palace of the Governors was still standing, but the rebels had converted it for their own use into a pueblo. They had added two floors to the original one-story structure, closed off the doors and windows, and entered the building down ladders placed in holes cut in the roof.

The Spanish reprisals were harsh. The victorious Vargas executed by firing squad seventy male Pueblo Indians involved in the revolt and distributed 400 women and children among the colonists as servants. Though these initial punishments were severe, the Spanish had learned a lesson from the revolt and the new government was more tolerant of native ways. Spanish rule was not as oppressive and efforts to eradicate Indian culture were less extreme. The practice of forced labor and tribute was abolished. In return, the Pueblo Indians supported the Spanish against marauding Plains Indians. For their part, the Franciscan missionaries moderated their zeal and tolerated the traditional religious practices of the Indians in their underground kivas. The pueblos were allowed more freedom and their inhabitants were allowed to keep many of their traditional cultural practices, though Catholicism was observed in the mission chapels.

On the other side, the Pueblo Indians also showed more tolerance. The two cultures operated with some independence, but learned to live with each other. The Spanish government guaranteed that Indian lands would not be violated and, in return, the Indians pledged loyalty to the Spanish crown.

The recapture of Santa Fe by the Spanish allowed the return of a popular tradition. In 1625 Father Alonso de Benavides, the head (*custos*) of the Franciscan missions in New Mexico, had brought with him to Santa Fe a small wooden statue of the Virgin Mary named *Nuestra Señora del Rosario* (Our Lady of the Rosary). The statue was lovingly called *La Conquistadora* (Our Lady of the Conquest), because she had arrived in the days of the conquistadors. Also known as Our Lady of the Assumption, she is known today as Our Lady of Peace. During the Pueblo Revolt, the retreating colonists were able to rescue *La Conquistadora* and take her with them to El Paso, even though her shrine that was attached to the Assumption parish at the east end of the Plaza was destroyed. When Diego de Vargas and the Spanish returned to Santa Fe after the Pueblo Revolt, they brought *La Conquistadora* back with them. Today the statue, dressed to look like a Spanish queen, has a permanent home in a small side-chapel (La Conquistadora Chapel) in the Cathedral Basilica of St. Francis of Assisi in downtown Santa Fe, as it has since 1714. Her Papal Crown of precious metals and jewels was recognized by Pope John XXIII in 1960 and donated by the people of New Mexico. The only time she leaves her permanent home in the chapel is to go for a week to Rosario Chapel in Rosario Catholic Cemetery in Santa Fe to celebrate her blessing for the relatively bloodless re-conquest of New Mexico.

When Diego de Vargas returned to Santa Fe after the Pueblo Revolt, he brought with him *La Conquistadora*, also known as Our Lady of Peace, who was first brought to Santa Fe by Father Alonso Benevides in 1625, but was removed to El Paso to safety during the Revolt. She now has a permanent home in a side-chapel in the Cathedral Basilica of St. Francis of Assisi in Santa Fe.

By 1692, the Spanish had reoccupied most of the area surrounding Santa Fe. On December 29, 1693, however, a small group of Indians counterattacked. The Spanish, aided by 140 fighting men from Pecos Pueblo, drove off the attackers. The rebels were not well organized and the Spanish defeated them easily. In April of 1695 Vargas was able to found the second Spanish town in the colony, Santa Cruz de la Cañada, thirty miles north of Santa Fe, close to the Tewa pueblos.

Sporadic revolts continued to break out, but they were quickly suppressed. On June 4, 1696, Pueblo Indians revolted again, killing five friars and twenty-one settlers. At the pueblo of San Cristóbal, fray José de Arvisu and fray Antonio Carboneli were clubbed to death. At Nambé, two friars asleep in the convent were killed when Indians barricaded the windows and doors and set the church on fire. At Jemez, fray Francisco Casañas de Jesús María was clubbed to death.

The Spanish were quick to respond to these hostilities and rapidly overcame the opposition, but peace did not follow immediately. Vargas continued to ride back and forth until he had defeated the rebels. Pueblo resistance carried on until the end of 1696 with several bloody battles. One major success for the Spanish occurred when one of Vargas' troops killed a leader named Lucas Naranjo, from the San Juan and Santa Clara pueblos, with a lucky shot. The Pecos Indians cut off his head and took it back to their pueblo as a trophy. By December of 1696, Vargas had re-conquered New Mexico for good.

In spite of the bloody conflict, the Pueblo Revolt did achieve results. After the re-conquest there was a reduction of mission influence in the 1700s. The *encomiendas* and *repartimiento* were eliminated. The Pueblos were allowed to govern themselves and elect their own officials. They were finally allowed to practice their katsina religion again and much of their culture was kept intact, including dances, songs, and language.

After the re-conquest in 1692, Spanish missionaries re-established missions at many of the Indian Pueblos. However, these were merely churches, unlike the missions that the Spanish later established in California where Indians were gathered together and worked in large manufacturing complexes that required the services of many priests.

The Hopi and Zuni villages were never re-conquered and remained independent. The Hopi pueblo of Awatovi was the only Hopi village that accepted the Spanish and built a new mission after the re-conquest. Seventy-three of the villagers became converts. Men from the other Hopi pueblos ordered the missionaries out. When they refused, Indian raiders attacked and set fire to Awatovi and destroyed everything connected with mission. They killed the men and moved most of the women and children to other pueblos. In all, 700 men, women, and children, Christians and non–Christians alike, were killed. Awatovi was never reoccupied.[56]

Vargas' successor was Pedro Rodríguez Cubero. He arrested Vargas on charges of graft, favoritism, and misgovernment. Vargas was put under house arrest then sent to Mexico City to account for himself. He was exonerated and reappointed governor of New Mexico. Vargas died campaigning against the Apache in 1704, but not from the heroic wounds of battle. He died from dysentery, an inflammatory disease of the bowels.[57]

Chapter Six

New Spain Expands

Three main routes to the north from Mexico City funneled missionaries, soldiers, and their families to Spanish settlements that sprang up in western Texas, New Mexico, southern Colorado, southern Arizona, and southern California. One route, established in 1697, went northwest through the Mexican provinces of Sinaloa and Sonora, and then continued by water across the Sea of Cortez to Baja California (Antigua California) and north to upper California. An alternate branch went directly to California (Nueva California), established in 1769. A second, central, route, established in 1629, continued through Nueva Vizcaya to New Mexico and Santa Fe, with a branch west to the Hopi pueblos of north-central Arizona. The third route, established in 1689, went north through Nuevo León and Coahuila to Texas.

Texas

The first European to reach Texas was believed to be Alonso Alvarez de Piñeda, who mapped the Texas coast in 1519, thus establishing a vague Spanish claim to the land. Álvar Núñez Cabeza de Vaca landed near Galveston in 1528, and subsequently wandered the West, as described in Chapter One. In 1598, Juan de Oñate formally claimed Texas for Spain, though the first mission was not established until 1682. In reality, then, the Spanish did not do much more than establish a few missions and settlements in Texas close to the coast.

In 1682 the Spanish established their first mission, Corpus Christi de la Islate, and a permanent settlement in Texas at Ysleta, near El Paso. The population around El Paso was about 4,000 and the area contained, vineyards, orchards, and cornfields. El Paso also produced wine (known among Americans as "pass wine") as a profitable trade item. Some of this was distilled to make brandy ("pass whiskey").[1]

Spanish conquistadors who penetrated the country northeast of Mexico in their constant search for riches were constantly harassed by the Tejas Indians, a name which ironically came from an Indian word meaning "friends." This eventually resulted in the area being named Texas. Bringing these Indians into Spanish society meant that they had to be converted to Catholicism.

The Spanish did not like having empty regions in Texas because of their concerns over the presence of advancing Russian, British, and French colonists in North America. In the early 1700s the French, in particular, were contemplating how they might profit from the riches of the silver mining areas of northern New Spain and so established a colony and trading post at Natchitoches on the Red River in 1714. Spain responded to French settlements in Texas and Louisiana by founding their own settlements. In retaliation, concerned officials in Mexico decided to construct a string of missions and presidios in Texas, both for protection against outsiders and to subdue and convert the Indian inhabitants. This strategy was similar to using colonization of New Mexico to reinforce Spanish claims to land in the Southwest and to act as a buffer against any incursion by foreigners from the north.[2]

It had not gone unnoticed by officials in Mexico City that French fur trappers and traders were interested in reaching Santa Fe to trade their goods for silver dollars from Mexico. This went against Spain's well-established policy of not allowing trade with foreign nations. New Mexico was expected to block these efforts. The mission outposts in Texas, therefore, were established originally primarily as a buffer against an incursion of French colonists from the Mississippi Valley. In 1716 officials in Mexico sent an expedition into eastern Texas and within a year had established a presidio and four missions, one of them at San Miguel de los Adaes, only twelve miles from the French colony at Natchitoches.

The nomadic tribes of Texas, such as the Hasinai, the Apache, and the Comanche did not accept baptism, refused to be converted, and did not want to live under the restricted lifestyle of the missions. As a result, the mission system generally failed in Texas, except along the San Antonio River where five missions were founded between 1720 and 1731. Texas also failed to attract colonists. There were no rich finds of gold, no Indians population to act as laborers, and no particular trade opportunities. In spite of this, three dozen missions were eventually established in Texas.

One example of the mission failures was Nuestra Señora de la Purísma Concepción de Acuña, founded in 1716 in the Angelina River valley west of present day Nacogdoches. Drought, famine, disease, and Indians raids made the mission a failure at this location and it was moved to San Antonio in 1731. Here it did better and grew corn, beans, melons, watermelons, and pumpkins. The mission stock consisted of 900 head of cattle, 300 sheep, and 100 horses.

San Antonio

In 1710 fray Antonio de San Buenaventura y Olivares founded Mission San Francisco Solano in Texas. The mission was unsuccessful in its original location and was moved in 1718 to the San Antonio River, named in honor of St. Anthony. The new mission became Mission San Antonio de Valero. In 1718 the Spanish government also established a presidio nearby named San Antonio de Béxar, which eventually became the center of the town of San Antonio. The mission moved again after a devastating storm and construction began at the present site in 1724. The chapel was built of adobe mud, brush, and straw. The complex at San Antonio eventually consisted of the presidio, the surrounding town of San Fernando de Béxar, founded in 1731, and four missions.

The other missions that were established near San Antonio over the next thirteen years were Mission San José y San Miguel de Aguayo, Mission Nuestra Señora de la Purísma Concepción de Acuña, Mission San Juan Capistrano, and Mission San Francisco de la Espada. The missions were located about three miles apart on a twelve-mile stretch along the river south from San Antonio. This was the greatest concentration of Catholic missions in North America. Mission San José was known as the "Queen of the Missions," a nickname also later given to the California mission at Santa Barbara. Mission San José was the largest and one of the most successful of the Texas missions with more than 300 residents at its peak. The mission, founded in 1720, was surrounded by thousands of acres of farmland, and included a gristmill and a granary.

The three later missions were started in various locations, but were consolidated and moved to San Antonio after an agreement with France realigned the international border. Mission Concepción, built in 1755, was noted for a mysterious, unexplained sun-like image on the ceiling known as "The Eye of God." Mission San Juan Capistrano, originally built as San José de los Nazonis, was moved to the San Antonio River and renamed in 1731. San Juan was a flourishing farm of orchards and gardens that supplied much of the local area with produce, as well as shipping surplus farm products to Mexico. Peaches, peppers, grapes, corn, beans, and squash were among its many crops. Its herds of sheep and cattle were said to number around 7,000 animals. Mission Espada, the southernmost of the mission chain, was founded in 1690 as San Francisco de los Tejas. It was moved in 1731 to the San Antonio River and renamed San Francisco de la Espada. It grew to be a large self-contained compound, complete with blacksmith's shops and other workrooms.

These missions, built as walled compounds to protect against marauding Apache and Comanche, were intended to start settlement in the region to act as a buffer against invasion by other nations from the north, to protect the frontier against marauding Indians, and to spread Christianity to the mission Indians. In return for labor at the missions, the Indians received food, housing, and protection from raiders.

Life in the Spanish missions of the Southwest was intended to be similar to living in villages in Spain, with the objective of teaching the mission Indians to eventually live like Europeans. Each mission was intended to be self-sufficient through its farm and livestock activities. Sheep, goats, and cattle were sold or traded to local presidios, to other missions, and to surrounding settlements to increase the income of the missions. Hides and cloth woven from the wool of the animals was an important source of revenue. Maintenance of the mission and its farms, as in New Mexico and California, was carried out by mission Indians. Blacksmith shops were built to make and repair farm implements. Carpentry, stone-cutting, masonry, and similar skills served to build and maintain the mission buildings. Water was distributed through a series of ditches (*acequias*) for drinking, washing, irrigation, and powering grist mills for grinding grain. In case the local presidio was unable to provide adequate protection for the missions, Christianized mission Indians were taught to use firearms in order to be able to protect their communities from outside raiders. The use of firearms was essential as the Apaches in Texas were armed with long lances, which gave them a considerable advantage over the Spanish soldiers who were armed with only short swords (*espadas anchas*).

The days of the mission Indians were highly structured. Mission bells determined a daily routine that included church services three times a day, meals, prayers, and the schedule for religious instruction. The church bells were also rung to summon troops from the presidio to assist with defense in case of Indian attack.

Mission Indians had to learn two new languages: Spanish for everyday conversation and Latin, which was the language of the church. The time between religious activities was spent in work on the farms and ranches, and in the mission workshops. Men and boys worked in the fields or in the carpentry and blacksmith shops at the tasks required to build and maintain the mission structures. Women and girls took on tasks such as cooking, cleaning, sewing, making pottery, and processing fat from cattle into soap and candles.

Not all of the routine was pleasant for the mission Indians. Many of the Indians were not eager to accept the Spanish way of life and the friars often complained that they were slow and careless. Some Indians ran away, but were usually soon caught and subjected to harsh punishment. Dissent was constant between the military at the presidio, the missionaries, and the local landowners over land, water, and how best to use the Indian laborers. On top of that the missions were under constant harassment from Apache and Comanche raids, though the mission environment did indeed provide protection for the less aggressive mission neophytes.

Indian raids and killings continued, however, and the Spanish made little headway. For example, in 1757 Diego Ortiz Parrila had founded the Presidio de San Luis de las Amarillas on the San Sabá River and planned a mission nearby on the northern border of the Mexican province of Coahuila. The Apache Indians did not flock to the mission as expected and converts were few. In March of 1758 Comanche Indians raided and burned the mission and killed two of the friars and two soldiers. A 380-man expedition with Indian allies sent to punish the Indians was defeated and retreated to San Antonio.

In 1761 France persuaded Spain to become its ally in a war with England. In 1762 France transferred ownership of the Louisiana Territory to Spain as compensation for entering the war and in an effort to keep Louisiana out of British hands. Spain, however, was not strong enough to establish a firm rule, and Comanche and Apache warriors continued to regularly raid Spanish missions in eastern and central Texas. By the time the French ceded their claims to the Spanish in 1762, the town beside the presidio of San Antonio de Béxar and the Mission San Antonio de Valero (that would later become commonly known as the Alamo) was the sole center of the Texas frontier province. By 1772 Spain had abandoned four missions and two presidios in eastern Texas and fallen back to San Antonio, which was made the center of Spanish government in Texas. The total remaining Hispanic population was around 1,800.

The peak of the San Antonio missions lasted from the mid-1700s to the mid-1770s, when Indian conflicts intensified. Decline was mostly complete by the early 1800s. Spanish efforts failed due to the devastating results of European diseases on the native people, an inability to conquer the local Indians or convert them to Christianity and mission life, and changes in the local culture that included European assimilation and intermarriage. Colonization efforts had been mediocre, in any case, as no substantial riches, such as gold, had been found for easy exploitation. Only cattle ranching survived to later result in the legendary Texas ranches and cattle drives to the railheads in Kansas.

In 1821, when Mexico achieved independence from Spain, the new regime in Mexico City made local government and church officials revoke any allegiance to their former homeland. Many of the friars in Texas refused, abandoned their missions, and left the country. Their departure resulted in the collapse of the Texas mission system.

By 1824 the missions had been secularized and the mission lands and buildings had either been turned over to the mission Indians or sold to local residents. The churches and the religious activities continued, but as local Catholic parish churches rather than the property of the missionary orders.

Texas Independence

Apache and Comanche Indians continued to be a problem. The Spanish missions in Texas always existed in a type of isolation as it was difficult to cross the Great Plains because of these marauding Indians. Spanish soldiers and missionaries who needed to travel from Texas to New Mexico had to go south to Durango, Mexico, then across Mexican territory before heading back up to New Mexico and Santa Fe. It was not safe to travel directly between the two.³ In response, officials in Mexico City proposed to locate strategic colonies in Texas as a buffer that was strong enough to hold back the Indians, and to repel disreputable squatters and land grabbers. Only the *Norte Americanos* ("North Americans"), as Spanish called the citizens of the United States, were interested in pursuing serious colonization.

Governor Martínez recommended a man named Moses Austin to head the effort. Accordingly, American colonization started under Austin just before the Mexican Revolution. Moses Austin died of pneumonia before he could complete negotiations with the new government, but colonization efforts continued under his son Stephen F. Austin, who negotiated a land grant from Mexico on the Colorado and Brazos Rivers. In order to remain in Texas, settlers had to become Mexican citizens and convert to Roman Catholicism. But, by 1830, with 8,000 or so Americans in Texas, religious, cultural, and political tensions had grown between Mexico and the settlers, and the Mexican government suspended further immigration. The government was concerned about the future trend of this influx of foreigners who brought with them their own customs, language, and ambitions for the country.

In 1833 Austin went to Mexico to try to negotiate a separate government. Though he reached a nominal agreement, he was jailed for inciting insurrection. When he was released and returned to Texas in 1835, the American colonists were on the verge of a revolution that did indeed break out before the end of the year. Austin commanded the troops that fought the Mexican army at San Antonio. In 1836 the Republic of Texas had been formed and declared its independence from Mexico. The new government claimed the Rio Grande to its source as its western boundary, even though there was no historical basis for that assumption.

The Alamo

The Alamo was the remaining part of Mission San Antonio de Valero. The mission reached its peak of development in the 1780s, but by 1793 was completely closed and secularized. In 1803 Spanish cavalry troops were stationed at the Alamo as a military garrison to guard against American invasion and protect against Indian attacks. The troops, under the command of San José y Santiago del Alamo de Parras, were known as the Alamo Company, and so their post became known as the Alamo.⁴ In 1805 the upper level of the old *convento* was turned into a military infirmary (which also treated civilians), making it San Antonio's first hospital. After Mexico gained independence from Spain, the building continued as a military fort.

The Alamo was a dilapidated ruin in 1835 when it was taken over by Texas revolutionaries who played a memorable role in the fight for Texas Independence during the Battle

The Alamo was the remaining part of Mission San Antonio de Valero. The mission was completely closed by 1793. The Alamo was taken over by Texas revolutionaries hoping to delay the advance of Mexican troops, but the defenders were killed on March 6, 1836. Ever since, the Alamo has been a symbol of the sacrifices made to gain Texas Independence. In 1845 the army took over the mission building as a quartermaster depot and the peak of the new roof was hidden by adding the iconic curved parapet in front of it (Library of Congress).

of the Alamo in 1836. They fought hoping to delay the advance of Mexican troops until Sam Houston could finish raising an army to resist the Mexicans.

William Barret Travis and 187 Texans under his command barricaded themselves in the old mission compound at the Alamo on February 23, 1836, to make a stand against Gen. Antonio López de Santa Anna, the self-proclaimed President of Mexico, and his army. After a thirteen-day siege, Santa Anna decided to destroy the Alamo and attacked on March 5 with 5,000 men. The final assault lasted for five-hours and resulted in the deaths of 600 Mexican soldiers. Travis, Davy Crockett, James Bowie, and the other defenders were all killed on March 6, 1836. Santa Anna had the bodies burned so that the battleground would not become a memorial. Ever since, the Alamo has been a symbol of the sacrifices made to gain Texas independence and the Texans' heroic last stand inspired the cry, "Remember the Alamo."

The battle of the Alamo has become a legend that has grown throughout the years. For example, Travis drawing a line in the dirt and asking men who would stay to cross it is a part of the legend that did not take place. Another part of the legend is the Bowie knife. Contrary to popular stories, the Bowie knife, the famous style of large, wicked-looking hunting knife used on the frontier for defense and all-around use, was not designed by Jim

Bowie, but by his brother Rezin Pleasant Bowie. Brother Jim was the one who made it famous.

The Alamo, badly damaged from the battle, remained deserted for the next nine years. In 1845, as Texas was about to be annexed to the United States, the army took over the mission building as a quartermaster depot. They repaired the walls and put a new wooden roof on the mission church to protect the military supplies stored inside. The peak of the new roof was hidden in 1850 by adding a curved parapet in front of it. This iconic addition has become part of the symbol of the building.

In 1855 the Catholic Church took possession of the immediate land around the church after winning a legal fight against the city of San Antonio and the United States army over its custody. Civilian building were constructed on the property and the compound's outer walls were taken down. The church sold the *convento* to a wholesale grocer named Honoré Grenet and leased the church to him. In 1883, the State of Texas bought the church as a memorial to those killed in the battle. It has since been repaired and restored.

The Fight for Independence Continues

After his victory at the Alamo, Santa Anna moved on to Goliad where he captured and executed 371 Anglo prisoners. Then he made the mistake of dividing his army and was subsequently surprised by Gen. Sam Houston. On April 21, 1836, Houston and 900 Texans attacked Santa Anna and 1,200 of his soldiers at the San Jacinto River near Houston, routed them, and took the Mexican general prisoner. The Texans killed more than 600 Mexican troops and forced Santa Anna to sign a treaty granting independence to Texas. This ended the Mexican War of Independence and the Texans felt avenged for the massacre at the Alamo. The United States recognized the separate Republic of Texas on March 3, 1837.

By the 1840s Texas was still unstable and Indian attacks on traders continued. In 1841 Texas marched troops into New Mexico in an attempt to annex part of the province and profit from the growing and lucrative trade between the United States and Mexico. The attack was poorly conceived and failed as a result. The ragged band of Texas soldiers were disarmed at San Miguel del Vado, New Mexico, and were marched south to Mexico City. Here they were released to find their own way home.[5]

Skirmishes back and forth between Texas and Mexico continued for several years. One infamous incident that occurred during the ongoing war became known as the Black Bean episode. In 1843 Nicholas Dawson led a group of fifty-three volunteers to San Antonio to fight against the Mexicans. They were surrounded by 400 Mexican troops and 36 of the Americans were killed in the fight. The rest, except for three who escaped, were captured. To avenge them, 700 men from the Texas militia marched to attack the Mexican soldiers. Four hundred of them eventually marched back to San Antonio, while the other 300 went on to attack the Mexican town of Mier. They were also poorly-organized. Believing that they were outnumbered by Mexican troops, the men rapidly surrendered and were started on the journey to prison in Mexico City. During the march, 175 of the prisoners overpowered their guards and escaped, but were soon recaptured. In retaliation, Santa Anna decreed that one out of every ten of the escapees was to be executed. In a random lottery, 159 white beans and 17 black beans were put into a pot and each of the men had to draw one. Those who pulled out a black bean were put before a firing squad and shot on March 25, 1843.[6]

Arizona

The Spanish were the first Europeans to visit Arizona. Initial forays, however, were not promising. One wilderness section in Arizona was so deserted, even by Indians, that the Spanish named it *el despoblado*, or "the desolate place."[7]

In 1736 an important silver strike occurred near an Indian village called *Ali-Shonak* ("Place of the Small Springs"), southwest of Nogales. The Spanish miners who mined the area corrupted the name to *Arizonac*. When Anglos arrived they further corrupted the name to Arizona, which eventually became the name of the state.[8]

The only major Spanish settlements in Arizona were at Tucson and Tubac. Similar to the history of Santa Fe, the Santa Cruz valley around Tucson contained early pithouse dwellers. As in New Mexico, these Indians traded with Mesoamerica and the Mexican coast to the southwest. Ancient irrigation canals were used to water squash, beans, maize, and cotton as part of a sophisticated agricultural operation.

Spanish Tucson was not built as a capital or a town, but as a presidio. It housed 1,015 soldiers, settlers, and Indians. Mission San Agustín del Tucson was founded by fray Francisco Garcés close to the Tohono O'odham village of Chuk-Shon, near the Santa Cruz River in 1771. Similar to the New Mexico missions, the complex included a church, a granary, a *convento*, and walled-in gardens. The presidio, built in 1775 to protect settlers from raiding Apaches, was located across the river, north of today's Congress Street. The presidio was built in the shape of a square, each of the four walls about 700 feet long, twelve feet high, and three feet thick.

Another presidio was built at Tubac, ten miles south of Tucson. This was home to 600 men, women, and children. The Presidio de San Ignacio de Tubac was built on what had been a Pima village before becoming the mission farm. It was established in 1752 after a revolt by the local Pima Indians. Fifty soldiers were stationed there with the task of controlling the Pima and the Apache, and to conduct on-going exploration of the Southwest.

The first Spanish missionary to explore Arizona was Father Eusebio Francisco Kino, a German-educated Italian Jesuit priest, who arrived in Mexico in June of 1681. After Spanish missionaries such as Kino arrived, they had to be self-sufficient in order to survive. They quickly taught the natives how to use adobe for construction, how to farm and ranch with cattle, sheep, and goats, and how to make handcrafted items.

Kino founded his first Arizona mission church, San Xavier del Bac, near the Tohono O'odham village of Bac in 1692 on the Santa Cruz River, about nine miles south of Tucson. Juan Bautista de Velderrain started to build the present church at San Xavier del Bac in 1783. It was a solid building, made from fired brick and lime mortar. Velderrain's successor, fray Juan Bautista Llorens, finished the church during the 1790s, except for the dome of one of the towers. Work on the east tower stopped in 1797 when building funds ran out and it was never completed. The bell-tower remains unrestored to today to maintain historical accuracy. The impressive pure white building is sometimes called "The White Dove of the Desert."

In 1691 Kino established a mission on the Santa Cruz River that was named San Cayetano de Tumacácori, and later renamed San José de Tumacácori. Kino founded another mission close by in 1701 at the village of Guevavi, near Nogales, which became San Gabriel de Guevavi. Tumacácori was established as a missionary outpost with no resident mission-

The Arizona mission church of San Xavier del Bac, near the village of Bac, was started in 1692 about nine miles south of Tucson. Construction started on the present church in 1783 with fired brick and lime mortar. The church was finished during the 1790s, except for the dome of the east tower when building funds ran out. The bell-tower remains incomplete and unrestored today to maintain historical accuracy. The impressive pure white building is sometimes called "The White Dove of the Desert."

aries, but in 1771 was made the head mission of the district. The mission church was built in stages between 1803 and 1825 near a spot visited earlier by Father Kino, with construction supervised by fray Ramón Liberos. The mission included housing, classrooms, workshops, and granaries. The *convento* was typical for the period, containing a large central patio surrounded by living quarters for the priests, storerooms, workshops, classrooms, and granaries. An orchard and a cemetery were located nearby. The mission was secularized in 1821 with Mexican Independence. Continued Apache raids finally drove off remaining residents in 1848. Anglo ranchers moved in after the United States acquired the territory in 1854. They used the cemetery for a corral and allowed the mission buildings to deteriorate. The present buildings at Tumacácori are the ruins of three missions built between late 1600s and early 1800s.

Between 1687 and 1711 Kino built a chain of twenty-four mission villages in the Southwest where he introduced grains, fruits, and European livestock. He was an energetic man and mapped much of northern Sonora and southern Arizona during forty expeditions. The map he made during a trip to Baja California showed that it was not an island separated from the mainland by the mythical Straits of Anian, which was the traditional belief at the time, but was instead a peninsula. The pueblo at Casa Grande was already in ruins when Father Kino first saw it in 1694.

In the late 1800s a popular belief existed that the Anasazi ruins spread across the Southwest were built by the Aztecs of central Mexico. Early settlers had heard stories of Cortés' conquest of Mexico and assumed that the Aztecs had built these structures also. This was the reason for the name of the pueblo ruins located at Aztec in northern New Mexico, though they were not built by the Aztecs of Mexico and there was no connection between the two. Similarly, the early settlers in the Verde Valley of central Arizona were so convinced that the five-story ruin of a twenty-room cliff-dwelling built in a cliff alcove above Beaver Creek was built by the Aztec leader Montezuma that they named it Montezuma Castle. In reality, the structure was built by the Sinagua Indians who migrated there in the 1100s. The Sinagua were dryland farmers, hence the name given them by the Spanish means "without water."

Colorado

Colorado, which lay directly to the north of the New Mexican settlements of the upper Rio Grande valley, was the object of exploration by the Spanish. Among many pieces of evidence for Spanish incursion were the bones of a Spanish soldier that were found near Deadman Creek and the headstone of a padre who died in 1660 on Ute Creek in Costilla County.[9]

In 1594 an expedition under the leadership of Juan Hermana in search of the legendary Seven Cities of Gold disappeared in southern Colorado. A second expedition later found their bones alongside a river where they had apparently been killed by Indians. As the dead soldiers had no priest traveling with them, they had died without the last rites and their souls were thought to be doomed to roam in Purgatory. In their honor, the Spanish named the river *El Rio de las Animas Perdidas en Purgatorio* ("The River of the Lost Souls in Purgatory"). The name was later shortened to the Las Animas River, the Purgatory, or the Purgatoire, and was eventually further corrupted by Anglo cowboys into the Picketwire.[10]

When slaves from mission villages in New Mexico ran away, the Spaniards pursued them and used force if necessary to recapture them. Though the earliest recorded expeditions into Colorado were intended to find runaways, they also increased Spanish knowledge of the land to the north. One such expedition was led by Juan de Archuleta in 1650, when he pursued and brought back Indians who had fled from Taos Pueblo. The escapees had settled on the eastern Plains about 100 miles from Pueblo, Colorado. During the course of the expedition, Archuleta discovered the Arkansas River, which ran from Pueblo east to Kansas. He called it the Nepesta River (sometimes also spelled as Napestle or Nepestle).

In 1706 Juan de Ulibarri marched north from New Mexico into eastern Colorado to recapture another group of runaways. He traveled east of Pueblo to a vague location named *El Cuartelejo*, which was possibly as far away as southwest Kansas. During the trip he took formal possession of the country in the name of the King of Spain. The Royal Ensign Francisco de Valdéz asked if anybody objected. Nobody did, so Ulibarri cut the air in all four directions with his sword. The surrounding crowd threw their hats in the air and discharged their guns. In their minds, Spain now owned Colorado.[11]

During the expedition Ulibarri was the first European to see the Spanish Peaks, two cone-shaped mountains of gray rock located south of the town of La Veta (Spanish for "The Vein"), Colorado. The Ute Indians named them *Huajatolla* (also written as *Wahatoya* or *Guajatoyah*, depending on how the phonetic name was spelled on paper), which meant the "Breasts of the Earth."[12] The Spanish more delicately called them *Los Dos Hermanos* ("The Two Brothers"). The Utes believed these two mountains to be the home of fearsome ghosts and vengeful gods. Spanish explorers were in awe of the mountains also, one observer even claiming that he had seen fire and steam shooting from the summits. Certainly the summer thunderstorms that often formed near the two summits were taken as evidence of rain gods living there.

These isolated granite peaks became the northern limit of the Spanish empire. The two mountains were an important landmark for Spanish explorers, and for later travelers on the Santa Fe Trail. In 1719 Governor Valverde camped with 600 soldiers near the town of La Veta while they were searching for troublesome Indians.[13] Also in 1719, Don Pedro de Villasur erected a military supply depot at La Veta, which was thought to be the first structure built by white men in Colorado. The first recorded Spanish expedition along the Rio Grande into Colorado was that under Juan Maria Antonio de Rivera in 1761. In 1765 Rivera led expeditions north from Santa Fe to explore southwest Colorado and southeast Utah for precious metals.

The boundary between Spanish land and American territory was uncertain and the Spanish looked upon Anglos from the East as intruders. To safeguard their claims and lands, the Spanish built forts on important passes into their territory. One such fortification was built on Sangre de Cristo Pass in southern Colorado in 1819. Sangre de Cristo Pass (a few hundred yards north of North La Veta Pass on present U.S. Highway 160) was an old trail originally used by Comanche Indians to travel between their home in eastern Colorado and New Mexico to trade with the Taos Indians and the Spanish. In 1768 it was used by Governor Juan Bautista de Anza to cross the Sangre de Cristo mountains while pursuing Comanche raiders.

One story says that the pass was named by Anza when he traveled it in 1779.[14] Supposedly as he camped out, a brilliant sunset colored the nearby mountain range with a radiant blood-red glow and he called it the *Sangre de Cristo* or "Blood of Christ" mountains.[15] Another version of the naming of the pass attributes the name to Francisco Torres, a missionary to the Pueblo Indians who was wounded during a skirmish. Supposedly as he lay dying the mountains turned blood red with the setting sun and he murmured "*Sangre de Cristo*."[16] A third version attributes the name under similar circumstances to New Mexico governor Valverde.[17]

These two cone-shaped mountains in southern Colorado, named the Spanish Peaks, were well-known to the Spanish. They served as an important landmark for explorers, but were also rumored to be one source of Aztec gold and the location of lost gold mines. The Ute Indians believed the mountains to be the home of gods, and the intense summer storms that gathered on the peaks were a sign of their displeasure.

This pass was the chosen route through that part of the mountains for the next hundred years. It became so well used by trappers and traders that became known as the "Taos Trail" or the "Trapper's Trail." The pass was certainly known to have been used in 1749 by French fur trappers.

De Anza also named other passes in the area, such as Poncha Pass (meaning "a low gap in the mountains") at the north end of the San Luis Valley of Colorado. Medano Pass meant "sand hill," because it led into the Great Sand Dunes of Colorado. Raton Pass on the New Mexico-Colorado border meant "mouse pass." Mosca Pass entering the San Luis Valley near the Great Sand Dunes received its name from *mosca*, the Spanish word for "fly," probably due to the persistent presence in summer of pesky flies, ticks, and mosquitoes in the area.

Spanish Settlement

Spanish interests also focused on expanding the border of New Mexico further north from Santa Fe into Colorado. After Mexico gained independence from Spain, the new government encouraged permanent settlement in southern Colorado to provide a buffer against invaders. To assist in this, the government issued generous land grants to colonists willing to plant crops and raise stock. Spanish settlement was slow, but a few colonists persisted. To speed the process, land grants were made to Spanish people who would settle in northern New Mexico and southern Colorado in order to maintain a claim to the territory by colonization, and thus secure it against Texan or American claims.

The Spanish colonized southern Colorado mostly along the Rio Grande and its tributaries. The San Luis Valley and the Rio Grande valley still contain a large population of Spanish-Americans, many of whose ancestors settled there prior to the Mexican War of Independence. These pioneer settlers came primarily from Taos, Santa Fe, and Abiquiu. The first were of Spanish descent. The later ones were *mestizos* of mixed Spanish and Indian blood, and some were Indians. When Thomas Jefferson Farnam passed through South Park in 1839, he commented that he met Indians who spoke Spanish.[18]

There is evidence that the Amidor Sanchez family lived in the San Luis Valley as early as 1763. It was unlikely that this family lived in an isolated house, as Indian raids were rampant in the area. It was more typical, and therefore more likely, that several families lived in a colony of houses built around a central courtyard (*placita*) for defense against marauding Indians.[19]

The first official settlement in Colorado was the town of San Luis, a walled colony on the Rio Culebra founded under the direction of Carlos Beaubien, the owner of the Sangre de Cristo Land Grant. In 1851 six families moved in, thus making San Luis the oldest town in Colorado. The settlers built their adobe houses around a square courtyard for protection against raiding Indians. Interior doors and windows faced into the courtyard and the outer walls typically only had one opening, barred in case of attack by a heavy gate. In this way valuable livestock, such as horses, mules, and cattle, could be driven into the courtyard and the gate sealed during raids, until such time as it was safe to come out again.

Settlers wishing to live in San Luis were required to appear before the local judge, had to qualify as good citizens, and had to pay for a town lot, the price of which was to be turned over to the church for its use. In keeping with Spanish tradition, a tract of land of 633 acres was reserved as a town commons, called *La Vega* ("The Meadow"), where the settlers could graze their horses, cattle, and sheep. This was said to be the largest remaining commons in the nation besides Boston. The R&R Grocery store in San Luis, founded in 1857, is the oldest operating business establishment in Colorado.

In the same area, the village of San Pedro was settled in 1852, and San Acacio, nearby to the west, in 1853. The little town of San Acacio is the home of the oldest continuously used church in Colorado, which was built in 1856. The Mission San Acacio was built by townspeople who prayed for rescue to their patron saint, San Acacio, as they were about to be attacked by Indians. They promised to build a church if they were saved. At the last possible moment, the Indians were scared away by what they thought was a huge vision in the sky of a soldier protecting the villagers. The shaken Indians retreated and the grateful villagers kept their promise and built the church.

The towns of Chama and San Francisco were also founded in the early 1850s in the San Luis Valley by families who migrated from the Taos–Arroyo Hondo–Arroyo Seco area. Other small Spanish-American villages, such as Conejos, were founded on the west side of the valley by settlers from the lower Rio Chama valley. In 1852 Fort Massachusetts was built at the base of the Sangre de Cristo Mountains to protect the mostly Spanish-speaking colonists.

Houses were built from adobe with clay and gravel roofs, and whitewashed plastered walls. Some houses in the area were built with *jacal* construction. These structures were crude, but sturdy. The furniture inside was often homemade. The bed might be only a sack filled with straw or corn shucks.

These homes were often clustered around a central town square in the Spanish style. The villages consisted of sun-baked plazas, flat-roofed adobe houses, irrigation ditches running along unpaved streets, churches with crosses on their tops, and yards containing little grass but perhaps a few hollyhocks and peach trees. The farmers dug irrigation ditches, used crude wooden ploughs, and raised crops of wheat, corn, and beans. They also raised cattle, horses, sheep, and goats.

Settlers gave many of the rivers and creeks in southern Colorado Spanish names, such as Piedra (stone or gravel), Los Pinos (the pines), Las Animas (the souls), La Plata (the silver), Mancos (lame) and Rio Grande (large or grand river). Colorado itself, in fact, is named for the mighty Colorado River, which means "red" in Spanish, because of the muddy red runoff after the thaw of snowbanks high in the mountains in the spring.

The Great Sand Dunes

In the southern part of Colorado, on the west edge of the San Luis Valley, is an area of eighty square miles covered by dunes of sand, some of towering more than 700 feet above the valley floor. Legend and superstition surrounded the Great Sand Dunes even before Juan de Zaldivar and a group of Spanish explorers saw them as they passed through the San Luis Valley in 1599. The Apache and Cheyenne called the dunes the "Singing Sands," because of the rustling, whispering noise the tiny grains of sand made as the wind constantly moved them back and forth. Eerie wailing noises sometimes whistled across the dunes, now explained by scientists as the wind funneling down from the appropriately-named Music Pass to the northeast. A group of miners who camped on top of the pass in the 1860s swore that they had heard violin music penetrating the darkness of the night.[20] Local Indian legend said that the moaning came from the eternal restlessness of the sand.

As Explorer Zebulon Pike described the dunes in his journal when he was trying to determine the international boundary between the United States and Spain, "Their appearance was exactly that of the sea in a storm, (except as to color) not the least sign of vegetation existing thereon."[21] When Pike entered the valley via Medano Pass and followed it down Medano Creek past the Sand Dunes in 1807, he came across an old road on the west side of the pass that was known as the "Spanish Road." The presence of a road, rather than just a trail, indicated the use of earlier wheeled vehicles, which would in turn suggest some Spanish settlement in the area.[22]

There are legends of huge phantom palomino horses with webbed feet galloping across the sand in the moonlight, playing with the wind. This may have had some vague basis in fact as wild bands of horses descended from those left by the Spanish had roamed the dunes in the past. Other legends were more recent, such as the story of the wagon train that came over Mosca Pass to the east and stopped for the night by Medano Creek, which runs along the south edge of the main dune-field. The drivers unhitched the mules and bedded down for the night. In the morning all the wagons and mules had mysteriously disappeared into the sand. Flocks of sheep and their herders are said to have been swallowed up by the shifting sand.

The Green Horn Incident

Frequent Indian raids on the Spanish settlements of northern New Mexico continued to be carried out by Comanche Indians who lived along the Arkansas River in southern Colorado. Typical of these incidents involved a party of Comanche who visited Taos in 1751 to trade their furs for trinkets and food. Along the way they raided Galisteo, south of Santa Fe, where they killed many of the Spanish settlers and stole their horses and other possessions. In response, Governor Cachupin set off in pursuit, caught them on the Arkansas River, and killed a hundred of the Comanche.

In 1771 more than a hundred residents of New Mexico were killed by Indians and thousands of horses, mules, cattle, sheep were stolen. In 1773 Spanish soldiers pursued a band of Comanche horse thieves and caught up with them alongside the Conejos River in the San Luis Valley of Colorado, where they recovered 200 horses. In 1774 the Comanche made five devastating large scale raids on Spanish settlers in New Mexico, driving off livestock, killing sheep and their herders, and carrying away women and children.[23]

In 1778 one of the mandates of the governor of New Mexico, Juan Bautista de Anza, was to stop Comanche raiding and, better yet, to try and make an alliance with them.[24] An additional personal motive for him was that the Comanche had killed Anza's father.[25]

One of the fiercest of the Comanche war leaders was *Cuerno Verde*, or Green Horn. His name came from a green-painted buffalo horn that was mounted on his war bonnet.[26] Cuerno Verde's hatred of the Spanish started when his father was killed in battle. After that he took revenge on the Spanish in battle whenever he could and killed any survivors in cold blood. Anza felt the best course of action to make the Comanche realize the power of the Spanish was to go after Green Horn and defeat him in battle.

On August 15, 1779, Anza, accompanied by 600 soldiers and friendly fighting men from the Ute and Jicarilla Apache tribes, mounted a military expedition against the Comanche. The punitive expedition entered the San Luis Valley in south-central Colorado, crossed Poncha Pass and the Arkansas River near Salida, then continued north into South Park in the center of the state.[27] They continued east around Pikes Peak (whose Spanish name was "*El Capitán*"), traveled the old Indian trail down Ute Pass, and continued south.[28] The plan was to attack Cuerno Verde and his men from behind in an ambush on his home territory. And it worked.

Anza surprised the Comanche on Fountain Creek, south of Colorado Springs, on August 21. During the resulting surprise fight, several Comanche warriors were killed and sixty women and children were captured, along with 500 horses. Cuerno Verde escaped and the chase continued to the south. In a second battle, Anza caught up with the Comanche on the plains between Colorado Springs and Pueblo, and Cuerno Verde was killed in the ensuing fight on September 3.[29] Eighteen more warriors were killed and dozens of women and children were taken captive. Nearby Greenhorn Creek and 12,349-foot high Greenhorn Mountain took their names from the Indian chief. Successful in his mission, Anza and his troops continued south to New Mexico. He and his men had traveled 615 miles, but had accomplished what he set out to do. Anza said afterwards, "A larger number might have been killed, but I preferred the death of this chief even more than those who escaped, because of his being constantly in this region and his cruel scourge of this kingdom, and because he had exterminated many pueblos, killing hundreds and making as many prisoners whom he afterwards sacrificed in cold blood."[30]

After this decisive defeat, Comanche raids on the Spanish declined significantly. Several years later the Spanish made a treaty with the Comanche, in which the Indians promised to give up their nomadic life and settle down. In 1787 Anza set up a village named San Carlos de los Yupes along the Arkansas River in southeastern Colorado, probably near Pueblo. Here the Indians, with the assistance of Mexican labor supplied by Anza, built nineteen houses, planted crops, dug irrigation ditches, and raised sheep and cattle supplied by the Spanish. The eventual failure of the project a year later may have been because one of the Comanche women died and tradition dictated that her family and friends had to abandon the site.[31] The Indians left and wouldn't come back. This was the first and last attempt by the Spanish to try to assimilate the Comanche and found a colony in Colorado.[32]

Winter snow on the Mount of the Holy Cross in central Colorado collects in two intersecting crevices at the top of the mountain to form a giant white cross that lingers each summer until July. Several legends tell how early Spanish explorers lost during raging snowstorms found new strength and inspiration when they sighted the giant snowy cross in the wilderness in front of them (Library of Congress).

Turquoise

Turquoise was one of the gem materials found in quantity in Colorado that was prized by the Indians for its great social and religious importance. This spectacular bright blue-green stone was used for jewelry among the Anasazi and later Indians of the area. Spanish conquistadors routinely reported seeing Indians with lumps of turquoise adorning their noses, as well as their ears. The gem was also used as a trade item. It was not, however, valued by the Spanish.

Colorado's San Luis Valley had at least two turquoise mines, one of which may be the oldest mine worked by prehistoric people in North America. The workings were nine miles east of Manassa, Colorado, and are now called the King Mine. At one time this was the largest producer of turquoise in the world, though it is not worked much now. Other significant turquoise deposits in Colorado included the Hall Mine, five miles northwest of Villa Grove. This also appears to have been worked by Indians, as prehistoric tools have been found at the site.[33]

Mount of the Holy Cross

Colorado was the location of the Spanish legends of the 14,005 foot Mount of the Holy Cross, located in the central part of the state. Two intersecting crevices in the mountain, twenty-five to fifty feet wide and fifty to eighty feet deep, formed a giant cross. The horizontal section was 750 feet wide and the vertical segment was 1,500 feet long. Snow that collected in these crevices during winter formed a giant white cross that lasted until it melted in July.

Spanish legends swirl around the mountain like the clouds. Several of the legends deal with the sighting of the cross by early Spanish explorers. One tells that two Spanish priests from New Mexico lost their way during a raging snowstorm. They were close to death when suddenly the clouds parted and they saw the giant snowy cross in front of them. They gained such new inspiration and strength from the sight of this religious symbol that they were eventually able to find their way back to New Mexico. The popularity of the mountain and making pilgrimages to see it was so great that in 1929 the cross was declared a National Monument. Eventually, due to difficulty of access and a general decline in interest, the monument was abolished in 1950.

CHAPTER SEVEN

The Lure of Pacific Shores

When Hernán Cortés lost official control of the land he had conquered, he returned to exploration. From 1532 to 1539 he sailed up and down the west coast of Mexico, hoping to find a suitable shortcut to the Orient. The accepted thinking of the time was that Baja (Lower) California was an island and it might be possible to find a direct sea-route between it and the mainland. The hoped-for sea route did not exist but, in the process of looking for it, Cortés explored Baja California and proved that it was a peninsula and not an island. Cortés continued to sail up and down the Gulf of California (alternately named the Sea of Cortez after him) looking for elusive gold and following the legends of the Amazon women. However, finding neither gold nor the women of legend, but only plagues, shipwrecks, and hostile Indians, Cortés gave up his dreams of finding another rich kingdom to conquer. He was the loser in a power struggle with Viceroy Mendoza and sailed back to Spain in 1540. He eventually fell out of favor with King Charles of Spain and died from pleurisy in Castilleja de la Cuesta in 1547 at age 62.

Baja California was a hot, dry wilderness that supported only enough deer, rabbits, and bighorn sheep for scattered tribes of Indians to survive. Their arrowheads and stone tools have been found almost everywhere on the peninsula. Many examples of rock art, preserved by the dry climate and isolation from civilization, have been found in shallow caves and under rock overhangs.

The coastal Indians lived primarily on the abundant shellfish that they found in the shallow waters along the shores of the Gulf. Shell middens scattered along both coasts showed that ancient hunter-gatherers had lived in Baja California for at least 6,000 years. These piles of ancient seashells consisted mostly of clam and scallop shells, and the carapaces (upper shells) of giant sea turtles.[1] These were simple people who lived each day trying to survive their precarious existence under difficult environmental conditions.

The missionary headquarters for all of California was at Loreto, founded in 1697 by Juan Mariá de Salvatierra on the lower east side of the Baja Peninsula. Though Jesuit priests established missions in Baja California, missionary activity was not particularly successful because the 50,000 Indian inhabitants of the peninsula were widely scattered. Another reason was that these Indians did not understand the concept of abstract ideas, which made conversion to Christianity difficult.

The Jesuits were also charged with map-making and exploration of the Baja Peninsula in order to define and mark the new territory. In addition, two conditions were imposed by the king. One was that all expenses had to be paid by the Jesuits and the other was that the entire conquest was to be made in the name of the king. As a result, the Jesuits lived in their missions in poverty and loneliness, valiantly working their difficult task at great

Primitive tribes of coastal Indians lived in Baja California, primarily on the abundant shellfish that they found in the shallow waters along the shores of the Gulf. Middens of clam and scallop shells, such as this one in the center of the photograph, can still be found scattered along both coasts. Spanish missionaries tried to convert these nomadic groups to Christianity, but found it a difficult task to bring abstract religious ideas to these simple people who lived each day trying to merely survive their precarious existence.

personal sacrifice. The dry, hostile conditions of Baja California were hard on the missionaries. The barren land did not allow the missions to grow much more food than was required for bare subsistence levels.

The Society of Jesus was eventually expelled and removed to Spain by King Charles III in 1767 with no explanation, apparently because he feared the growing influence of the Jesuit priests. One associated reason is alleged to have been that he felt that the sixteen priests at the missions of Baja California were somehow withholding gold, pearls, and other riches that were due to the king. This would seem unlikely as Baja California was a barren, inhospitable land populated by hostile natives, and there was little chance for the priests to amass any riches. After the Jesuits were expelled, the monarch decided that the Franciscan order should take their place and the first Franciscans arrived in Baja California in 1768. The king transferred the established missions in the New World to the Franciscans. They occupied the old missions and established new ones. The Franciscans were eager to expand their empire of Indian conversion and operated the missions in the same manner as the Jesuits.

In 1541, the same year that Coronado left the Southwest, Spanish explorer Juan Rodríguez Cabrillo was the first to sail up the coast of Southern California.[2] Experienced in campaigns in Cuba, Mexico, and Honduras, he was looking for a route by sea from the Atlantic to the Pacific to simplify trade with the Indies. Cabrillo sailed into the harbor at San Diego on the day of St. Michael the Archangel in 1542, so he named it San Miguel (St. Michael). The landing is commemorated by Cabrillo National Monument at the southern tip of Point Loma in San Diego.

After naming San Miguel, Cabrillo continued up the Pacific Coast. His next landing was at San Pedro, just south of Los Angeles, which he named *Bahía de los Fumos* ("Bay of the Smokes") after seeing plumes of smoke from Indian campfires on shore. Waiting out the winter on Santa Catalina Island, he broke his leg (or possibly his arm, depending on the source) and died from a massive infection of the wound. He was buried on a nearby island.

The expedition continued on under Bartolomé Ferrer, Cabrillo's chief pilot, but missed Monterey Bay and the harbor at San Francisco's Golden Gate, which was the entrance to one of the greatest landlocked ship anchorages in the world. This was not surprising. Other Spanish and Portuguese navigators had sailed up and down California's shores for years, but thick fogs and the jagged shoreline often concealed the entrance to San Francisco Bay. There is evidence that the British freebooter Sir Francis Drake first discovered the Bay and claimed it for England, but the British took no further action and the harbor was left undisturbed. The vast bay was not discovered again until 1769, when a land expedition under Gaspar de Portolá, headed for Monterey, stumbled onto it when he overshot their destination. The first Spanish ship to sail through the Golden Gate was the *San Carlos* under Captain Juan Manuel de Alaya, who was the first to explore the inner reaches of San Francisco Bay in August of 1775.

In spite of missing San Francisco Bay, Cabrillo's expedition under Ferrer continued to a few miles north of the California-Oregon border, then turned around. Although Cabrillo's expedition claimed California for Spain, the Spanish showed no real interest in their property until 200 years later, when they started building missions.

The harbor at San Miguel was later renamed San Diego by Basque seaman Sebastián Vizcaíno, who explored the California coast in 1602 and 1603. He went ashore on September 28, on what he thought was the feast day of St. Diego, hence the name he gave to the town. He actually landed the day before the correct day, but the name remained. Vizcaíno also named Point Reyes Puerto de los Reyes (more commonly known simply as Point Reyes) further up the coast, after the Sacred Day of the Three Kings. When land grants were later handed out by the Spanish government, thousand of acres of Point Reyes became cattle ranches. Vizcaíno explored as far north as Cape Mendocino in northern California, then turned back south due to harsh weather and illness among his crew members.

Presidios and Missions

Spanish missionary activity in the Southwest took place in three primary areas, in New Mexico, Texas, and California. One area stretched from Socorro, New Mexico, north to Taos along the Rio Grande river, and was centered around Santa Fe. The second was in

Texas from the Gulf Coast inland to San Antonio. The third was along the Pacific Coast from San Diego to San Francisco.

Missions in California became the center of Spanish activity along the west coast. The primary purpose of the missions was to convert the local Indians to Christianity, but the Spanish Crown also hoped that their establishment would increase Spanish colonization.

Founding of the missions in California started in 1768 when Spain perceived a new threat to its holdings in North America. Russians who had arrived in Alaska from Siberia to follow the fur trade for seal and otter pelts had started to move down the West Coast. The British in Western Canada were also considering ownership of the region. An additional perceived threat were the ships of English and French freebooters who threatened Spanish ships plying the coastal waters.

Worried by rumors of proposed British and Russian expansion on the northern Pacific Coast that had already moved as far south as Oregon, concerned officials in Mexico City ordered Gaspar de Portolá, the governor of Baja California, to establish a series of missions and settlements along the Pacific Coast in Alta California. Portolá had originally been assigned to Baja California in 1867 to arrest and expel the Jesuits. Spanish Alta (Upper or present-day) California stretched from San Diego north to San Francisco. Spanish Baja (Lower or Old) California was considered to lie along the coast from San Diego down to the southern tip of the Baja Peninsula.

Land along the Alta California coastline was well suited to farming and cattle ranching. And missions. The grasslands were green and lush, the climate was mild, and the local Indians were peaceable hunter-gatherers who could be easily assimilated into the Spanish missionary world.

Missionary activity in California started in the spring of 1769 when an expedition of soldiers and settlers led by Portolá marched north from Baja California into Alta California. They were accompanied by several Franciscan monks led by fray Junípero Serra, who had orders to establish missions at San Diego and Monterey. After a six week journey the group reached San Diego and rendezvoused with a group of colonists who had arrived by sea carrying supplies for the missions that Serra would establish. The first of Serra's missions built in California was San Diego de Alcalá, founded in 1769. San Diego would continue on to become one of the California missions with the most converts. By 1797 the mission had 1,405 Christian Indians.

Over the next fifty-four years, twenty more missions were built, largely the work of Serra, who founded nine of them. Legend has it that the missions were deliberately spaced along the coast a day's journey from each other to allow easy travel between them for the friars. This statement is questionable because the spacing was actually about sixty-five miles. That would be a long day's trip even on a horse. More likely the missions were spaced such that travelers could find a hospitable place to recuperate after several days' travel.

The Spanish missions and presidios up and down the coast were connected by a primitive road called *El Camino Real*, or "The Royal Highway" (part of which is now Highway 101). This was a common name for roads, such as the other *Camino Real* between Santa Fe and Mexico City. In fact, any connecting road used by the Spanish in the New World was technically a *camino real* or "highway of the king." Hence *camino reals* are found in several places.

Portolá continued north from San Diego with Monterey as his next goal. He reached

Monterey Bay and decided that, though beautiful, it was not the potentially great seaport that he had been told it was. Thinking he had not arrived at his destination yet, he and his group continued north and eventually found the bay at San Francisco almost by accident. He then realized that he was too far north and had overshot his goal. He turned back south again to San Diego.

In 1770 he tried again. He successfully established a presidio at Monterey and established his headquarters there. He claimed Alta California for Spain and made ready to defend the Spanish empire against what the Mexican government believed to be an imminent Russian attack. In reality the attack never came.

Junípero Serra joined Portolá at Monterey and founded Mission San Carlos Borromeo in 1770. In 1771 he moved the mission three miles down the coast to a location near the river at Carmel that was better suited to farming. Carmel was named for three Carmelite friars who accompanied Spanish settlers in the early 1700s. Serra remained at Monterey until his death and burial there in 1784.

The first missions in California were built near bays so that they could be easily supplied from ships. Monterey Bay was first discovered and named in 1602 by Spanish explorer Sebastián Vizcaíno as he sailed up the Pacific coast. He named the bay and surrounding area for Gaspar de Zúñiga y Acevedo, the *conde* (Count) of Monterrey, the new Viceroy of New Spain.[3] The name was later changed to simply Monterey. In 1775 the settlement was recognized by the King of Spain as the capital of California.

Monterey Bay was ideal for protecting shipping, with a white sandy beach, and pine and oak forests nearby for shipbuilding and repairs. The bay at San Francisco was a better harbor, but it was often shrouded with heavy fog and had treacherous rocks around its narrow entrance. As a result, San Diego and Monterey became the major seaports on the west coast of California. The two presidios divided command of the entire region. As the seat of government for Alta California, the town of Monterey was the location of the custom house that was a required stopping point for every ship wanting to trade on the coast.

The power of the government lay with the governor, who was appointed by the central government in Mexico City. The governor was the chief civil and military officer. Under him, each town had a commandant who was the chief military officer and was in charge of the presidio. As courts to settle legal matters had not yet been established, small issues were dealt with by civil officers. Capital cases were handled directly by the governor.

Presidios were built by the Mexican government near the first missions in order to provide protection from local Indians. Presidios were built at San Diego (1769), Monterey (1770), San Francisco (1776), and the fourth and final presidio at Santa Barbara (1786). The early presidios were of simple construction that consisted primarily of a crude log stockade for protection from Indian attack. By the late 1700s, these had been replaced by better construction of stone and adobe. The presidio at Monterey consisted of four rows of one-story plastered buildings surrounding an open square in the center.

Settlers were quick to build their houses around the presidios for their own protection and lived in small towns that contained traders, soldiers married to mission Indians, and other settlers who lived in the area. A number of American and English traders also married Californian women, became Catholics, and settled in California.

Houses in Monterey were mostly plain buildings, one story high with red-tiled roofs. They were made of whitewashed adobe bricks cemented together with mortar made from the same material. Walls were up to five feet thick in order to keep the buildings cool in summer and warm in winter. The floors of the common laborers were compacted earth and windows were grated without glass. The wealthy, however, had boards on their floors and glass in their windows. Generally houses did not have fireplaces and chimneys because they were not required in the moderate climate. Cooking was performed in a cook-house that was separated from the main house. Early cooking and eating utensils were made from bone, wood, and horn. The arrival of the Spanish brought metal cooking implements, along with iron pots and tin cups. As in Santa Fe, outdoor ovens of adobe (*hornos*) were commonly used for baking bread and other food.

A String of Missions

The primary aim of the Spanish missions was to Christianize natives who had not heard the true word of God. But part of their goal was economic development and social discipline. The missions, which also served as defensive fortresses, later developed into commercial trade centers as well as serving as social and cultural meeting places for the area. In 1773 each early California mission had about forty cattle (for a total of about 200), along with sheep, goats, pigs. By 1800 this had grown to about 150,000 head of livestock.[4]

The buildings themselves blended several standardized architectural features that became known as the California mission style. For example, they were often built around a central patio with covered arcades running around the four sides. Another characteristic feature was whitewashed walls with heavy red tiles on the roof.

The missions established in Alta California were different from those built in New Mexico. In New Mexico, priests built missions and churches on (and sometimes literally on top of) already established Indian pueblos. The Indians of California lived in peaceful tribes in small, scattered semipermanent villages along the coast before the Spanish arrived. They were seldom hungry in the mild southern coastal climate and lived on shellfish, plants, fish, and grubs. They also hunted small game. In the warm climate of southern California they wore few clothes. Then the missionaries arrived to Christianize and enlighten the Indians. In order to control them better, the priests rounded them up and forced them to live on the mission grounds. Here they baptized them and tried to teach them the European way of living. By 1833 about 31,000 Indians lived at the missions.

The Indians were made to work on mission farms, which was a significant change for these hunter-gatherer tribes. Many accepted the lifestyle changes imposed by the Spanish; however, not all of them did and several violent uprisings occurred. As in New Mexico, these were immediately suppressed by the superior military forces of the Spanish.

The Franciscan priests had authority over the missions and their affairs. The local military commander was in charge of other matters, including crime. Punishments decided by the superior officer (*comandante*) at the presidio usually consisted of floggings of various degrees. The Indians were forced to stay close to the missions. If they escaped, the military force from the presidio was used to hunt them down and return them for punishment, which consisted primarily of whipping and spending time locked up in the stocks.

Seeds were brought by the friars to start the mission crops. Mission Indians planted and harvested wheat, grapes, corn, beans, oranges, and other crops for food, and raised cows, pigs, horses, goats, and sheep. In addition, food crops included vegetables, along with wild nuts and fruits gathered from the surrounding countryside. The friars also brought seeds from oranges, lemons, and grapefruit, which eventually became the basis for California's citrus industry.[5]

Many of the same problems plagued the California missions that were rampant in New Mexico. For example, both mission systems faced the same problems with water supplies. Insufficient rain led to drought and crop failure. Too much rain washed away the crops and flooded the buildings. Missions typically produced surpluses of livestock and food that were sold to raise money. Even though the conversion of Indians in California was only marginally successful, the missions became powerful forces in the economy.

Another crop that came with the Spanish was grapes, which grew out of the need for sacramental wine at the missions. The first grape cuttings, a variety of *Vitis vinifera* or the "common black grape," were brought to the New World by Cortés. The wine made from them was used in church services, as well as for daily use. The grapes were known as "mission grapes," because of their relationship with the church.

California's abundance of sunshine and moderate rainfall made the climate ideal for growing grapes and this eventually evolved into the California wine industry. The first California winemakers were the Spanish missionaries who introduced European cuttings to Mission San Gabriel in 1771. The communion wine made from them was heavy and bitter, and was not popular for recreational consumption. Other wines of the early 1800s were fortified with brandy to reduce spoilage in the warm climate.

The first of the large vineyards was established in the late 1850s after the United States took over California. Until about 1860, California white and red wines were made from the original grapevines that the missionaries had brought with them. After the mid–1860s

Mission San Gabriel, northeast of Los Angeles, shown here in 1909, was founded in 1771. The largest of the six bells seen in the wall weighed more than a ton. It was said that the bells could be heard up to ten miles away. The first California wine-makers were the Spanish missionaries who brought European cuttings to Mission San Gabriel when it was founded (Library of Congress).

other varieties of grapes were also planted. American winemakers introduced European varieties of grape that were more acceptable for recreational drinking.

Grapes flourished in the California climate. In 1820 a Mexican woman named Maria Felix planted a vine in Santa Barbara, California, that eventually grew to be a foot in diameter at the base and yielded 1,200 pounds of grapes at each harvest.[6]

The production of wine was not always a benefit. One early priest who observed the use of alcohol by the Indians reported that "Lewdness, adulteries, incests, and several other crimes which decency keeps me from naming, are the usual disorders which are committed through the trade in brandy, of which some traders make use in order to abuse the Indian women, who yield themselves readily during their drunkenness to all kinds of indecency." He added that "Injures [sic], quarrels, homicides, murders, parricides are to this day the sad consequences of the trade in brandy."[7]

At the end of the 1700s, the missions of Alta California had more than 20,000 neophytes. Their mortality rate, however, was high. The Indians suffered from the change in their diet to mission food and from confinement in close quarters inside the missions. Under these conditions, they were unable to ward off the white man's diseases and died in large numbers from dysentery, unknown fevers, and venereal disease. After 1769, over the next sixty years or so, the native population of California declined severely due to illness and forced labor. During one smallpox epidemic at Mission San Juan Bautista, records state that the appalling smell from the graveyard saturated the entire Mission building.

Mission San Gabriel Arcángel was founded in 1771. Mission San Gabriel had six bells, the largest of which weighed more than a ton. Bells were used at the missions to indicate when it was time to eat and pray, or to perform other activities. It was said that the bells at San Gabriel could be heard from ten miles away. Earthquakes at this mission were sometimes so strong that they shook the Spanish off their feet. In 1781, a small town sprang up to the southwest of the mission, settled by forty-six people that the mission friars considered to be lazy and corrupt, and interested mainly in drinking, gambling, and pursuing women. The settlement was called El Pueblo de Nuestra Senora La Reina de Los Angeles de Porciucula, better known today simply as Los Angeles.[8] Nuestra Señora La Reina de Los Angeles, built between 1818 and 1822 is still an active parish church.

The mission at San Juan Capistrano, founded in 1776 and built in the shape of a cross, was one of the most beautiful of the California missions. It contained the oldest building in California, a chapel built in 1782, that is still in use. Mission grapes planted here were used to produce wine by 1783. The mission was famous for its population of swallows that nested in the ruins of the old church. They departed on their annual southern migration on St. John's Day (October 23) and returned on St. Joseph's Day (March 19).[9] The roof and belfry collapsed during an earthquake in 1812.

The town of Santa Barbara was the social capital of early Spanish California. Mission Santa Barbara, the tenth in the California chain, was called the "Queen of the Missions." The present church, completed in 1820, served at one time as a beacon for sailing ships.

Mission San Buenaventura in Ventura (the town's real name is San Buenaventura like the mission) was founded in 1782 as Junípero Serra's ninth and last California mission. Mission La Purisma Concepción was founded in 1787, but was moved to a new location east of Lompoc after it was destroyed by an earthquake in 1812. The new location had more fertile soil and a mild climate for growing crops. The mission was secularized in the 1830s.

The Spanish missions and presidios up and down the California coast were connected by a primitive road system named *El Camino Real*, or "The Royal Highway." The presidio at Santa Barbara was founded in 1786. The mission, shown here, was founded in 1782 as the tenth in the California mission chain, and was known as the "Queen of the Missions." The present church, completed in 1820, served at one time as a beacon for sailing ships in the Pacific Ocean. The later town of Santa Barbara became the social capital of early Spanish California.

One of the most prosperous missions was Mission San Juan Bautista, north of Monterey Bay, which had thousands of cattle, sheep, and horses, and fertile fields of wheat. It also had a treasury full of gold. San Juan Bautista was the largest mission built by the Franciscans, begun in 1797 and completed in 1812. The great cathedral there was built on Spanish and Moorish patterns, with thick adobe walls.

Mission Nuestra Señora de la Soledad, in California's fertile Salinas Valley, was one of the smaller missions, but by the 1820s was home to 500 Indian neophytes and 15,000 head of livestock. The most northerly of the missions was Mission San Francisco Solano.

Though the Indians of the northern California missions appeared to be peaceful, native tribes around the southern missions were not. Attacks by hostile Indians occurred at Mission San Diego and Mission San Gabriel with some regularity.

Life at the Missions

Each mission functioned as a church, home, fortress, town, farm, and government outpost. Missions were built as a walled compound that contained the church, workshops, the *convento*, Indian dwellings, processing for the mission's cattle, and a granary.

Newly baptized Indians were given Spanish names and forced to live on the mission farms in housing that was segregated by gender, even for husband and wife. The missionaries tried to convert the Indians to the Christian faith, but also attempted to turn them into Spanish citizens who followed the European way of life.

Work for the Indians included making adobe bricks and roof tiles for the mission buildings, and acting as the labor force for the missions. This was no easy task as building a mission church took several years to complete. The friars kept these "neophytes," as they were called, continually busy. After construction was complete, the neophytes performed any necessary maintenance on the buildings.

Other tasks around the missions included tending the livestock, and acting as cooks, servants, and gardeners. In addition, the neophytes were subject to religious instruction, mandatory attendance at church services, and learning such trades as blacksmithing, carpentry, construction, and weaving. Cattle provided hides, soap, and tallow for mission use and for trade. Blankets and clothing were made from the wool of mission sheep. Candles, ropes, cloth, woven goods, and shoes were made in the mission workshops. Neophytes were also taught to play musical instruments and to sing both for church services and secular concerts. Mission San José had a band of thirty Indian musicians that included flutes and violins. Mission San Juan Bautista had a choir of Indian singers who gave public performances.

A small detachment of soldiers was stationed in a presidio close by each of the early missions to guard the mission inhabitants and settlers against Indian attacks, and to help keep the peace. The soldiers stood guard, protected the priests and mission buildings, maintained horses and weapons, and acted as an escort for the friars when they left the mission grounds. The Spanish staff was small. The number of soldiers in Alta California numbered only about sixty, with eleven Franciscans friars, making the whole Spanish scheme of settlement somewhat precarious. Each mission typically had two missionaries, a corporal (*cabo*), and only three or four common soldiers to form the guard (*escolta*) and control several thousand Indians.[10] This resulted in too few soldiers to guard the missions and themselves. Support from the central government, both financial and in terms of morale, was often lacking.

There were only around 3,300 people of Spanish origin in California. Life for them, though, was generally pleasant by the 1820s. The climate was mild and the mission Indians were generally peaceful. The population was small and Spanish estates were large, supporting large herds of longhorned cattle, along with cornfields, orchards, and gardens. Entertainment consisted of horse races, cockfights, and dances. Horses were plentiful. Most ran wild, but were branded with the owner's mark and had long leather ropes (*lazos*) around their necks that dragged behind them. A man would catch a horse in the morning, ride it all day, then turn it loose at night. He would catch another the next morning for the day's use.[11]

In spite of this idyllic-sounding lifestyle, life at the missions and presidios had a dark side for the neophytes. Spanish soldiers were not always as upright and professional as they might have been and abuse of the Indians was frequent. Morale among the troops was often low and their morals lower, resulting in frequent cases of abuse against Indian women at the missions. As one authority aptly put it, the behavior of soldiers stationed on the Spanish frontier was often "open and uninhibited." Abuse of the mission Indians by the staff was not uncommon, as most of the Spanish soldiers were bachelors expecting the spoils of lust from their conquest.

In all fairness, it was a difficult situation. The soldiers, young active men with natural desires, had no recourse to Spanish women, so they often turned to local Indian women for sexual release. Some married Indians converts at the missions. Other, in more direct fashion, routinely molested Indian women, sometimes in gang rapes.[12] For lack of suitable partners others violated men and young boys. Father Cambon at San Gabriel was horrified when he saw a soldier sodomizing an Indian inside the mission. He also claimed that young boys in the mission were routinely molested by the soldiers.[13] One desperate young soldier was caught in a compromising situation with a mule. As punishment for what was considered handiwork of the devil, both were killed and their bodies burned.[14]

Though attempts were made to try to attract single women and married couples to the missions, they were not particularly successful. It was the same at all the Spanish outposts. As one observer of Spanish soldiers in Florida noted, morale fell and many sank to "inordinate Use of Ardent Spirits and bad Wine … and promiscuous Intercourse with lewd Women."[15]

Another unpleasant fact of life for the neophytes was that they had to do as they were told or face beatings and time in the stocks. As in New Mexico, if the neophytes ran away, they were pursued, hunted down, and beaten. On the dark side, women were whipped, as well as men. Both male and female neophytes were subject to the stocks, rape, and other corporal punishment. The friars considered this type of punishment to be a great kindness, as it forced the natives along the pathway to salvation instead of consigning them to the eternal damnation that was reserved for nonbelievers. These punishments were not taken lightly by the Indians, however. At Santa Cruz, for example, a priest who was too vigorous in his beatings was murdered.[16] Generally, though, the neophytes were helpless to rebel under the superior power of the Spanish soldiers.

Passive resistance by the workers ranged from slowdowns on the job to telling each other dirty jokes about the friars. Religious items that have been excavated from the missions showed that the spiritual practices of the natives were still carried on in secret, even within the mission walls.

In the late 1700s in an attempt to boost colonization, which was the key to success in the Spanish provinces, officials turned to other sources. Married convicts, prostitutes, and orphans were sent to try to boost the population. Such a mix of undesirables gave California the reputation of the Spanish equivalent of Botany Bay, after similar later attempts in Australia. This practice further served to discourage legitimate colonists from settling in California.[17]

The Hide Trade

Cattle reproduced and spread so rapidly in the New World that even as early as the 1550s there were more cattle than there was demand for meat. As a consequence, more cattle were raised for their valuable hides and tallow than they were for eating. It has been estimated that 1,250,000 hides were exported from California between 1831 and 1848.[18] This high demand for leather fueled the growth of ranches, but much of the meat went to waste. The demand for hides also created further demand for more vaqueros to care for the growing herds.

With Mexican Independence in 1821, American ships owned by large Boston mercantile companies came to California on a regular basis. The journey to California was not an easy one at the time. Ships from New England and the East Coast had to fight their way through the foul weather around Cape Horn at the southern tip of South America, and then sail up the west coast of California. Along the way they traded for cowhides, leather, and tallow. Many of the Eastern companies had permanent agents in California so that they could deal directly and easily with the prosperous California missions. Nicknamed "Bostons," these agents were headquartered in the presidio at Los Angeles and in the provincial capital at Monterey. From these two locations they traveled up and down the Pacific Coast making contracts for hides for New England boot makers.

There were no banks and no credit system, and investments were made only in cattle. Silver coinage and hides were the media of exchange in circulation. Hides were so widely used instead of currency that they were nicknamed "California bank notes" and "leather dollars."[19]

Soon a brisk trade in cattle hides developed between the missions, the ranches, and the ships of many nations. By 1842 Monterey had become a small, but prosperous, shipping center for American buyers. The hides were so bulky and individually low in value that it was only profitable to transport them by ship.[20] Yankee sea captains anchored along the coast and traded hides, horns, and tallow for supplies with local ranchers and the Franciscan friars at the missions, who owned nearly all the cattle. First, however, all the Yankee ships had to dock at Monterey to obtain a license and to pay duty on goods for barter and sale.

The cattle were roped by the neck and back feet, similar to modern rodeo, and then butchered. For excitement, those riders who were very good made butchering into a type of sport and killed the cattle from horseback with a knife.[21] Skinners took off the hide and cut up the best meat on the carcass for salt beef or jerky (*carne seca*).

To extract the tallow, the outer fat under the hide, which amounted to seventy-five to a hundred pounds, was removed and melted in large metal kettles. The hot, liquefied fat was poured into leather bags (*botas*), allowed to cool, and the bags were sewn up for sale to traders. Five hundred pounds of fat in a bag was a standard measure of trade with the ships. Women gathered the inner fat for use in domestic cooking. Some of it was made into soap and candles.

Fresh hides had to be well-cured to withstand the long trip to Boston. First, all the remaining meat and fat was cut off. Then the hides were soaked in sea water for several days to soften and clean them. One simple way of doing this was to stretch out and stake the hides in the sand at low tide and let the ocean water come in and cover them. The hides were left for forty-eight hours, then rolled up and soaked in vats of brine to further cure them and pickle the hides. The brine was simply seawater with large amounts of salt mixed in it. After forty-eight hours the hides were removed, spread out, and staked down on the ground. While the hide was still wet and soft, workers scraped away any remaining flesh and removed the ears, so that the hides could be stacked more evenly. The hides were allowed to sit in the sun for twenty-four hours to smooth the leather and make sure they were dry. If there was residual moisture, the hides would rot. The final step was to beat the hide with a flail (a free-swinging stick attached to the end of another stick) to remove any dirt and dust. After the hides had been cleaned, cured, scraped, dried, and beaten in this fashion, they were ready for storage in a warehouse. Curing the hides required a hot, dry climate, so most of work was done around San Diego.

When a Yankee ship sailed into the bay to trade, the hides were carried down to the shore in oxcarts or on mules' backs, or were thrown from the tops of the sea cliffs onto the beach. From here they were loaded into rowboats, carried through the breakers on the sailors' heads to keep them dry. The hide was doubled over lengthwise with the hair side in and stored flat in the ship's hold. After a full cargo of hides filled the ship, they were transported back to Boston to be made into shoes, many of which were later sold back to Californians. A typical cattle hide weighed about twenty-three pounds and each hide was worth 12½ cents a pound in Boston. At the end of the voyage, the ship's captain received 2 percent of the total value of the cargo.[22]

One irony of the system was that the Californians bought shoes and boots made from their own leather that had been carried twice around Cape Horn. Hides were valued at $2 to $3. The cost of shipment to and from Boston was about $3 or $4. Then the boots were manufactured, made a return trip, and were sold in California for $15, which was about three times the price in Boston. This high price was partly due to the heavy duties imposed by the government and partly due to the expenses of shipping by sea.

The trade in cow hides and tallow was brisk. American ships went up and down the coast collecting wherever they could, buying or trading with the locals. A round trip from Boston typically lasted from twelve to twenty-four months. Though the Boston owners of the ships made a good profit, for their sailors it was monotonous, tough, dirty hard work.

The American ships also traded tea, coffee, sugar, spices, raisins, molasses, hardware, crockery, tin goods, cutlery, clothing, boots and shoes, jewelry, and furniture. Among the more unusual trade items were fireworks from China and wheels for carts from England.[23]

The Pathfinders

One of the problems faced by the California missions was maintaining contact with the rest of the provinces of New Spain. The capital of Alta California at Monterey was more than a thousand miles from Santa Fe. The accepted method to travel to the California missions from New Mexico was to travel overland to the Gulf of California and then proceed by ship up the coast. This was a long, difficult, and tedious journey. To make communication, travel, and trade between the two colonies easier, an overland route was needed to tie the California presidio and mission outposts to New Mexico.

In 1774 Juan Bautista de Anza was ordered by the viceroy to explore a route to the California missions and thereby pioneered an overland trail from Sonora to Monterey. Anza set out from Tubac, near Tucson, where he was garrison commander, accompanied by fray Francisco Garcés, twenty soldiers, and fourteen servants, and traveled through southern Arizona. The group followed the Mojave River, and in March successfully reached Mission San Gabriel, northeast of Los Angeles. They took five months to reach the presidio at Monterey in California, but by achieving this Anza opened a trail from Tucson to California, called the Gila Trail, thus eliminating the need for the perilous sea journey from Baja California. It was not the easiest route, however. Even though the route followed the Gila River for some of the way, there were merciless sections of arid desert in Arizona and California with no grazing for animals.

Anza repeated the journey in September of 1775 with a group of 242 settlers, including soldiers, muleteers, women, and children, to establish a presidio and mission in the San Francisco area. The staging area for the expedition was again at Tubac. This type of travel was not an easy undertaking as the expedition had to carry all their supplies with them. Their food included six tons of flour, beans, cornmeal, and sugar (and the chocolate that Mexicans loved) that had to be loaded off the mules every night and then reloaded the next day. The expedition included 695 horses and mules, and 355 head of cattle.[24]

Anza traveled north past the Casa Grande ruins in south-central Arizona, turned west along the Gila River towards the Colorado River at Yuma, then northwest to Borrego Springs and Mission San Gabriel. After a short stay there, the group traveled on to Monterey.[25] Anza achieved the remarkable goal of guiding the expedition safely over an unknown route through barren, hostile country. The route he pioneered continued in use for several hundred years for soldiers, missionaries, gold seekers, stagecoaches, and traders. Trading with New Mexico was mostly manufactured goods that were exchanged for California horses and mules.

His task successfully accomplished, Anza left his second-in-command, José Joaquín Moraga, in charge. Moraga, accompanied by some of the colonists and soldiers, carried on to San Francisco several weeks later and established a mission and presidio overlooking the Bay in 1776. Anza meanwhile returned to Mexico City to report. While there he was promoted to Governor of New Mexico.

Another well-known, though unsuccessful, exploration to find a route to the West Coast was the Domínguez-Escalante expedition. Their expedition started in July of 1776 when a party of seven Spanish soldiers led by two Franciscan priests set out from Santa Fe. They hoped to find a better, more northerly route to Monterey that would avoid the hot and difficult desert wilderness crossings experienced by Anza, and provide better forage for animals.

The leader of the expedition was Francisco Atanasio Domínguez, the Commissary

Visitor of the Custody of the Conversion of St. Paul. The title of Commissary Visitor was given to only the best of the clergymen, one to whom a special task was assigned. Among other duties, Domínguez was charged with performing formal inspections of the New Mexico missions, inspecting the archives in Santa Fe to determine their historical accuracy, and finally establishing an overland route to link Santa Fe to Monterey for economic, defensive, and military reasons. His companion, fray Francisco Silvestre Vélez de Escalante, was a priest of Our Lady of Guadalupe at Zuni Pueblo, and accompanied the expedition as the record keeper. Though second in church rank to Domínguez, Escalante is generally regarded by historians as being the practical leader of the expedition.

Father Escalante had previously traveled in the West, including visiting the Hopi pueblo of Walpi in Arizona in 1775. The Hopi were never re-conquered by the Spanish after the Pueblo Revolt of 1680 and thus maintained their *katsina* religion. Escalante was horrified when he watched the native ceremonial masked dancers and drummers. He mentioned in his journal that each of the dancers was naked except for a small feather attached to the end of his penis, and went on to say, "This horrifying spectacle saddened me so that I arranged my departure for the following day."[26]

The Domínguez-Escalante expedition traveled northwest from Santa Fe, and headed for the Montezuma Valley, northeast of Cortez, Colorado. After several weeks of travel they camped by a river that they named *El Rio de Nuestra Señora de los Dolores* ("The River of Our Lady of Sorrows"). Settlers later shortened the name to the River of Sorrows or the Dolores River. On the south bank, overlooking the river, they found the remains of two abandoned Indian villages, both of which had been built and occupied by the Anasazi during the 1120s.

The ruined pueblos became known as the Escalante ruin and the Dominguez ruin. The Escalante ruin sat on top of a high hill overlooking the Dolores River. Built in the 1120s, it was the larger of the two pueblos, consisting of a double row of rooms in a rectangular layout surrounding a kiva. The Dominguez ruin was one of several small pueblos at the foot of the hill below the Escalante ruin. The part of the ruins visible today was a four-room structure that probably housed four to eight people, or one family. The design included a kiva and was typical of pueblo households of the time, consisting of a small row of rooms with southern exposure that faced a kiva. The walls were made in *jacal* style from upright poles, a brush top, and adobe clay.

The expedition continued north through Colorado and then turned west. The men traveled as far as Utah Lake, south of Provo, making them the first Europeans to see Utah. At Provo they turned back south, going to Cedar City and the Arizona border.

When the snows of winter started, the two leaders had to decide whether to press on to California or to return to New Mexico. There were no existing maps, they had no guide, and they did not really know where they were, so they decided to return to Santa Fe.

When the exploration party reached the Colorado River from the west, they were hard-pressed to find a crossing, let alone a safe one. They finally decided to chop steps into the sandstone walls above Padre Creek, then lowered their supplies and animals by ropes and slings in order to be able to cross Glen Canyon. The place where they crossed became known as "The Crossing of the Fathers."[27] On their way back, the group spent one night sheltered by the high cliffs of El Morro. No inscription from them has been found, probably because it was too cold and the snows of December were too deep.

The remains of the Escalante ruin, named after Father Escalante, were discovered while he and Father Domingez were searching for a better route to Mission San Gabriel near Los Angeles in California. The ruin contains rectangular rooms built next to a large circular *kiva*. The rectangular shaft in the foreground provides ventilation for the underground interior fireplace.

The bedraggled party reached Santa Fe on January 2, 1777. During their journey of five months they traveled a huge circle through New Mexico, Colorado, Utah, Arizona, and then back to Santa Fe, covering 2,000 miles of the most challenging terrain in the Southwest. Though Domínguez and Escalante did not finish the route they were looking for and failed to find a suitable passage to California, they accomplished the exploration of a large area of unknown country and returned with valuable information about the Southwest.

Following the expedition, Domínguez was recalled to Mexico to answer charges of misconduct leveled at him by disgruntled fellow friars. He spent the next thirty years in missionary assignments in New Mexico. Escalante remained in New Mexico for several years, then died at age thirty in 1780 having returned to Mexico for medical treatment.[28] Escalante's name is remembered today by the Escalante River, the Escalante Desert, and the town of Escalante in Utah. Domínguez's name was not so widespread, but is remembered by features such as Domínguez Canyon in western Colorado.

Decline of the Missions

By the time Mexico separated from Spain, the missions had effectively become huge cattle ranches. In 1833 the Mexican government secularized the missions of Upper and Lower California. The missions were converted into local parishes and the missionary priests were replaced by local clergymen. The churches remained as religious buildings, but were no longer the former large estates that generated vast revenue. When the ranches were secularized, they evolved into vast cattle ranches under the control of favored Spanish noblemen (*hidalgos*). The Indians were emancipated and had no more obligation to work on them or maintain them.

When the United States took over California, ownership of the missions passed into government hands and they became part of the public domain.[29] The missions at San Juan, Carmel, San Francisco Solano, and San Juan Capistrano were put up for auction. The rest, except Santa Barbara, were rented out. Most of the mission land was sold, given away by grant, or retained by the government.

Social Banditry

When the United States took over California with the Treaty of Guadalupe Hidalgo, one of the provisions was that every male citizen of Mexico in the appropriated area could either retain their Mexican citizenship or become a citizen of the United States. The American concept of Manifest Destiny, however, meant that ownership of the land by Mexicans was not recognized by the invading pioneers.[30] As a result social banditry flourished. A social bandit was one who was a criminal in the eyes of the law, but a hero in the eyes of the people. This hero was supposed to right all wrongs and was the one who avenged injustices done to the "little people" or the common man.

This concept goes back to the promotion of early common bandit-heroes in English literature, such as Robin Hood, Dick Turpin, and Guy Fawkes. One movie version of Robin

Hood expressed this concept well in the prolog when the screen said, "In times of tyranny and injustice when law oppresses the people, the outlaw takes his place in history."[31] The best known examples of social banditry in the United States were the real life Jesse James and the Younger Brothers, and the fictional character of Deadwood Dick. Though cast by newspapers, dime novels, and motion pictures into the role of a folk hero, the real life James was one of Quantrill's raiders during the Civil War and a cold-blooded killer after the war ended.

The most famous of the Spanish social bandits in California was Joaquín (or Joachim) Murrieta (or Murieta), a semifictional hero who was famous for his exploits against supposed tyranny imposed on Mexican immigrants in the early 1850s. The legend that grew up around him said that his family had been attacked by a group of Yankees who tied him up, beat him, and raped his wife. He escaped and vowed revenge. This was similar to the legends that grew up around the fictional Zorro in California.

The real Murrieta and his outlaw band terrorized the Anglo community in California. The governor finally called in bounty hunter Harry Love to track him down. In 1853, Love and his posse tracked down a series of Mexican bandits who had the name of Joaquín and dispatched them. Love brought back the head of the alleged outlaw leader, pickled in whiskey, for identification. It was never conclusively proven that this was the outlaw chief who was causing all the problems, but the ghoulish trophy was displayed to curious Californians in a saloon in San Francisco for an admission price of a dollar.

Zorro

The story of Spanish settlement of California would not be complete without a brief mention of Zorro, a fictional social bandit who created erroneous images that many people have used to visualize the Spanish in California. Zorro was not a real person, but sprang from the concept of the noble but oppressed outlaw that was used by dime novelists and early Hollywood to promote the good badman as a heroic character. Zorro was one of the fictional Masked Avengers of the Old West. None of the books and movies that recounted his exploits, however, showed the real history of California. The story of Zorro was pure Hollywood adventure. Even his pseudonym, which means "foxy person," was part of the fictional image.

The basic plot was that a swashbuckling hero, disguised by a mask, tried to avenge wrongs perpetuated on the native people by the Spanish government in early California. Behind the character of Zorro was the disguised Don Diego Vargas, supposedly a squeamish landowning aristocrat who hated violence by day, but was a masked avenger of the people at night.

The fictional character of Zorro first appeared in installments in "The Curse of Capistrano" by Johnston McCulley in the pulp magazine *All Story Weekly* in 1919. The cover described the story as taking place "When Romance and Rapiers Ruled in Old California." It was a simple tale of a masked man who rode around early California avenging wrongs committed on the peons by an unscrupulous governor. The hero's identity was not revealed until the conclusion. The first movie character of Zorro, played by the genuinely athletic Douglas Fairbanks, appeared the next year in *The Mark of Zorro* (1920), a tale that was characterized by stirring swordfights, dazzling acrobatics, fast chases, and Fairbanks' trademark feats involving swinging from balconies, leaping over walls and roofs, and stunts with wagons.

The popularity of the character and movie started a cycle of similar Zorro films. Typical was the motion picture *The Bold Caballero* (1937), in which Zorro came to the rescue of Indians burdened with excessive taxes. In true melodramatic Hollywood style, the first title blazed across the screen as "Spain's conquest of California was a saga written in blood," and continued somewhat ungrammatically as, "As though in answer to their prayers arose Zorro—a masked, incredibly daring hero—led them in a desperate revolt which provided freedom."

The Mask of Zorro (1998) further confused the real and the fictional by making Alejandro Murrieta into Zorro. In the film he is the screen brother of Joaquín Murrieta, who indeed gets his head lopped off by the villain.

McCulley went on to write sixty-five Zorro stories and Hollywood went on to make many Zorro movies. Among the odder versions was the comedy *Zorro, the Gay Blade* (1981) with two Zorros, one of whom was decidedly unusual.

Zorro should not be taken seriously as the history of California. The legend of Zorro simply reflected a yearning for the mythical romance and charm of old Spanish California in a series of nostalgic tales with right prevailing over injustice and tyranny. Similar stories are found in the dime novels of the late 1800s, with mythical versions of outlaw heroes such as Jesse James, Billy the Kid, and Deadwood Dick. In Europe, the outlaw Robin Hood, the highwayman Dick Turpin, and the swashbuckling Scarlet Pimpernel played similar folk hero roles. In more recent times, a similar theme was perpetuated by Batman and other superheroes who were secret avengers hiding behind the facade of shallow individuals to avoid suspicion of their real law-enforcing activities.

CHAPTER EIGHT

Indian Horsemen and Spanish Cowboys

Two important elements that shaped the history of the West after the arrival of the Spanish conquistadors were the gun and the horse. Arguably the greatest influence that the Spanish had on the native population of the Southwest was the introduction of the horse.

Spanish colonists introduced three important animals, cattle, sheep, and horses, to New Spain, then brought them north to the semi-arid climate of New Mexico. All three appeared in Mexico as early as 1519 after the arrival of Cortes and all multiplied successfully in an environment that was similar to Spain. As fray Alonso de Benevides noted in 1634, "As for our cows, horses [and sheep] ... that have been brought over from Europe already, they breed very profusely."[1] In 1818, for example, the mission at Tumacácori in Arizona had 5,000 cattle, 2,500 sheep, and 600 horses, along with other domestic stock.[2] The missions were so successful in raising herds that they sold excess stock to add to mission wealth.

All three of these animals were quickly adopted by the nomadic Indian tribes, such as the Apache, Comanche, Navajo, and Utes, and incorporated into their lifestyles.

Indian raids claimed many of the Spanish settlers' sheep to build Indian herds. One Comanche raid netted 300 head of livestock, mostly sheep, near Albuquerque in 1774.[3] Sheep did better in dry conditions than cattle and were thus well suited to the dry desert country of the Navajo and the Hopi. Sheep vastly outnumbered cattle during the colonial times and Spanish sheep became very important to the Navajo. The Navajo were originally farmers who lived in the manner of the Pueblo Indians. When the Spanish arrived, however, the Navajo learned to raise sheep and goats, and use the wool to produce their characteristic wool blankets, which were splashed with bright colors and striking geometric patterns. The Navajo became world famous for their skill as weavers, producing blankets and rugs with complex angular patterns of diamonds and crosses. Looms and weaving skills that Navajos still use were derived from ancient pueblo Indian techniques.

Sheep and goats were also of great economic value to the Spanish settlers. Goats were angora goats, which yielded good yarn. Hispanic households produced much of their own woven cloth on rough-hewn looms, using the wool of sheep and goats. Men sheared the flocks, while the women washed and carded the fleece. From this they made rugs, blankets, ponchos, bedding, serapes, shawls, and trousers, as well as lighter material made into sheets, shirts, skirts, curtains, bedspreads, and table covers. The wool was colored with dyes made from leaves, flower petals, and roots.[4]

The original sheep brought by the Spanish in 1540 were churros, a breed that produced

A lucrative trade in cattle hides developed between California and shoe merchants in the East. Traders came in ships with necessities for isolated California missions and traded for cattle hides and tallow, which they carried around Cape Horn to Boston. Because of a lack of cash, hides were so commonly used for trade and as currency that they became known as "leather dollars."

tasty meat and long coarse wool that was suitable for weaving. Adult churro sheep typically weighed between sixty-five and eighty pounds. As they multiplied, they quickly became the province's most important domestic stock animal. By 1800 the number of sheep was estimated to be over 200,000 not including those owned by Indians.[5] By the mid–1880s Anglo-Americans crossbred churros with larger breeds, especially the French merino, to produce heavier bodies with better meat and better fleeces. The sheep industry in the West grew after the California gold rush created a high demand for meat.

Cattle had a similar importance to the later inhabitants of the Southwest. The first cattle were brought to Mexico with an expedition led by Gregorio de Villalobos.[6] Given the temperate climate of Mexico and few predators, cattle multiplied freely. The free roaming descendants of these original Spanish cattle and other breeds that followed them with Anglo settlers eventually formed the large Texas herds that resulted in the great Western cattle industry and drives of the 1870s and 1880s.[7]

Spanish Horses

More important than both sheep and cattle was the horse, whose speed, stamina, and durability made it indispensable in the West. The Spanish pony was considered to be the finest and fastest riding horse at the time and was extensively used for working with cattle in Spain. Horses were also valuable for inspiring fear in the natives. Today's quarter horses used for riding and working with cattle are partially descended from this early Spanish stock.

The first horses arrived on the North American continent in 1541 with de Soto and, by the 1780s, horses had spread among the Plains Indians.[8] This hardy stock was descended from the Moorish desert horses of Arabia and North Africa, which were selectively bred in Spain for excellence in hand-to-hand combat, surviving grueling cavalry marches, and herding Spanish bulls.[9] They were tough animals that could live on meager food supplies.

The first horses in the New World were twenty-four stallions and ten mares brought to Hispaniola by Christopher Columbus in 1494.[10] Their descendants were transported with expeditions to Florida and Mexico. Many horses were slaughtered for food and others were turned loose at the end of an expedition when the explorers had no further need for them.

Cortés and his conquistadors brought domesticated horses with them to New Mexico. At the time of the arrival of the Spanish, there were no horses in the West. A type of small wild horse had originally flourished on the North American continent, but for some unknown reason the breed died out and became extinct about 7,000 years ago. Cortés found that horses enhanced the image of the Spanish as gods and were valuable in inspiring fear in the natives. Horses also allowed the Spanish to travel great distances during exploratory and conquering expeditions. The use of the horse allowed soldiers to wear heavier armor than they could have used on foot, an important defensive strategy that saved many of them during Indian attacks.

Horses flourished in the climate and environment of the Southwest. Spanish horses were either mares or stallions, as gelding was not practiced at the time.[11] Stallions were preferred to mares and, in Spanish tradition, no gentleman or lady would ride a mare. Stallions were considered by the Spanish with their male cultural emphasis to be more powerful than mares and their power and strength was judged by the size of their testicles. Mares were reserved for breeding stock and each *rancho* had a herd of brood mares and an appropriate number of stallions.

The typical Indian pony, with its shaggy coat and small size, evolved from the half Andalusian, half Arab stock that Spanish had brought with them to the New World. Indian horses had an interesting advantage over those of the Europeans. When the United States army fought the Indian Wars in the West between 1865 and 1890, soldiers had to be accompanied by a supply train to carry corn and oats to feed the larger cavalry horses during field campaigns. The smaller and hardier Indian ponies could eat summer prairie grasses and feed off the land. The Indians, however, were at a disadvantage during winter when their ponies only had willow bark to eat, and their horses often became malnourished until spring when the wild grasses returned.

The Plains Indians, such as the Apache and Comanche, were the primary beneficiaries of the arrival of the horse and quickly adapted to a lifestyle that relied on horses. By the early 1830s, the Comanche collectively owned tens of thousands of horses and mules that they had obtained by trading and stealing.[12] After the Comanche mastered the horse, they fought other Indians as well as the Spanish. By 1750 the Comanche controlled former Apache territory in central Texas and eastern New Mexico, where the Spanish seldom penetrated. The Comanche prospered on the vast herds of buffalo and raided Spanish and Indian settlements at will. The Indians soon learned that making surprise attacks on Spanish settlements was an easy way to obtain horses.

Some horses escaped from captivity and some were abandoned and left to fend for themselves if they became injured or crippled. As the Spanish did not practice gelding, the escaped horses multiplied so fast on the Plains that soon Indians were able to obtain what they needed from wild herds. Over the next hundred years or so, the horse population grew into vast herds of tens of thousands. These wild, unclaimed horses of the Southwest Plains were known as mustangs, from the Spanish *mesteño*. Mustangs were smaller than other horses, most Indian ponies being about fourteen hands high.[13] In California so many unbranded mustangs multiplied in the wild that they were periodically rounded up and slaughtered to protect the grazing land for domestic horses and cattle, and to stop them from bothering tame stock.

Later American settlers sometimes captured mustangs by "creasing" them. In this technique, the horse was shot through the upper crease of the neck, above the cervical vertebrae. If done correctly, the bullet shocked a nerve in the neck and the horse fell down senseless long enough to be captured, then recovered quickly. If the bullet was too low, it fractured a vertebra in the neck and killed the horse instantly.

Travelers crossing the prairie were sometimes forced to eat the meat of mustangs if they ran out of food. It was said that when young, mustangs were edible. But when they were old, the meat was said to be exceedingly rancid, particularly if the horse was fat. Fat animals were sometimes hunted for their oil content.

Another source of horses for the Indians was the Spanish themselves. As early as the arrivals of Coronado and Oñate, Indians had been stealing horses from Spanish ranches. The Indians of the Southwest who had been in contact with the Spanish since they arrived were the first to own horses. By the early 1600s, through trading and raiding, the Plains tribes had the beginnings of their own herds. By 1770 almost all the Plains tribes had their own horses. Among the Plains Indians, the horse became a symbol of wealth and status, a medium of exchange, a means of hunting buffalo, and an improved method of carrying out lightning raids against their neighbors. When courting, the wealth of a suitor was judged by the number of horses he owned, and horses were often part of the price for a bride.

The horse made mounted Indians superior to tribes that did not have horses. By giving the Plains warriors greater mobility, the horse changed their life in several ways. Now the Indians could catch more game and range further across the Plains to hunt. Before the Indians had horses, vast herds of buffalo had roamed the country from Florida to Oregon and New York to California.[14] Estimates of the number have ranged from 30 million to 70 million. When the Indians obtained horses and were able to follow the buffalo more easily, tribes such as the Cheyenne, Comanche, and Apache became nomadic hunters. Instead of running after the buffalo on foot, they killed the animals from horseback in larger numbers than before and the size of the herds started to decline. By using a horse, a hunter could pursue and kill enough buffalo to feed his family for months. Though the wholesale slaughter of buffalo started when the Anglo-Americans arrived, the Indians had already started the trend.

The most important hunting and war weapon of the Plains Indians was the bow and arrow. Bows ranged from three to five feet long, and were made from juniper or hickory. The shorter bows were preferable for use on horseback. Bow strings were made from twisted sinew. Arrows were made from the twigs of willow or current bushes that were peeled and straightened, with turkey or turkey vulture feathers fastened to the shaft with sinew. Arrow tips were made from flint or bone. After the arrival of the Spanish and the later Anglos they were made from metal, such as barrel hoops.

The bow and arrow had an effective range of about forty to seventy yards.[15] Its use was enhanced when shooting from horseback, as a hunter or warrior could move closer to his prey or adversary. Another important weapon was the lance, a pole that was six or seven feet long, tipped with a flint or metal point bound to the shaft with sinew. This weapon was easier to use for hunting buffalo when it was used from a horse.

Horses spread to the Plains tribes, reaching all of them between 1650 and 1770. By the time Anglo settlers arrived from the East, the Indian way of life had changed. Two hundred years of contact with the Spanish had made them expert horsemen.

The use of horses upset the old territorial boundaries. When the Utes received horses and guns, they were able to travel out onto the Plains. By the same token, the Comanche and Kiowa with horses now hunted in the mountains. Indians continued to selectively breed for speed, agility, intelligence, and endurance, both for buffalo hunting and as war ponies.

Some of the best horses were reputed to be the Appaloosas. The American version of the breed was developed by the Nez Percé Indians of Idaho. Spanish ponies were interbred with various European bloodlines, resulting in a breed that had a coat with spotted patterns. Subsequent theft and trade resulted in the wide spread of this type of horse.[16] Pinto is a Spanish word meaning "painted" and was applied to black-and-white, bay-and-white, and brown-and-white horses used by Indians.

Though the Plains Indians quickly incorporated horses into their lifestyle, horses did not spread as rapidly to the Pueblo Indians because horses were reserved for the Spanish.

The Pueblo Indians were not allowed to own or ride horses, as the Spanish realized that they could maintain an advantage if they could retain control of all the horses. The Pueblo Indians were limited to helping the Spanish care for their horses.

After the Pueblo Revolt of 1680, many Spanish horses were either stolen by the Apache or were driven off to run wild by Pueblo Indians who had no need of them. The result was the spread of a large number of horses among the nomadic tribes of the Southwest and the Great Plains. Horses helped the Plains Indians, such as the Apache, to obtain what they needed by raiding Pueblo Indians and Spanish settlements. By the 1740s, bands of Apache, Comanche, and Navajo mounted on horses were carrying out swift surprise raids on Spanish ranches, settlements, and missions. Punitive expeditions were sent in retaliation, but the Spanish found it basically impossible to stop these lightning raids.

By the 1700s, the Indians along the Rio Grande had acquired horses by trade and by theft from Spanish herds during attacks on settlers. The use of horses quickly spread up through the Rockies to Oregon. The Kiowa had horses by 1682, the Pawnee by 1700, and the Comanche by 1714.[17] The Comanche, Shoshone, and Blackfeet quickly learned the use of horses. The Sioux were also excellent horsemen. Horses traveled north to Montana by 1690 via the Navajo, Ute, Shoshone, Crow, and Nez Percé.

Indian Dogs

Before horses became commonplace among the Plains Indians, some tribes used tame dogs for hunting companions, and as pack and draft animals. The tribes of the Great Plains used dogs as beasts of burden to transport their goods from camp to camp as part of their nomadic lifestyle. One method they used to carry household possessions was to simply tie a pack onto a dog's back. A Spanish chronicler described the practice in this fashion, "These people [the Apache] have dogs similar to those of this land [Mexico], except that that they are somewhat larger. They load these dogs like beasts of burden and make light pack-saddles for them like our pack-saddles, cinching them with leather straps."[18]

Another method of using dogs for transporting goods was with a travois, which consisted of one end of a pole tied to each side of the dog, with the other ends trailing on the ground. The load was lashed between them. A large dog could drag as much as fifty pounds. This type of carrier was still used, adapted on a larger scale for use with horses, in the early 1600s.

The Plains Indians initially called horses "big dogs." They also called them "spirit dogs" and "medicine dogs."[19] The Lakota Sioux called horses *sunkakham*, or "holy dogs," and prized their horses above all their other possessions. They trained their horses for different uses. Some horses were dedicated to hunting and were trained to run close to the buffalo to allow an easier kill. Others were trained for war. Some were even trained to run over the owners' enemies if they happened to be on foot.

Raiders on Horseback

After they obtained horses, the Apache specialized in raiding the Pueblo people to steal food. They also captured Pueblo people who were traded or sold as slaves. They then expanded their raids to Spanish settlements to steal horses, sheep, and cattle. The Apache drove some communities out of existence during the period of Spanish expansion. The Apache were not after wealth, but only took what they needed to survive. In retaliation, the Spanish, and later the Mexicans, captured and enslaved as many Apache as possible. Even when the United States took over the Southwest, the raiding continued. In 1866 between 2,000 and 10,000 Apache were held as slaves by the Anglos, with more in Mexico.

Probably the most profound transition brought about by the introduction of the horse was to the Comanche, whose lifestyle changed from hunters on foot to that of far-ranging and effective mounted hunters and raiders. In adopting the horse, the Comanche turned out to be unwitting allies of the Spanish, as this new capability helped to resist the southward expansion of the British and the French from Canada.

Of all the Plains Indians, the Comanche became some of the most skilled horsemen. They were accomplished horse breeders and owned more than any other tribe. They were also experts at capturing and taming wild horses. A warrior would run a wild horse down and slip a loop of rope around its neck. He would then place his hand over its eyes and breathe into its nostrils to help to calm it.[20] There may also have been religious reasons for doing this, as a Cheyenne warrior believed that by breathing into a horse's nostrils he could impart some of his spirit into it. The gentling process included tying a newly caught wild horse to a previously tamed horse. This was followed by petting and gradually putting a light load on the horse's back until it was ready to accept a rider.[21] Though the Comanche enjoyed catching horses, they also liked to steal horses from other tribes.

When the Spanish built missions in California they also tried to keep horses away from the Indians. Spanish law stated that Indians could not even ride horses. Based on their prior experience in New Mexico, the Spanish knew that unfriendly Indians on horseback could pose a serious threat. However, the friars soon found that the herds of cattle at the missions were multiplying to the point where there were not enough *vaqueros* (Mexican cowboys) to take care of them. By 1834 the number of mission cattle in California was estimated to be 423,000.[22] And an additional number of cattle were multiplying out of control on the open range.

Some of the Indians in California, however, never took to the concept of horses. They ate them instead, and became known as the Horse-Eaters.[23]

Donkeys and Their Offspring

As well as pure-bred horses, other animals with horse-like characteristics were used by the Spanish. One important one was the donkey, a domestic animal that resembled a horse, but was much smaller, had long ears, and a shorter mane. The Spanish called them a burro; others called them an ass. A male donkey was further known as a jack and the female as a jenny. A cross between a burro and a horse resulted in two different animals, both of which could not reproduce further. A mule was the sterile offspring of a male donkey and a female horse, sure-footed and a better forager than a horse, and a hinny was the sterile offspring of a female donkey and a male horse, known for its stamina. Burros were excellent beasts of burden. They could carry a load of up to 300 pounds, or nearly double that of a horse. One problem was that though burros could swim, they often did not and drowned while crossing rivers.

The Appearance of Cattle

As well as a lack of indigenous horses, North America had no indigenous cattle before the Spanish brought them. Cattle from Andalusia in southern Spain were brought to Hispaniola, along with horses, as part of the cargo on Columbus' second expedition. Cattle were first transported from the West Indies to New Spain in 1521 and other shipments soon followed. By 1540 these cattle had multiplied naturally on the Yucatán Peninsula in Mexico. The Spanish started cattle ranching in Mexico and so the *vaquero*, or Spanish cowboy, was born.

Cattle came north to New Mexico with Coronado in 1540 and formed the nucleus of the Spanish cattle business. Cattle continued to move northwards with Spanish settlers and missionaries as ranching spread into New Mexico, California, Texas, and Arizona.

The Spanish were familiar with cattle, but not with wild buffalo. In October of 1598, Vicente de Zaldívar had the idea that he could develop a market for buffalo hides and meat, so he tried to domesticate some of them. Riders herded a group of buffalo together towards a huge corral, but the animals became upset and turned on them. The animals quickly gored the horses and their riders, and the Spanish gave up the idea of buffalo ranching.

The first of the cattle, the Spanish longhorns, were black. They were mixture of two breeds, Andalusian and Moorish. They were descended from cattle tended by the Moors on the arid plains of northern Africa and southern Spain. As their name implied, longhorns had long, wicked-looking horns that could grow up to seven feet from tip to tip. These lean, mean cows were called Mexican cattle or Spanish cattle. Later longhorns were colored with almost every combination of black, red, and white, as a result of interbreeding with other stock.

By 1821 these cattle had spread all over what is now southern Texas. Their descendents did well in the wild, becoming heavier and taller as they fed on the scrubby vegetation. The meat, however, was lean, stringy, and tough, and the longhorn did not reach a mature weight until about ten years of age. In time, interbreeding occurred with American cattle and eventually ranchers of the West deliberately crossbred the rangy Texas longhorns with fatter European short-horned cattle that had tender meat, such as Herefords, also known commonly as the "whiteface." The other advantage was that these domestic crosses were hornless (polled), which made herding and shipping them safer and easier by reducing the possibility of injuries from the long horns.

Spanish cattle were hardy and adapted well to the hot, dry country of Texas, Arizona, and New Mexico. These cattle could go without water for up to four days and could survive on the poor forage of the tangled dense thickets in the thorny bush country of southern Texas.

When the Spanish colonized the Southwest they developed the open-range method of pasturing cattle and horses. The stock was generally left alone to fend for themselves in the wild, though they were checked by riders every few weeks. Cattle roamed on the unfenced grassland, then were rounded up and separated by each owner's brand, and the calves were branded and accounted for. The brand was traditionally placed on the left hip, so that a cowboy would know where to see it clearly in groups of milling cattle. This roundup was called the *rodear*, which in Spanish means "to round up" or "to encircle," a word that eventually changed into "rodeo," the modern sport where contestants compete in various exhibitions of riding and roping skills.

Before the modern techniques of lassoing cattle were developed, the rider put the loop of his *lazo* on the end of a long pole and dropped it over the steer's horns. The technique of throwing the loop over the horns from a distance was not developed until later.

Cattle were slaughtered (the *matanza*) in late summer when they weighed the most. The hides were stripped away for trade or use as leather, the fat was used for cooking and for tallow, and the meat was carved for steaks or fried.

Part of the decline of the Texas missions was brought about by the difficulty of capturing and branding mission cattle in the rough brush country of south Texas. As a result, many of the half-wild cattle went unbranded. In 1778, the Crown declared that all unbranded cattle were its property and would be subject to taxation. This caused the vast herds of free ranging cattle formerly owned by the missions to decline to only a few hundred. As the herds declined, so did the mission revenue, and eventually the missions themselves.

Meanwhile, the descendents of bulls and cows brought by Spanish conquistadors, along with those that escaped from the missions and those stolen from the missions by Indians, continued to multiply almost unnoticed on grasslands of southeast Texas. From the time of the Texas revolution to the Civil War cattle grew wild and multiplied at a rapid rate. Estimates are that by 1830 there were 100,000 longhorns running wild in the Texas brush country.[24]

The original cattle brought north from Mexico to New Mexico and California were longhorns, whose wicked-looking horns could be as wide as seven feet from tip to tip. These animals were descended from Andalusian and Moorish cattle. Other breeds were later cross-bred with them to produce better meat and more docile cattle. These were the cattle raised at the missions and which eventually spread over southern Texas to form the nucleus of the early Texas livestock industry.

Attempts were made to round up some of the cattle and sell them in New Orleans in the 1830s and 1840s, and in California during the gold rush, but sales were irregular and of no particular consequence. The big cattle drives did not really start until after the Civil War, when a big cattle market developed to supply the demand for meat in the North.

By the 1850s, Texans had taken over the cattle business, with most of the large herds centered around San Antonio, Corpus Christi, and Laredo. The country was open, the grass was plentiful, the climate was mild, water was good, and there was no snow. Mexican longhorns and Spanish horses did so well that the American cowboy was born.

Branding

The practice of branding cattle for identification dates back to Biblical times, and was practiced by the ancient Egyptians and the Chinese. A permanent and distinctive mark burned into the animal's hide by a branding iron became the mark of legal ownership. The methods of rounding up and branding cattle introduced to the West by Spanish ranchers were used extensively by Mexican and later American ranchers.

Each animal had to have an earmark, an ownership brand, and sale brand. The earmark consisted of removing part of the ear with a cut or series of cuts that formed a distinctive design in one or both ears. By law, each rancher had to also have his own brand that was recorded in the official brand book. He petitioned the local *alcalde* (mayor), who decided whether or not the rancher was worthy. If approved, the rancher had to have an *el fierro para herar los ganados*, a regular iron to brand his stock, and *el fierro para ventear*, an iron used to cancel the original brand if the stock was sold or transferred.

When an animal was sold, the new owner put his brand on it. To prove that the transfer was legitimate, the original owner "vented" (from the Spanish *venta* or "sale") the original brand by burning a bar across it. Cows that had been sold many times might have many different brands on them. Today, because of the value of hides, cattle usually only have a single brand.

Cattle brands in the Old West consisted of a combination of letters, numbers, and symbols. Brands were read from top to bottom and left to right. The brand "/-K," for example would be read "slash bar K." Sometimes letters and numerals were applied in the conventional direction with some parts reversed, such as "reverse K" or "reverse 3." One example of a brand that read from to to bottom was the "R bar backward C." Other brands were placed on their side in a configuration called "lazy," such as "lazy B" or "lazy 5." A brand burned at an angle was read as "tumbling," as in "tumbling K" or "tumbling 3 bar J." Other brands consisted of symbols, such as a rocking chair, a bell, or two hearts. The explorer Cortés, for example, used a brand that consisted of three Christian crosses placed side-by-side.

The First Cowboys

The first Spanish cowboys appeared in Alta California around 1769. The modern American cowboy originated in Texas in the 1850s, but Spanish and Mexican *vaqueros* had been herding cattle long before that. The Spanish name *vaquero* is a combination of the

Spanish word *vaca* (cow) and the suffix *-ero*, which means "one engaged in a given occupation." Thus *vaqueros* were men whose job was tending cattle. Texans adapted many of the *vaquero's* techniques and customs for their own use, and created their own Texas cowboy culture. The Spanish name *vaquero* (one alternate spelling is *vacquero*) became later corrupted into the American word "buckaroo" for a cowboy.

Perversely, early *vaqueros* were often Indians. From the earliest days in Mexico to the late Spanish colonial days, there were no Anglo *vaqueros*. Most of the missionaries did not like dealing with cattle and felt that such work was beneath their dignity. Out of necessity, then, needing men to raise and guard the cattle, the missionaries often ignored the rule of Indians not riding horses and trained some of the mission converts to be *vaqueros*. The civil authorities understood the practical need for this and overlooked the letter of the law. These California *vaqueros* became America's first cowboys. They were taught how to saddle and care for horses, how to ride and rope, how to build a branding fire and brand cattle, and how to cut an earmark. They also learned how to shoe horses, do simple blacksmithing, and make branding irons.

This was not a glamorous job, and was not romanticized as later dime novelists did with the American cowboy. These were simply poor laborers who happened to perform their work on horseback. Eventually, however, their style of clothing was modified to meet the demands of their job. The use of hats with oversized brims, for example, grew out of a need for the *vaqueros* to shade their faces and keep their heads cool in the hot sun, and so the sombrero was born.

Many Spanish and Mexican words were adopted later by the American cowboys. The expression "savvy" comes from *sabe usted* or "do you understand?" The Spanish word *caballero* was used for "horseman." A herd of saddle horses, such as those accompanying a cattle drive, were called a *remuda*, from the Spanish word which means "remount." The name "bronco" for a rough horse came originally from the Spanish *broncho*, a name for a wild and untamed horse. The name was often contracted to "bronc" and applied to an unbroken horse. *Arroyo* was the name given to a dried-out streambed that temporarily became a riverbed after a heavy rain then dried out again. *Fiesta* was a religious festival, holiday, or carnival. *Hombre* was the Spanish word for a man, a rough, tough man, but also used to describe a "real man."

Vaquero Paraphernalia

The *vaqueros* developed most of the clothing, techniques, and terms used later by American cowboys.

Saddles

Vaquero saddles evolved from the Spanish war saddles (*silla de montar*) that were brought to the New World with Cortés and the conquistadors. This heavy and cumbersome rig eventually evolved into the more comfortable and practical saddles used by the *vaqueros*. These "Spanish saddles" were further modified by Texans to become today's roping saddles, which weighed about forty to fifty pounds.

The original Mexican saddle was single-rigged, using a single cinch, or strap under the horse's belly. The early California *vaqueros* experimented with moving the single cinch back and forth to try to prevent chafing the horse's belly, until they found what they considered to be the optimum position around the horse. During the later boom in the Texas cattle industry, cowboys roping large cows in rugged country added a second cinch further back. This type of saddle was called double-rigged. The double-rigged saddle had the advantage of staying in place when the cow came to the end of the lariat used to rope it, and pulled with a hard jerk on the saddle and horn.

The Western saddle originated in Mexico before it found its way across the border into Texas and California. Early Mexican saddles had very small saddle horns and, as a consequence, ropes used for catching and controlling cattle were tied either to a cinch ring or directly to the tail of the horse. In the late 1700s the horn became larger and stronger to allow *vaqueros* to anchor the rope to the saddle instead with a hitch around the horn. The saddle tree was made from wood and had a high horn to anchor the rope. A thick leather pad and two blankets were under the tree. On top of the tree was a large leather sheet (*mochila*) that was often embossed with fancy designs.

The concept of the *mochila* as a Spanish saddle covering was later modified into a type of leather saddlebag by riders for the Pony Express, who added a pouch for the mail on either side. This saddlebag was dropped into position across the horn and cantle of a regular saddle like the *mochila* and held on by its own weight. This way the mail could be easily and quickly transferred from one saddle to another when the rider changed mounts at each relay station.

The original Spanish ring bit for controlling the horse was a cruel type of bit that cut into the horse's mouth. The ring part of the bit went through the horse's mouth and encircled the lower jaw. Texas cowboys later modified this into the gentler spade bit that controlled the animal through pressure on the horse's mouth and tongue.

Rope

Cowboy names for ropes came from the Spanish names for *vaquero*

The original Spanish saddles incorporated single rigging, the strap underneath the horse's belly. The saddles used in Alta California retained the *mochila*, the large leather sheet seen here thrown on top of the saddle. The large leather *tapaderas* over the stirrups protected the rider's feet from cactus thorns and chaparral.

ropes. The word "lariat" came from the Spanish *la reata*, meaning "the rope." The word "lasso" came from *lazo*, meaning a snare or noose. Originally the *reata* and the *lazo* were different types of rope that served different purposes. The lariat was a short rope made of horsehair and was used for bridles and picketing horses, while the lasso was a longer rope made of leather, with a loop at the end for catching cattle. Eventually both names came to simply mean a cowboy's rope. The *honda* or *hondo* was a small loop or eyelet at the end of a lariat, through which the rope was pulled to tighten the noose. The name is derived from the Spanish term *hondón*, or eyelet. The cowboy word "McCarty" for a rope came from the Spanish *mecate*, which means a fine horsehair rope attached to a bit.

Ropes for catching cattle were made from various materials. Most common was untanned cowhide that was cut into thin strips, then braided together in four to eight strands to form a rope about half-an-inch in diameter and anywhere from forty to sixty feet long. Some ropes were as long as a hundred feet. Rawhide lariats were preferable for roping, as the stiffness of the leather held the loop open when it was thrown. When a cow was caught and ran to the end of the rope, ropes made from braided rawhide stretched, thus lessening the jerk on the horse and the cow.

Horsehair ropes were made of strands of horse hair twisted tightly together. These ropes were strong and were easy to make. Horse hair for ropes was traditionally gathered from the mares, as it was felt that long tails were how the mares recognized the stallions and for breeding purposes should be left intact.[25] Horsehair lariats were not as common or popular as rawhide ropes, however, as they were very light in weight and not as strong as cowhide.[26] But they were commonly used for picket ropes.

A few ropes found in southwest Texas were made of fibers from the maguey cactus. Maguey ropes held a loop well, but tended to disintegrate in wet weather, so they were typically only used for light work in dry climates.[27] The most popular of the later American cowboy ropes were made of manila hemp with three strands. Ropes for catching cattle were hung from a croup or thongs attached to the pommel of the saddle.

Vaqueros were skilled in using their *reata* to rope steers. For catching a cow or an ox, the rope was thrown to land around the animal's horns. The *reata*'s near end was then looped around the saddle horn (pommel) with a hitch to anchor the rope. The *vaquero*'s name for doing this was *dar la vuelta*, which meant to give a twist or turn around something. This was eventually corrupted to "dally," the American cowboy's term for wrapping the end of his lariat around the saddle horn after he roped a steer. The technique was more convenient than tying the rope directly to the saddle horn as the dally could be easily and quickly released when the cow was set free again. This was also the origin of the American expression "dilly-dally," a duplicated form of "dally" meaning to waste time in hesitation.

Clothing

The early *vaqueros* wore short breeches called *calzones*, made from leather, wool, or cotton. Others wore a long type of pantaloon called *calzoneras*, which had the bottom outer part of the leg open. These pants were slit up the side and buttoned, and were sometimes decorated with a fancy filigree. The fashionable way to wear them was open at the bottom to show the wearer's long underdrawers, which in the case of everyday workers were not always particularly white. By contrast, the drawers underneath a ranch owner's velveteen pants were sparkling white, which marked him as a man of wealth who could afford a laundress. Heavy leather leggings (*botas*) were often tied with garters around the lower legs for protection of the ankles and calves from bushes. Unlike the wealthy Spanish owners of the ranches, some early *vaqueros* who could not afford footwear often did not wear shoes or boots, but went barefooted.

In cool weather, the *vaquero's* outfit might be completed with a *serape*, which was a small blanket that covered the shoulders and torso, donned by putting the head through a slit in middle and letting the cloth drape over the wearer's front and back. Alternately a *vaquero* might wear a cloth or leather jacket (*chaqueta*).

Originally leg protection from thorny bushes was provided by a large piece of cowhide or buckskin called an *arma* that was draped across the saddle horn like a loose apron and tied around the waist and knees with thongs. The name was derived from *arma*, a defensive weapon or shield. The original design was large enough that it could be also tied around the breast of the horse, if desired, to protect it. The *arma* was eventually made smaller and lighter to cover only the legs. This garment was called by the diminutive *armita* meaning "short leg armor." Often a knife was tucked into the top for eating and slaughtering cattle. *Armitas* were also called "chinks" as a shortened version of *chinkaderos*. They were tied to the leg by thongs that held them in place. Various animal skins were used, such as goat, sheep, bear, wolf, or mountain lion pelts.

This protective gear further evolved into a closed type of leather leggings that were worn from the torso down, like a pair of pants legs attached by only a belt at the waist. These Spanish *chaperreras* or *chaperejos* ("chaps") were leather breeches developed to protect the thighs and lower legs from cactus or other thorny plants and bushes, such as mesquite and prickly pear, and the abrasive brush of Baja California. Alta California did not have the same problems with cactus, but there was plenty of chaparral and brush that made leg protection necessary. These cowhide chaps provided protection from rain and bites from irritable bulls or horses. Chaps in California were sometimes made from the skin of bears with the hair still attached to provide some additional warmth in the cooler climate of the northern part of the state. These were not always popular as they were hot in the summer and smelled terrible when wet.

The *tapadera* (from Spanish *tapar*, to cover) was a wedge-shaped piece of leather that shielded the wearer's boot from cactus thorns and chaparral to protect the feet in brushy country. It covered the stirrup at the front and side, but was open at the rear to allow easy entry of a boot.

Hats

The *vaquero's* outfit was topped (literally) by a low-crowned hat with a wide brim called a *sombrero* from the word *sombra*, which means "shade" in Spanish. The wealthier Spaniards had hats brightly decorated with gold or silver bands. The brims and crowns might be embroidered with intricate designs. A type of hat with a wide brim and a low crown that came to Texas from Mexico in the mid–1700s was called a *poblano*.

Regardless of the particular style, the *sombrero* had a wide, floppy brim to provide shade from the sun while the rider spent long hours in the saddle or to protect his head when it rained. Hats were commonly made from leather or felt, though some were made from the woven straw of the Mexican farmers. This design was sometimes cumbersome, but it was eminently practical in the hot sun of the Southwest. Along the Mexican border, the *sombrero* had a steeple shape with a large brim like a saucer. Further north, higher crowns and narrower brims were more common.

The hats of the later American cowboys were adapted directly from the Spanish *sombrero*. They were wide-brimmed with a small, peaked crown, commonly black or brown in color, and were made from leather, straw, cheap felt, or palm fiber. Cowboys in the Southwest liked the high crown and wide brim of the Mexican *sombrero* to protect their heads from the intense sun of the desert and to keep it cool. Northern cowboys preferred a lower, flatter crown and narrower brim that stayed in place better during high winds and did not blow off as easily in the climates of North Dakota and Montana. Eminently practical was John Stetson's Boss of the Plains design, which had a narrow four-inch brim and low, rounded four-inch crown.

Spurs

Horsemen have worn spurs since the knights of medieval times. Though used to control a horse while riding, spurs were also worn by knights as a badge of honor. Spurs came to the New World with Cortés and his conquistadors, and blacksmiths started making spurs in New Spain as early as 1598. Spurs were later adopted by the *vaqueros* and were worn as a symbol of status to signify their line of work. Even *vaqueros* who did not wear boots usually wore spurs, even strapping them to their bare feet if they had no boots.

A spur consisted of a rounded metal band that encircled the heel of a boot and was fastened in front by a chain or a leather strap. A circular rowel (the rotating disc with sharp projections mounted on the shank at the back) was used to prod the horse's side to guide him and make him go faster. Spurs were commonly made of iron, though rich ranch owners might have fancy spurs of silver. *Vaquero* spurs had extremely large rowels. The shanks were typically three to five inches long, with the rowels sometimes as large as six or seven inches in diameter. Some rowels were so big that they made walking impossible, as the wearer couldn't put his foot flat on the ground. These designs were so cumbersome that riders often removed them when

Spanish spurs encircled the back of the wearer's boot and usually had extremely large rowels, the pointed metal spikes that form the shape of a wheel. The spikes were often so long, such as these, that they dug into the ground when the wearer was out of the saddle and he could not walk wearing them. As a result, many riders took off their spurs when they were on foot.

dismounted. The spokes on later American rowels were typically narrow and blunt to prevent injury to the horse from a sharp spur. The fancier spurs had little metal pendants called "danglers" or "jingle-bobs," which jangled when the wearer walked.

Vaquero Games

Before the days of the gold rush of 1849, entertainment in Spanish California had a down-to-earth nature. When the province was still an outpost of Mexico, bullfights, gambling halls, and fandangos were popular forms of entertainment. They were rough amusements for rough men in a rough country.

Bullfights, cockfights, bear-baiting, horse racing, and other displays of horsemanship were staples of the *vaquero* lifestyle. The *vaqueros* had swift, well-trained horses and they liked to show off their riding skills. Horse races and other displays of horsemanship were particularly popular. One competitive game was to see who could pick up a small coin from the ground while riding at full gallop.[28] Another was to show off individual skills and dexterity with the *lazo* and to perform rope tricks. Some displays were games of pure horsemanship, such as pressing a coin under each knee against the saddle and then seeing if the rider could hold them there while jumping over hurdles.

One test of riding skills was the *carrera del gallo* ("the chicken race"). This involved burying a live chicken in the dirt with only its head and neck exposed above the surface of the ground. The rider galloped past it while leaning over the side of the horse and tried to grab the chicken by the neck and pull it out of the ground. The winner was the rider who accomplished this without falling off his horse. If the chicken was buried too deep in the ground or packed in too tightly, the rider might be unseated. As might be expected, this game often resulted in unfortunate fatal injuries to the chicken. In later years a gunny sack was substituted for the chicken as being more humane.

Cock Fighting

Though bear fights and bull fights were the most notorious, many other animals were pitted against each other for the entertainment of spectators and betting men. Cock fighting was an early sport imported from Mexico for entertainment. Hundreds of dollars could change hands during a well promoted match. When betting was complete, the owner or manager of each rooster put his bird on the ground in front of the other one. The roosters jumped at each other and tried to slash their opponent with the sharp, spiked spurs on the backs of their lower legs. One bird usually bled to death from these claw wounds and the other was declared to be the winner. If a bird refused to fight—which seldom happened—the other one was considered the winner.

Bullfights

Bullfights were popular and fights were staged pitting a matador against a bull. Fighting aggressive bulls in an arena carried a special connotation of masculinity for Californians of Spanish descent, and bullfights were regularly staged as entertainment. An early form of the sport of rodeo involved mounted *vaqueros* competing in front of audiences as they showed off their skills at roping bulls in an arena.

The fights in which a man was pitted against bull were patterned after Spanish bullfights. The bullfighters who took part in these contests were nearly always male. In an attempt to draw in larger audiences, lady bullfighters were occasionally promoted. In one performance at the mining camp of Sonora, California, a Mexican woman—at least so described by onlookers—fought and killed a bull. J.D. Borthwick described a similar bullfight at the gold camp of Columbia in California, where a Señorita Ramona Pérez fought a bull. After dispatching the animal, Señorita Pérez curtseyed then ran out of the arena blowing kisses. Though the act was very popular, it turned out afterwards that the Señorita was actually a Señor—a male bullfighter in woman's clothing.[29]

A related popular pastime was called *corrida de toros*, or "coursing the bull." The event was staged like a bullfight on horseback. The rider darted in and tried to get the bull to charge a bullfighting cape (*capa*) or a serape. Those skilled in the technique ducked out of the way while distracting the bull's attention with the cape. Those who were not so skilled often had accidents. Another part of the entertainment might be to "tail the bull," which involved chasing a bull, grabbing its tail, and flipping it over.[30]

Bull and Bear Fights

Popular recreational events were the bull-and-bear fights that came north as a Mexican cultural entertainment. This spectator event had its origins in the earlier sport of bear-baiting, which originally came to the East Coast of the United States from England.

Bull-versus-bear fights were particularly popular among the Mexican population as spectators placed bets on which animal would survive to the end of the fight. The cruel sport was well-suited to the California mountain country, because black and grizzly bears were plentiful in the foothills and mean bulls could always be found at a nearby cattle ranch. Grizzly bears were preferred for these fights because they had a nastier disposition than black bears and fights involving black bears were reported to be less exciting. To supply the animals, a group of *vaqueros* would ride out and capture a grizzly bear (*Ursus horribilis, Ursus arctos*) by roping its neck and feet. Even this preliminary capture was dangerous and the *vaqueros* had to be skilled with their *reatas* to avoid injury.

The bear was tied by a hind leg to a post in the middle of the arena with ten to twenty feet of slack rope or chain. Then the bull was released to attack it. The bull fought by charging his opponent and trying to hook it with his horns, whereas the bear attempted to bite and hold on with his teeth while trying to pull the bull down.[31] The bear was chained to prevent a habit of trying to escape and chase after spectators. The bull might or might not be restrained and promoters sometimes sawed off the tips of the bull's horns to avoid accidents and prolong the fight. Sometime a rope was tied to the bear with the other end tied to the bull's foreleg. The bull had its horns, the bear had its claws. Sometimes the bull won. Sometimes the bear won. Though this practice was inhumane, it also arose out of a practical necessity. Estimates were that there were 10,000 wild bears living in the valleys along the coastal areas.[32] These bears preyed on stock, killed and ate cattle, and had to be removed. Sometime a similar fight was staged as a mountain lion versus a bull. In California, another "sport" consisted of having a dog harass a bear to enjoy the reaction of the tormented animal.

After the initial rush of gold seekers in 1849, bull-and-bear fights remained a favorite of the California gold miners. Saloon owners in the mining town of Columbia, California, in the foothills of the Sierra Nevada mountains, for example, commonly staged these colorful events. The object of these animal fights was to make money for the sponsors, so crafty promoters built circular arenas of wood with raised tiers of seats and a high fence to keep out people who didn't pay to see the event.

Fandangos

Another popular recreational activity was the fandango, or dance event. Fandangos were popular, though the musical festivities might be accompanied by only a couple of guitars and two or three violins.[33] Not all of the musicians were good, but they were usually enthusiastic. Civil war soldier Ovando Hollister, attending a New Mexico fandango, expressed his displeasure when he claimed that, "Whether it comes from a one-stringed cornstalk fiddle, violin or guitar, Mexican music is all the same, screeching, mechanical, see-sawing, without feeling in composition or execution."[34]

Before the California gold rush of 1849, the name "fandango" referred to the dance itself, rather than the place in which it was held. The term eventually changed to "fandango saloon" or "fandango house," meaning a dance hall, then became shortened to the simple name of "fandango." Like other dancehalls in the West, these establishments eventually became places of gambling and prostitution. One early observer in New Mexico, Josiah Gregg, commented that the name fandango "is never applied to any particular dance, but is the usual designation for those ordinary assemblies where dancing and frolicking are carried on."[35] Fandangos were popular among the poorer inhabitants of Mexican California and New Mexico, who often went to watch American men dancing with Mexican women.

Though fandangos were popular among the local residents, they were not always accepted by the government. In San Antonio, one official claimed that fandangos "excite lust" and "give very serious offence to God."[36] Most gained a reputation among *Americanos* for their uninhibited ways. In the mining town of Sonora, California, the local newspaper noted that at the end of the evening the men often left with the women dancers, and hinted not too subtly of the poor moral character found in these places. The offended reporter also noted that men and women danced very close.

James Pattie, attending a fandango in Santa Fe, New Mexico, in 1827 noted: "When the ball broke up, it seemed to be expected of us, that we should each escort a lady home, in whose company we passed the night, and we none of us brought charges of severity against our fair companions."[37] Hollister noted the same in 1862 when he said, "In the ballroom there are some fine looking women, but they are generally ignorant and sensual. Virtue is comparatively unknown among them." But as he philosophically added, "All things have their use, and the Pike's Peakers [the soldiers] used the fandango to the best advantage, and were doubtless pleased and satisfied."[38]

For added excitement, fandango houses were periodically the scene of violence and other crime. The *San Joaquin Republican* of July 30, 1851, reported a murder that had taken place at *Casa de los Amigos*, a fandango house in Stockton, California, which was then a mining supply town. Apparently Caleb Ruggles and James McCabe hadn't realized that they were in an establishment that in Spanish meant "House of the Friends," and quarreled over who would go home with dancer Luz Parilla. The subsequent fight involved a Bowie knife and a gun, with the result that McCabe shot Ruggles. Even though the event was determined to be self-defense, a year later the city prohibited fandango saloons. In the mining town of Volcano, the paper reported that a "Spanish dance house" was closed when the owner was arrested for grand larceny.

Chapter Nine

The Spanish Falter

At the time of Coronado's arrival in the New World in 1540, Spain was at the height of its might and culture, and was the most powerful nation in Europe. Its monarch, Charles I, had been elected Holy Roman Emperor in 1519. But Spain lost her fleet in 1588 to the British, lost several wars in Europe, and by the 1670s had declined as a world power.

In the Southwest of North America, the first Spanish colonial period in New Mexico lasted from 1598 to 1680, from the colonizing expedition of Oñate until the Pueblo Revolt. The second colonial period lasted from 1692 to 1821, from the re-conquest of Santa Fe by Vargas until the people of New Spain rebelled against their Spanish rulers and the Republic of Mexico succeeded in winning Independence. After 1821 Spain's rule ended and its influence on the Southwest faded away.

Even before Mexican Independence, Spanish rule in the New World was plagued with difficulties as the far-flung northern provinces became harder to manage. In California, the string of missions spread up and down the coast were essentially independent and autonomous because of their distance from Mexico City. New Mexico was in a similar situation, with the additional problem that the colonists and missions were still subject to constant raids by hostile Indians. The Spanish viceroys in Mexico City found themselves unable to effectively govern the distant provinces and make suitable decisions from hundreds of miles away. They were not on the scene of events and were not directly involved in the often rapidly changing volatile situations that arose. Even if the viceroy could make an appropriate decision, the time required to communicate questions and decisions back and forth were lengthy. The situation had probably already changed by the time any directives were received. This isolation did have the advantage that New Mexico was spared the ten years of turmoil and revolt that accompanied the fight for Independence in Mexico. New Mexico maintained a relatively stable political entity, with one notable exception being the Chimayó Rebellion of 1837.

However, at the same time, various pressures were exerted on Mexico by other nations. The Russians had advanced down the coast in the upper part of California and settled as far south as Fort Ross, just north of San Francisco. Though this small fur-hunting colony was never a real threat to the Spanish, a Russian presence was perceived as dangerous by government officials in Mexico City. New Mexicans, on the other hand, feared an Anglo-American invasion that threatened from the East, and Florida was under pressure from the British in the Carolinas.

Spanish outposts established at Nacogdoches in 1716 and San Antonio de Béxar in 1718 were intended to guard against French and English threats from the Mississippi Valley, but their position was precarious.[1] In Texas, as elsewhere, the Indians had proven to be

By the time Mexico gained its Independence, the Spanish legacy included a series of churches spread out over the Southwest. This is the beautiful little church of El Santuario de Chimayó. The church is often called the "Lourdes of America," as it is famous for its reputed healing powers. As many as 30,000 people still flock to the Santuario at Easter time, many of these pilgrims walking along the highways, some carrying wooden crosses on their shoulders.

intractable. In addition, the discipline and routine of the mission system in Texas had seen little long-term success and only lasted for about fifteen years. As a result the missions in Texas were closing and settlers leaving.

The northern edge of the Spanish border was threatened by Indians. Apache, Comanche, Ute, and others were still creating havoc. Yet it was essential for the Spanish to secure the northern border to protect the rich silver mines of Mexico. Their outpouring of wealth had sustained the economy of New Spain and had helped with the increasing tax burden demanded by Spain.

Some of these problems might have been resolved by a larger Spanish colonial population. Spain had only a few thousand soldiers in the New World to control vast areas of land and the civilian population never amounted to more than a few tens of thousands. Arizona never had more than a thousand or so Spanish inhabitants at its peak. Santa Fe had only about eighty soldiers to protect the capital and patrol the surrounding area, though their capabilities were supplemented by friendly Indians and civilian militia. The large population centers were few. They consisted of San Antonio and El Paso in Texas, Santa Fe in New Mexico, and San Diego and Monterey in California. In practice, though, Santa Fe and San Antonio were only very isolated outposts.

Many of the magnificent remaining churches of the Southwest feature elaborately carved and painted altar screens (*reredos*), such as this one in the Chapel of San Miguel in Santa Fe. Religious icons and paintings several centuries old adorn the walls. This beautiful altar backdrop was renovated and restored in 1955.

One of the important impacts of colonization was the introduction of horses, though the horse also had negative aspects for the Spanish because of the way it changed the way of life of the Plains Indians. With horses, these sedentary farmers could follow buffalo and other game, hunting as they migrated across the Plains. This led to an increased food supply and, with better food supplies, Indian populations increased. This increased population became more belligerent towards colonists and resulted in an increase in intertribal warfare. Tribes preyed on each other and the weaker ones were either enslaved or migrated to quieter areas.

After the United States took over the Southwest, the Indians still raided and fought, but now with Anglo-American settlers and the United States army rather than with the Spanish. This new government's goal was to confine the Indians to reservations and, by this means, open up the Western land for "productive use," which was considered to be settlement, ranching, and farming.

Political Changes

Through most of the 1600s, the only significant Spanish settlement in the southwestern United States was the province of New Mexico. The Franciscans had briefly extended their conversion efforts to the pueblos of the Hopi in northwest Arizona, but with the Pueblo Revolt of 1680, the Franciscans were driven out and the Hopi remained resistant to further efforts to bring them back into the fold.

The Jesuits did not enter southern Arizona and convert the Pima tribes until the early 1700s. After the Jesuits were expelled from the New World in 1767, the Franciscans took over, but little additional Spanish colonization resulted, other than by a few miners and ranchers. The Spanish influence never really expanded outside the Santa Cruz River valley or north of Tucson. There were no strategic or economic incentives for further colonization, so these small Arizona outposts remained stagnant.

By the late 1700s, the concern of the government in Mexico shifted from expansion to defense of the northern border. When Juan de Ulibarri marched north into Colorado from New Mexico in 1706 to recapture escaped Indian slaves from the Picuris Pueblo, he returned with the news that French traders were already active on the western side of the Great Plains and trading with the Indians. In 1719 these reports were confirmed by New Mexico's governor Antonio Valverde during similar punitive expeditions against the Utes and the Comanche. As a result, the central government became more concerned about encroachment by the French than they were about a few raiding Indians.

By the mid–1700s, some of the concerns of foreign invasion died down as the French in Europe allied themselves with the Spanish against the English. Then in 1762, when France seemed likely to lose its claims in North America to Great Britain, Louis XV of France ceded the Louisiana Territory and all of France's other claims west of the Mississippi to Spain to prevent the land from falling into British hands. Another motive for the transfer was that the French colonies had not been a financial success and France was eager to rid itself of the continuing financial drain.[2] Spain, therefore, became the new owner of what was called Upper and Lower Louisiana. This ended the rivalry between France and Spain for the time being.

Nevertheless, in 1768, the Spanish Royal Corps of Engineers recommended a change in fortification of the frontier and the east-west links between New Mexico, Arizona, and California. As a result, the viceroy ordered the establishment of fifteen presidios stretching across the Southwest in a line from Bahía del Espíritu Santo, on the Gulf of Mexico southeast of San Antonio, to the Gulf of California. One step towards this goal was the founding of the presidio at San Diego in 1769 and the resulting increase in commerce and communications between California and New Mexico.

In the 1770s nomadic Indians continued stealing horses and cattle, and attacking and murdering settlers in Texas, Arizona, and New Mexico. Between 1771 and 1776 Indians in the province of Nueva Vizcaya in north-central Mexico murdered 1,674 people and stole 68,256 head of livestock.[3]

A little progress was made to settle differences with various Indian tribes. For example, after the defeat of Cuerno Verde and the Comanche in 1779, the Spanish and the Utes formed a military and trade agreement. The Utes agreed to trade only with official Spanish agents and the Spanish agreed to help the Utes against enemy tribes. By the early 1800s, however, the Utes became dissatisfied with the alliance when they realized that the Plains Indians were doing better by trading with the Americans.[4]

In 1800 Napoleon forced Spain to return land to his empire and Spain ceded the Louisiana Territory back to France. In 1803 Napoleon agreed to sell the entire Territory to the United States for $15,000,000 dollars. The final price, after the addition of other French obligations and interest, was $23,213,576 or about 4 cents an acre.[5] The size of the Louisiana Purchase was 909,000 square miles, which was 43,000 miles larger than the entire United States at the time of the purchase. One only half-humorous perspective on all these changes came from author George Hufsmith who pointed out that the Louisiana Territory was land that "…the United States had fairly recently bought from France, who never really owned it in the first place because they stole it from the Spanish who never really owned it either, insofar as they stole it from the Indians who had possession of it even earlier, but didn't really own it either."[6]

The Adventures of Zebulon Pike

America had purchased a vast area of empty land with the Louisiana Purchase, but really did not know what they had bought. In the summer of 1806, General James Wilkinson, the governor of Upper Lousiana and commander of the army, ordered Lt. Zebulon Montgomery Pike to explore the southern part of the newly-acquired Louisiana Territory. Pike, a veteran of a previous expedition in the West, was given the official mission of exploring the headwaters of the Arkansas River and the international boundary with Spain, the exact location of which was vague. The United States claimed that the border was the Rio Grande, but the Spanish insisted that it was the Red River. The name of the Red River, now called the Canadian, came from the Spanish *cañada*, meaning "canyon."

There is still controversy and speculation among historians about the real reason for Pike's trip. Wilkinson was legitimately governor of the Louisiana Territory and commander of the army, but during his tenure he sold information to the Spanish government about American plans for the Southwest.[7] He was also an acquaintance of Aaron Burr, Jefferson's vice-president. Both were masters of intrigue and deceit, and were both involved in a series of murky schemes.[8]

Burr and Wilkinson may have together planned Pike's expedition, as Burr had a scheme to separate the western states and the Louisiana Territory from the rest of the country, a plot that Wilkinson revealed to President Jefferson in 1806.[9] It is thought that Wilkinson and Burr may have sent Pike to gather intelligence about Spain's northern provinces along with information about fortifications and trails, for a possible invasion of Mexico. Alternately, they may have wanted Pike to explore and report on trade routes to Santa Fe for possible future commerce with Mexico. They may indeed have simply wanted a legitimate survey of the headwaters of rivers in the West in order to help to establish the international boundary between the United States and Mexico. Nobody really knows.

Because Wilkinson had ordered Pike's expedition, Pike also came under suspicion.[10] Pike's official orders were to avoid Spanish territory, but he may have had secret orders to spy on Spanish activities. There is still academic debate about whether Pike was really spying on the Spanish for the United States government or for Aaron Burr's personal schemes.[11] Whether Pike even knew the real reason for the expedition is also unknown.

Whatever motivated the expedition, Pike and twenty-one men set out from the army post at Bellefontaine, just north of St. Louis, in August, 1805, with clothing and supplies intended for a trip to last four months in mild weather. He had no maps, but there were well-worn trails to follow. The men moved west across Kansas and entered Colorado, as Pike had decided to find the source of the Red River and then follow it eastwards. Pike's route into Colorado followed the Arkansas River towards the Rockies on an old Spanish trail.

By the time Pike and his men reached Colorado, his activities had already been reported to Santa Fe and Spanish forces were watching his progress. As Pike worked his way into the mountains, he became confused and began to wonder if his "Red River" might in fact be the Arkansas River. Turning south into the San Luis Valley he found another "Red River," which in this case was the Rio Grande.

Hearing rumors that a Spanish expedition was looking for him, Pike built a stockade in the winter of 1806 five miles up the Rio Conejos, a tributary of the Rio Grande just north of the Colorado–New Mexico border. Pike planned this to be the expedition's fortification for the winter. He claimed "that four or five might defend [the stockade], against the insolence, cupidity, and barbarity of the savages...."[12] The stockade was about thirty-six feet square, surrounded by a moat with the outer walls made from logs twelve feet high placed on end. The inner part of the stockade was further protected by a layer of sharpened stakes slanted towards the outer wall. This was the first building set up by Americans in Spanish territory and resulted in the first American flag being flown in Colorado.

After the stockade was built, the volunteer surgeon for the expedition, Dr. John H. Robinson, set out by himself to the south to try and find Santa Fe. The reason he gave was that he was supposedly sent by merchant William Morrison to collect money owed to him by Baptiste LaLande, a trader who had previously absconded with Morrison's money after he financed a trading expedition in 1804. Robinson, however, was another close friend of James Wilkinson, thus his sudden departure for Santa Fe by himself was in itself suspicious. It has never been satisfactorily explained whether Pike's men really were in a desperate situation and Robinson legitimately left to seek help, or whether this was simply his excuse for going to Santa Fe to spy on the Spanish.[13]

In February of 1807 fifty-nine Spanish dragoons and fifty mounted militia arrived at the stockade and informed Pike that he was trespassing in Spanish territory. They politely claimed that the governor had sent them to "protect" Pike and his men and escort them back to Santa Fe. The reality was that they detained him and his men for trespassing on Spanish soil. Pike, by way of defense, claimed surprise that he was not at the Red River, but at the Rio Grande. Regardless, the Spanish troops insisted that he accompany them to Santa Fe where they kept him under virtual arrest. Pike and his men were not exactly prisoners, but they were not free to leave.

Pike and his men were eventually taken to the United States border near Natchitoches on the Mexican border on July 1, 1807, and released. He returned safely home to the United States without ever having found the source of the Red River. However, whatever Wilkinson's real purpose was for sending Pike, the expedition did increase the amount of known information about Spanish New Mexico and the Southwest. Luckily Pike had stuffed his notes from the expedition into the barrels of his men's muskets for safekeeping and was afterwards able to reconstruct the details of his journey. Whatever Pike's intended purpose had been, he was the first American to bring back so much useful information about Santa Fe. Pike's published account of the expedition was viewed with great interest as government officials wanted to encourage trade with New Spain.

In 1819 Spain and the United States finally agreed on an acceptable boundary between the two nations. The Adams-Onis Treaty placed the boundary along the Arkansas River. The land south and west of the Arkansas River belonged to Spain and, after Mexican Independence, to Mexico. In Colorado, the line ran up the Arkansas River to its source and then due north to the 42nd parallel. This remained the northern limit of Spanish and Mexican territory until the close of the war with Mexico in 1848. Soon after the boundary was established, Maj. Stephen H. Long led an expedition to explore the territory south of the Platte River and north of the Arkansas River.

In 1836, when Texas gained Independence from Mexico, the United States claimed that the western boundary was the Rio Grande. Mexico disputed this and the disagreement became part of the prelude that led in 1846 to a two-year war between Mexico and the United States.[14] Victory and takeover of the Southwest by the Americans forced Mexico to surrender all of its territories north of the Rio Grande. This included modern Arizona, New Mexico, Colorado, Utah, and parts of Nevada and Wyoming. The one-sided takeover by the Americans was not well accepted by most of the local citizens. New Mexicans in Taos rebelled in January of 1847 and killed the new American governor Charles Bent, as will be described further in Chapter 11.

Slavery Continues

With Mexican Independence after 1821, the Spanish alliance with the Utes was no longer valid. Trading with the Utes had always been for the usual items, but an added important trade item had been Indian slaves traded to the Spanish after they were captured during skirmishes between Indian tribes. This trade was still flourishing in the 1850s and there is evidence that the slave trade was carried on in the San Luis Valley of Colorado as late as the 1860s.[15] Indian Agent Albert Pfeiffer at Abiquiu reported that an expedition against the Navajo in 1858 brought back with them twenty-one small Navajo girls. Taking slaves was justified as retaliation for the Indian capture of Mexican boys.[16]

The acquisition of Indian servants, which is a polite way of saying that in reality they were slaves, began early during the colonization efforts. Some were Indians captured in battle who were donated to loyal citizens, but by the 1700s the character of slaving had changed and obtaining slaves was an important factor in the New Mexican economy. This was an accepted practice and many Anglos and Spanish households had slaves. Between 1700 and 1760, over 800 Apaches were placed in Spanish homes as servants. They were usually baptized as Catholics and given Spanish names. One of the principal markets was the trade fair at Taos, where a slave might be purchased for $500. Many of these slaves were captured Navajo children. Any remaining Indian servants were given their freedom after the Civil War.[17]

The Land Grants

One feature of the changing political scene and the practice of Spanish conquest was the awarding of large land grants in the Southwest. One advantage for the Spanish was that

This is the small church at San Acacio which was built in 1856, making it the oldest continuously-used church in Colorado. The church was built by the town citizens for their patron saint, San Acacio, after a fortunate rescue just as they were about to be attacked by Indians.

settlement of the northern area of the New Mexican province provided a protective buffer against any possible encroachment by outsiders, particularly American fur trappers and settlers. Some of the grants were so large that they extended into Colorado from New Mexico. The conditions of the grants were that grantees were to establish colonies and promote agriculture.

The land grants ranged in size from the small Pacheco grant of 1769 that was a mere 581 acres, to the huge Tierra Amarilla Grant that was made in 1832 and comprised 594,516 acres straddling the Rio Chama from Colorado into northern New Mexico. The Las Vegas Land Grant near Las Vegas, New Mexico, was awarded to a collective of twenty-nine individuals. Another large grant was the Sangre de Cristo Grant, made in 1843 and comprising 998,781 acres.[18] Later Mexican colonization laws limited the size of private grants to approximately 48,000 acres.[19]

The Treaty of Guadalupe Hidalgo, by which the United States took over the Southwest from Mexico in 1848, included a provision that private property rights would be respected, and the United States pledged to honor the original Mexican and Spanish land grants. However, Congress had to approve the grants after determining which were genuine and which were not. Sorting out these property rights took many years as the original ownership was often confused. For example, the descendants of the original Tierra Amarilla Grant settlers lost a large amount of their property due to a judicial error.[20] Congress did ratify the Sangre de Cristo Grant (about fourteen miles east of Alamosa, Colorado), the Maxwell Grant (northern New Mexico and southern Colorado), and the Tierra Amarilla Grant (about thirty-six miles west of Antonito, Colorado). Congress reduced the size of the Nolan, Vigil, and St. Vrain Grants. Settlement of the Conejos Grant dragged on for years until it was finally disallowed.

One of the original petitions for a land grant was proposed by Manuel Martinez in 1832 when he asked for land in the Chama River Valley. This later became the Tierra Amarilla Grant of southern Colorado, which was confirmed by Congress in 1860.

Thirteen-year-old Narciso Beaubien and Stephen Lee petitioned Governor Armijo for a little over a million acres in the San Luis Valley of southern Colorado. In return, they promised to colonize the land, raise cattle, and grow crops. The land was granted in 1844, but Narciso Beaubien and Lee were killed during the Taos Rebellion of 1847. As there was not enough money to settle Lee's estate, his half interest was sold to Carlos Beaubien, the father of Narciso, for $100. Carlos received his son's half by inheritance so, for only $100, he became owner of 1,038,195 acres of land.[21]

Carlos Beaubien was already part-owner of the Beaubien-Miranda Grant that sprawled over the northeastern part of New Mexico and over the border to the north into Colorado. The original owners were Carlos Beaubien and Guadalupe Miranda, two Mexican citizens living in New Mexico, who received the land from the Mexican government in reward for their pioneering efforts in New Mexico. The grant turned into an immense ranch of nearly two million acres on which they raised sheep, cattle, and horses, and farmed corn, wheat, and hay. They processed their own crops in a three-story grist mill that produced flour. They sold goods and services to travelers, they leased part of the land, and were involved in mining and banking. Important clients were the U.S. army and the Cimarron Indian Agency. With success at every turn, Beaubien had a palatial home with carpets, fine furniture, and four grand pianos. Miranda left for Mexico after the Taos Rebellion, so Beaubien ended up owning both the Beaubien-Miranda Grant and the Tierra Amarilla Grant for almost nothing. By 1854 he owned the largest piece of land owned by any one individual in the United States. Beaubien gave away much of his grant in 1853 in an effort to reduce the taxes that the new United States government was expected to impose.

Lucien Bonaparte Maxwell, the son-in-law of Carlos Beaubien, and also a former trapper, trader, explorer, Indian agent, mill owner, and land developer, became the owner and manager of the Beaubien-Miranda Land Grant. It was now a private land holding of 1.7 million acres in northern New Mexico and southern Colorado. He founded the town of Cimarron, which means "wild" or "untamed" in Spanish, in the heart of the grant. He built Maxwell's Aztec Flour Mill in Cimarron in 1864.

Three or four attempts were made to settle on the Conejos Grant, which was opened to settlers in 1832, but they were not successful. Each time the hopeful settlers were driven away by Indian attacks or their crops failed due to drought, so they finally gave up and went back to New Mexico. Because of this apparent "abandonment" of the land, the United States government rejected confirmation of the grant. Another factor was that no evidence of the original grant could be found. This was not unusual and many of the initial land titles were so vague that Congress disallowed many of them. The unfortunate original grant recipients living on them were then reduced to the status of homesteaders.

In 1823 Luis Maria de Baca was awarded a huge grant called Vegas Grandes, near Las Vegas, New Mexico. The original ownership was disputed, so Baca was allowed by Congress to select five other sites, called "floating grants," in exchange, and the grants were confirmed in 1860. One of these was the Baca Grant No. 4 that still exists northeast of Alamosa in the San Luis Valley of Colorado. Today the grant is about twelve miles square or around 92,000 acres.

Starting in 1843, colonists tried several times to settle the Sangre de Cristo Grant, but the Ute Indians continually drove them away. The first people to settle founded the town of Costilla, just south of the Colorado–New Mexico state line, but they were considered to be squatters and were evicted. Authorized colonists arrived in 1849 and finally established several clusters of homes. The grant was confirmed by Congress in 1860.

Not everyone was happy with what they considered to be Congressional meddling over land issues. Two of these were the Espinosa brothers, Vivian and Jose, who left a trail of death across southern and central Colorado in 1863, blaming the Spanish loss of New Mexico, and specifically the loss of their family land, to the Americans. The brothers' cousin, Felipe, left a note that was found after his death that said, "They ruined our family—they took everything in our house; first our beds and blankets, then our provisions. Seeing this we said, 'We would rather be dead than see such injuries committed on our families.' These were the reasons we had to go out and kill Americans."[22] Another reason that has been presented was that they wanted to gain revenge for relatives killed in the war between Mexico and the United States. Whatever the real cause was, the brothers decided to kill as many Americans as possible.

To accomplish their objective, the brothers left their home in San Rafael, Colorado, and rode through South Park in the central part of the state, randomly murdering and robbing whoever they met. Robbery of the victims after killing them made the stated purpose of revenge suspect. Whatever their real motive was, the random murders created panic, particularly among those who lived alone or had to travel in lonely places by themselves.

A posse finally tracked them down and killed Vivian when he tried to escape. Jose did escape and joined up with his sixteen-year-old cousin, Felipe, both of them continuing a path of revenge. Finally, the U.S. army hired mountain man Tom Tobin to track the two down. He killed them and took their heads to the commandant at Fort Garland as proof. According to Felipe, the brothers' final tally of dead victims was thirty-two.

Spanish Failure

The Spanish influence was most prominent in the Southwest between the establishment of the first colony in 1598 and 1848 when the Americans took over. The Spanish were successful as explorers, but not as successful as colonists. Spain's method of colonization was to conquer provinces, enslave the local people to do useful work, and convert them to Catholicism. Their sequence was to conquer, convert, exploit, and incorporate the natives. Conquest was done by conquistadors, conversion done by friars, and the *encomienda* exploited and made a profit from the natives.

Similar to European feudal methods, the foundation of the Spanish system was to have serfs to do the real work. No Spaniard produced his own wealth through manual labor, so Spain depended on the productivity and wealth of the Indians. In order for this system to succeed, there had to be a compliant native population to perform the labor. Without the Pueblo Indians the system would have failed.

Ultimately the *encomieda* system failed, the missions failed, and Spanish soldiers could not suppress the Plains Indians. One of the driving reasons for colonization was to make money for the crown. The Spanish needed a stable and docile work force to support their missions and colonies, so the sedentary Pueblo Indians were well-suited to their system of conquest, whereas the nomadic Plain Indians were not. The Plains Indians did not have property or land the Spanish could seize, they could not be conquered, they would not stay converted, and they refused to produce anything. The mission system worked well in California because the Indians there were docile and made good workers.

Another long-lasting problem for the Spanish was that the Southwest had nothing that they really wanted or could profit by. The hoped-for riches of the legendary cities were not found. There was no gold.

Early Trade in Santa Fe

To further create an atmosphere of isolation, New Mexico adhered to the well-established Spanish policy of not allowing trade with foreigners. Trappers and traders who ventured to Santa Fe or tried to trade with the New Mexicans were liable to be arrested, have their goods confiscated, and be thrown into jail. Anglos and other outsiders, however, eyed the potentially lucrative Santa Fe trade and tried to figure out how they could participate in some of it.

Some of the earliest foreign trading in Santa Fe was conducted by two French brothers, Pierre-Antoine and Paul Mallet, who traveled from Kaskaskia, Illinois, along the Arkansas River, and then to Santa Fe in 1739.[23] They hoped to develop some trade business and investigated the possibility of fur trapping, though they may have also been looking for gold. As this type of trade was not allowed and would-be traders were jailed, their budding venture did not develop. Unlike later would-be traders, they were simply allowed to leave. Other French traders reached Santa Fe again in 1750 and 1752. Occasional entrepreneurs came to Santa Fe after that to trade, but they had to sell their goods quickly and afterwards leave town in a hurry with their Mexican silver and furs to avoid arrest.

Baptiste LaLande, a French Creole who was sent west with merchandise by William Morrison, a merchant and fur trader from Illinois, brought trade goods to Santa Fe in 1804 to see if any business could be developed. LaLande sold the goods but, instead of returning to Illinois, kept the profits for himself, and set up his home in Santa Fe in a comfortable lifestyle.[24] Even at that time he noted the attraction of the seemingly exotic women of Santa Fe smoking, dancing, and drinking wine.

In Zebulon Pike's journal of his adventures after his arrest by the Spanish in 1807, he mentioned meeting LaLande and James Purcell in Santa Fe. Pike noted that LaLande may have been acting as a spy as a prelude to the American takeover of Santa Fe. Purcell (also known as James Pursley) was a former carpenter from Kentucky who had traveled to the southwest and become an Indian trader and fur trapper in South Park in Colorado around 1802. He was the first American known to have settled in Santa Fe and ended up staying there permanently after 1805.[25]

Another attempt to develop trading in New Mexico was made by Robert McKnight and his brothers, who owned a trading post in Franklin, Missouri. McKnight had heard about the inflated prices being paid for merchandise in Santa Fe, so he decided to assemble a mule caravan of goods and see if he could profit from it. McKnight, James Baird, and Samuel Chambers set out in April of 1812 with seven other men and a pack train of mules. They were not successful. When they reached Santa Fe, they were arrested, their mules and goods were confiscated, and they languished in prison in Chihuahua until after Mexican Independence in 1821.[26]

Though the Louisiana Purchase was complete, the boundary between the two nations remained in dispute. American traders tried to obtain permission from the Spanish to trap for furs in the disputed territory, but were refused. In 1817 a group of trappers gathering furs in southern Colorado was captured by Spanish troops who marched them and their furs to Santa Fe. They were imprisoned for forty-eight days. Finally, their furs and belongings were confiscated and they were expelled with only a horse for each of them. Ironically, only a few years later, after Mexican Independence in 1821, Americans were permitted to freely enter New Mexico for trapping.

Trade between the United States and New Mexico, particularly Santa Fe, did not develop until after Mexican Independence, when the new government welcomed the Americans and their goods.

The Remaining Colonies

In 1821, when Mexico achieved independence from Spain, the main outpost of the Spanish colonization efforts in the Southwest was New Mexico. Settlement in Arizona consisted of a small strip along the Santa Cruz River south from Tucson to the Mexican border.

Texas contained a similar strip of Spanish missions from San Antonio to Goliad and the coast, plus outposts at Nacogdoches, Laredo, and El Paso. In California, a string of missions remained along the coast from San Diego to San Francisco.

In New Mexico, major settlements stretched from Taos to the south, mostly along the Rio Grande valley to Socorro with some settlements spread out on either side. In Colorado, only a few small settlements dotted the southern part of the state, again mostly centered on the Rio Grande.

CHAPTER TEN

New Trails to Santa Fe

Under Spanish rule, commerce with foreign merchants by the provinces was prohibited. As a result, the residents of New Mexico were required to purchase their goods at inflated prices from Chihuahua City or other cities to the south. The event that reshaped the character of commerce and determined the future of Santa Fe occurred with Mexican Independence from Spain in August of 1821, which for the first time allowed the opening of trade with the United States. Santa Fe was the largest town in the northern part of New Spain and was the capital of the province, so it became Mexico's gateway for trade in the American Southwest and with the Americans. Ironically, Santa Fe actually played no part in the Independence movement and, because of its remote location, didn't even know that a change of government had taken place until several weeks after it occurred.

Early in the summer of 1822, an expedition of mountain men packed 1,100 pounds of furs from New Mexico to St. Louis. The partners had been trapping beaver in the mountains around Taos without competition from the great fur companies in the Northern Rockies. They traveled by way of the crude wagon road that went over Sangre de Cristo Pass in the San Luis Valley to the north of Taos. Anglo and French trappers were supposed to pay a tax to the Mexican government on the skins they collected, but many didn't bother or smuggled them out at night to avoid government officials.

The fur trade was so good that trappers, almost half of them of French extraction, swarmed into the area. So many came that in 1824 the central government decreed that only Mexican citizens could be awarded trapping licenses. Among these early mountain men was Antoine Robidoux, whose father had founded St. Joseph, Missouri. He arrived in 1824 after previously operating trading posts on the Uintah River in Utah and on the Gunnison River in Colorado. His supply trains traveled over Mosca Pass west of the Great Sand Dunes, which was another Spanish short cut across the Sangre de Cristo Mountains. He used this route so much that for a while it was called Robidoux Pass.[1]

As Taos was close to the mountains and the Santa Fe Trail, it became the center of the trapping and fur trade. One of the prominent mountain men who made Taos his home was Christopher "Kit" Carson, a small, wiry man who was an authentic scout, trapper, guide, and all-around Westerner. Married to a woman from Taos, Josefa Jaramillo, Carson settled there with his family. Some of the other trappers made their homes there, some came to gather new supplies before heading out into the mountains again, and some came to drink *aguardiente* (the strong whiskey called "Taos Lightning") and seek the company of women. When the fur trade started to collapse in the 1830s, many of the mountain men who had made Taos their base of operations married Mexican or Indian women and stayed on.

These men and their trails became part of the basis for the future business union between New Mexico and the United States.

Three main trails came together in Santa Fe. The most important was the Santa Fe Trail, which developed into an international wagon road from Missouri to Santa Fe. Another was the Old Spanish Trail to California, an important trade route with the West Coast. The third was *El Camino Real de Tierra Adentro* ("The Royal Road to the Interior Lands"), the main wagon road between Mexico City and Santa Fe. Dramatic growth occurred on all three trails after 1821 and Mexican Independence from Spain. Franklin, Missouri, was only 775 miles from Santa Fe via the Santa Fe Trail, whereas Mexico City was 1,600 miles via *El Camino Real*. These three trails made Santa Fe into a major trading hub. Through them merchants in Santa Fe could effectively do business with other markets across the nation and even with international customers in Paris and London.

The Santa Fe Trail

The most famous of the trade routes ran between Independence, Missouri, and Santa Fe, and thus aptly became named the Santa Fe Trail, a journey of 775 miles.[2] The Santa Fe Trail started to develop as a trade route in the 1820s. A broad array of merchandise came to New Mexico from the eastern United Sates and Europe on the Santa Fe Trail. Merchants took many of these products further south into Mexico on *El Camino Real*. As well as goods, American merchants brought in foreign ideas, culture, habits, and tastes.

When a financial panic swept the nation in 1819, businessman William Becknell in Missouri faced economic ruin. Becknell's commercial ventures had failed and he was left with many debts. He reasoned that he could salvage his financial affairs in the remote town of Santa Fe, so he advertised for a group of men to join him to go west to trade for horses and mules. He and five other men set out from Franklin, Missouri, on September 1, 1821, with pack horses and mules carrying trade goods. He had planned to trade with the Comanche for horses and mules, but it was too late in the season for Indian trading, so the group rode on to Santa Fe.

On November 13, a few days before they reached their destination, the group met 445 Mexican soldiers under the command of Capt. Pedro Ingacio Gallego at a place later named Kearny's Gap, just southwest of Las Vegas, New Mexico. Becknell was afraid that they might be arrested like others before them but, to his surprise, the meeting was cordial. Mexican Independence had already been achieved, so Gallegos welcomed the traders and encouraged them to proceed to Santa Fe to meet with Governor Melgares. The group finally arrived in Santa Fe, a town of about 5,000 residents at that time, on November 16, and started trading. Their merchandise was all gone in a month at a good profit. A sister of one man in the group was said to have made $900 on her $60 investment.[3]

Becknell sold his merchandise for a handsome profit and was able to pay off most of his debts. His venture was so successful that he returned to Franklin in January of 1822 with Spanish blankets and silver dollars to buy more trade goods. On his second trip to Santa Fe he took twenty-one men and three wagons fully loaded with trade goods. Others soon started to follow, but Becknell was considered the "Father of the Santa Fe Trail," because of his early trailblazing efforts.

Eighty-one small traders repeated the journey in the spring of 1824, traveling as a group for mutual protection against marauding Indians along the way. They brought goods worth $35,000, consisting of small tools, knives, hats, needles and thread, shirts, linen, hosiery, and similar popular merchandise. They returned to Missouri with $180,000 in gold, silver, Mexican silver coins, and $10,000 in furs, for a whopping profit of 600 percent.[4]

Spanish silver was a preferred item for Anglo traders. There was little circulating money in New Spain and currency was scarce. When they used coins, the New Mexicans used Spanish dollars, large silver coins with a milled edge called the *peso duro* (hard dollar), minted in Spain or the New World. Considered legal for use in the United States, the coins were also referred to as "eagle dollars," after the image of the eagle on one side.[5] One coin was worth eight *reales*. These large coins were regularly cut apart into quarters or eighths ("pieces of eight") to make change. Each eighth was called a "bit," and was worth 12½ cents. The old term "two bits" is still used in parts of the United States to describe 25 cents. These silver coins were often carried by merchants back to Missouri in rawhide bags for ease of transport. This flow of Spanish silver made Missouri one of the most stable states in the nation, and insulated it from the effects of the financial Depression of 1837.

With the lure of large profits, trade caravans continued to roll towards New Mexico. Items that were not readily available to the New Mexicans, such as textiles, lead, hardware, cutlery, champagne, canned oysters, and glassware, were traded in Santa Fe for silver, mules, horses, furs, hides, blankets, and other items that would sell well in the East. Early traders made three to five times their investment.

Trading for horses and mules to take back to "the States" was a popular part of the business as a mule worth $15 in Santa Fe could bring as much as $100 in Missouri.[6] The demand for horses was so great that huge herds were brought to Santa Fe.

Trading between Mexico and the States was so successful that in 1825 the American government commissioned a team under George C. Sibley to survey a practical route from Fort Osage, Missouri, to Santa Fe and Taos. After two years of work, the results of the survey were lost in some government office, the road was never built, and the whole project was dropped.[7]

In 1826 the government in New Mexico sent Manuel Escudero as an envoy to Washington to encourage trade. He returned with six wagons of goods from Missouri and made a handsome profit from the trip. Ezekial Williams led a caravan with great success to Santa Fe and back that was a mile long and consisted of fifty-three freight wagons and carriages, accompanied by 105 men.[8]

By the 1830s a steady stream of Missouri merchants left Independence or Westport Landing (now part of Kansas City) in the spring in order to reach Santa Fe by early summer. After they arrived, some traders rented stores and conducted retail sales themselves, some sold goods off the backs of their wagons, and some sold their goods at wholesale to local merchants. Many chose the latter method as they wanted to dispose of their goods as quickly as possible and return home to Missouri before the first snowfall.

Eventually so many merchants made the trek that Santa Fe could not absorb all the goods they brought. One caravan alone in 1831 consisted of 100 wagons and 200 men. When Santa Fe became saturated with goods, the excess items were shipped south to central Mexico to keep the trade going.

Early profits were typically 40 percent to 100 percent of the initial investment. Later profits diminished somewhat, but most could expect a return of at least 10 percent to 40 percent on their investment. Nevertheless, merchants needed substantial backing, as outfitting a wagon train was expensive. They had to pay for the merchandise, wagons to carry the goods, animals to pull the wagons, supplies for the trip, and wages for the drivers. As a result, small independent traders were eventually replaced by large merchants who had adequate financial resources. Some of the merchants stayed in Santa Fe through the winter and continued to sell. Others continued south to Chihuahua City to continue trading and selling their goods.

By the late 1830s, merchants in Mexico and New Mexico resented paying high prices and losing the substantial markup charged by American merchants on goods brought from the East. In response, several merchants from Santa Fe started their own wagon trains to Independence so that they could purchase their own goods for trade and sale in New Mexico.

Import duties were subject to the whim of the governor. In 1839 New Mexico governor Manuel Armijo started to charge an arbitrary import tax of $500 per wagon, regardless of its size or the value of its contents. In order to reduce this import duty, some traders stopped a short distance outside Santa Fe and packed as much as they could onto the least number of wagons that could carry the load. Other merchants reduced their tax by replacing their Missouri-built wagons with larger vehicles, such as the Conestoga wagons. Another trick was to consolidate goods in the wagons as food and other supplies brought from Missouri were consumed as the journey progressed. The excess wagons with their empty crates and barrels were simply burned beside the trail to avoid having to pay taxes on them. Veterans of travel on the Santa Fe Trail liked to scare newcomers by concocting tall tales of how these burned-out hulks were the remains of wagons burned during Indian attacks. The New Mexican government soon caught on to these tricks and started to send roving patrols backwards on the trail to escort the wagon trains to the customs inspection point before they could be repacked. These taxes largely supported the local economy when Mexico became independent.

Officials eventually levied a tax depending on an arbitrary assessment of what they thought the merchandise was worth, regardless of the invoice price. The duties were very high, anywhere from 10 percent to 100 percent of the actual cost of the goods. When Mexico became part of the United States, tariffs stopped for a while and then a duty proportional to the value of the imported goods was imposed.[9] By 1852 the tax was lifted, permitting free trade with Mexico.

Regardless of taxes, the amount of goods transported along the Santa Fe Trail mushroomed. In 1822, trade along the Trail was $15,000. In 1846 a total of 636 wagons with 750 teamsters and drovers carried $1,000,000 in goods to Santa Fe.[10] In 1860, the *New York Herald* reported that 16,439,134 pounds of goods had been transported to New Mexico. The paper detailed that this Herculean task involved 7,084 men, 6,147 mules, 27,920 yoke of oxen, and 3,033 wagons. Groceries, cotton goods, hats, bonnets, paper, window glass, and notions (items related to sewing, such as thread, needles, buttons, and ribbons) were popular. So were such exotic items as canned oysters and champagne. The reporter also noted that many of the wagons transported whiskey, which was in high demand and was the basis of large profits. Author David Noble has reported that the totals in 1860 were 2,170 wagons,

5,948 men, and 17,836 oxen transporting goods worth $3,500,000.[11] Whichever source contains the most accurate figures, the numbers were obviously large. In 1863, 15,000 tons of freight worth $40,000,000 were shipped over the Santa Fe Trail.[12]

Wagons returning to Missouri carried wool, buffalo robes, hides, dried buffalo meat, and gold and silver. Particularly prized by trappers, soldiers, and other frontiersman were Mexican candy cones (*piloncillos*), made from sugar, shaped like a cone and about three inches long. Sometimes a little cheese was added and the mixture used for food. They were a popular trade item carried back to Missouri for sale.

Business was good at the United States end of the trail. Augustus Storrs, for example, shipped goods from Franklin to Santa Fe that were worth $35,000 in Missouri. After he had sold and traded the merchandise, including cutlery, silk shawls, mirrors, books, pens, and paper, he had made $180,000.[13] The Old Pioneer Store at the Council Grove end of the Santa Fe Trail sold $400,000 of merchandise over a two year period in the early 1860s. Interestingly, of that, $12,000 was in whiskey sales and $15.40 in Bibles.[14]

The Route from Missouri

The Santa Fe Trail started in Missouri, wound across Indian Territory, then entered Mexico on the way to its northern capital of Santa Fe. The early "trail" was not a single road, but consisted of a series of roughly-parallel muddy tracks that meandered over the plains in the same general direction. The pathway was more of an amalgamation of old Indian trails and those used by earlier buffalo hunters. People, horses, wagons, mules, and oxen plodded for miles along these alternately dusty and muddy trails that were in places worn into deep ruts. On the wider parts of the trail, wagons were able to travel three or four abreast.

While freighters used the heavy Conestoga wagons, most westbound families used small farm wagons that required fewer horses or oxen to pull. Wagon boxes were made from hardwood to resist shrinking and the bottom of the bed was coated with tar to made it somewhat waterproof during river crossings. Hoops made from hardwood and soaked in water until they were pliable were made into a U-shape and held up the canvas top, or bonnet.

The wagon bed did not ride on springs—only the driver's seat did—so the ride in the wagon bed was rough and uncomfortable. The rumor spread by experienced travelers on the trail was that a man could fill a butter churn with milk in the morning and the rough ride would result in freshly-churned butter by the evening meal.

Several departure points for the trail were in western Missouri. Becknell started at the town of Franklin, which was established in 1817, named after Benjamin Franklin. The Missouri ends of the trail gradually became concentrated at Independence, as this town had the largest docks and warehouses to bring in and store goods that arrived by steamboat from the East. By the 1850s the majority of the freight business had moved to Westport Landing, about twelve miles west of Independence.[15] It was less crowded and so took over as major shipping and outfitting center for overland traders.

After leaving Independence or Westport, small caravans joined up with others at Council Grove, about 120 miles to the west. Here they formed into larger groups and elected a leader. Many of the travelers used the pause to cut trees to provide hardwood for wagon

The majority of transportation on the Santa Fe Trail was conducted with big Conestoga wagons, originally built by the Pennsylvania Dutch in the Conestoga Valley of Pennsylvania. These wagons could carry more freight than pack animals and could be loaded with up to two or three tons. From a distance the billowing canvas tops of the covered wagons looked like a fleet of ships, which gave them the common name of "prairie schooners."

repairs during the trip across the treeless plains. Typically these groups elected officers and drew up a list of rules for behavior on the trail. As the first part of the trip was through Indian country, the first caravans required military escorts. Later caravans armed themselves heavily for their own protection.

The wagons plodded across Kansas, going through Council Grove, Fort Larned, and Dodge City. In western Kansas the trail split. The shorter of the two branches, the Cimarron Branch (also called the Cimarron Cut-Off) headed southwest and followed the Cimarron River for part of the way. After leaving the river, there was a notable absence of water for the rest of the journey. Another problem was a lack of firewood for cooking and grass for animals. The journey between Missouri and Santa Fe via the Cimarron Branch typically took sixty-two days.

The other trail followed what was named the Mountain Branch. This trail led to Bent's Fort near La Junta, Colorado, then turned to the southwest and Trinidad, Colorado. This alternate branch of the trail was longer by about five days, but it offered water, better grazing, and a safer passage. The disadvantage was that it required crossing the 7,881 foot Raton

Pass between Colorado and northern New Mexico. The pass was rocky, steep, and rough, even for those on horseback. Wagon wheels routinely broke and in some sections the wagons had to be literally dragged up hilly sections. In some places, traveling 800 yards in a day was considered to be a good distance over the rocky terrain. The governor of New Mexico, Antonio Valverde y Cosio, crossed Raton Pass in 1719, and with great understatement described it as a "difficult trail."

Though the Cimarron Cut-Off was a shorter route and headed directly for Watrous and Fort Union in northern New Mexico, it was more dangerous to travel because of hostile Indians and the complete lack of water for one stretch of sixty miles. This long, dry stretch of short-grass prairie was called *La Jornada*, or alternately the Waterscrape. As Indian attacks became more common on the Cimarron Cut-Off, the Mountain Branch started to look more attractive. In spite of its challenges, estimates are that as much as 75 percent of the Santa Fe traffic traveled on the Cimarron Cut-Off.

The Mountain Branch became more popular after Raton Pass was graded and the general condition of the trail was improved to where a crossing by wagon was practical. In 1865 Richens Lacy "Uncle Dick" Wootton, mountain man, trapper, guide, rancher, and scout, blasted and graded an improved twenty-seven mile toll road across Raton Pass. He smoothed the roadbed and added bridges across some of the ravines. He set up a tollgate on the wagon road and charged $1.50 per wagon and 5 cent per head for livestock. Indians were allowed to pass at no charge.

In 1878 the Santa Fe Railroad offered Wootton $50,000 for the road. For his own reasons, he turned this large amount down, but sold it to them for $1 and a small monthly payment for him and his wife. In gratitude, the railroad named their most powerful locomotive "Uncle Dick" after him. Railroad tracks were laid across the pass to Raton, New Mexico, in 1879 and the railroad reached Lamy, seven miles south of Santa Fe in 1880.[16]

In New Mexico, the Mountain Branch and the Cimarron Cut-Off joined back together at the town of *La Junta* ("The Junction"), named for where the Mora and Sapello Rivers joined. The town was renamed Watrous, after local store-owner and rancher Samuel B. Watrous. The trail continued south to the town of Las Vegas (named for *las vegas*, "the meadows"), for the final push into Santa Fe. In 1541 Francisco Coronado had crossed the Gallinas River at Las Vegas when he explored northern New Mexico.[17] Wagons used the same crossing of the Gallinas River as Coronado, because that was the easiest place to cross the river between the canyons to the north and to the south.

The last great landmark on the Trail before entering Mexican territory was Wagon Mound, a large bluff that could be seen by travelers eager to end their journey. This natural promontory was named because it resembled the top of a covered wagon. Though this landmark was a popular camping spot for wagon trains, it was also well known as a place for ambushes by Apache and Ute Indians.

The first Mexican settlement of any note that travelers on the Santa Fe Trail encountered was San Miguel del Vado ("Saint Michael of the Ford"), founded in 1794 on a Spanish land grant of the same name. San Miguel contained the largest building on the trail after Bent's Fort. The town received its name *vado* ("ford" or "crossing") because this was one of the easier crossings of the Pecos River into Mexico. A small garrison of soldiers and the customs station for entry into Mexico were housed here. Arriving wagons were inventoried and import taxes levied on the freight. Construction of the Church of San Miguel was started in 1805 and finished in 1811. The church is still active and has hosted continuous services since it was built.

San Miguel declined after the American takeover of the southwest and the town of Las Vegas to the north became the major stopping point for westbound travelers. Spanish settlers had never been able to successfully settle *las vegas* due to constant harassment by Indians. But after the arrival of American trappers and wagons on the Santa Fe Trail, a settlement finally took hold and became the town of Las Vegas. By the 1860s some of the largest wool dealers stationed themselves in Las Vegas to handle the export trade of the millions of pounds of wool and hides that passed through the town. The town was dusty, dirty, raucous, and filled with saloons. As a result it became a popular stopping point for wagon trains.

The Trail ended at the Plaza in Santa Fe. Here wagonloads of goods from Missouri were unloaded and bargained to the local residents by traders hawking their wares. Eager buyers crowded and jostled each other in their enthusiasm to see and buy the new wares from the East. The weary freighters could find whatever entertainment they sought in the nearby dance halls, bordellos, and gambling dens. The Santa Fe end of the Trail is marked at the southwest corner of the plaza with a gray stone marker erected in 1910 by the Daughters of the American Revolution and the Territory of New Mexico.

With the increasing trade with the United States, Santa Fe became such an important town that on July 1, 1850, a monthly stagecoach started to run between Independence and Santa Fe. By 1857 the stage traveled twice a month.[18] By 1870, the railroad had reached southeast Colorado. In 1879 the Atchison, Topeka & Santa Fe chugged its way over Raton Pass to Las Vegas, New Mexico.[19] On February 9, 1880, the first train arrived in Santa Fe. From then on the days of the Santa Fe Trail were numbered because the railroad could carry freight cheaper, faster, and easier.

In the late 1800s and early 1900s, New Mexicans realized that they had a special character to their home and started to promote what we now call tourism by attracting visitors to visit their landscape and culture. Joining the bandwagon, in 1912 the AT&SF railroad started to offer tourists rates to visit Santa Fe and advertised the picturesque nature of the town. In addition, they started to adopt and promote the "Santa Fe style" in the architecture of their buildings along the line, for example in the Harvey House restaurants and the Harvey hotels associated with the railroad.

Inns (*fondas*) had existed in Santa Fe since the founding of the city, many of them still in the same location. A hotel, for example, has existed at the site of the current La Fonda hotel in Santa Fe since the town was established in 1610. The hotel hosted a Victory Ball after Gen. Kearny took over Santa Fe, and was used again by Gen. Ulysses Grant to celebrate the end of the Civil War. In 1919 the old adobe hotel was demolished and a new one was built on the previous location of the Exchange Hotel at the end of the Santa Fe Trail, adapting Spanish and Pueblo architecture to form its current iconic building.

Life on the Trail

Travel from Missouri across the Santa Fe Trail was slow, making the length of the trip about three months. Some traders, particularly those who packed out beaver furs, used mules, a cross between a female horse and a male donkey. Mules made the best pack animals for moving goods, but unfortunately Indians liked to steal them as they were worth a lot in trade. Mule teams were the primary beast of burden until 1829 when the army introduced oxen for pulling wagons. Oxen, castrated adult male cattle, were large sturdy animals that were good for pulling heavy wagons.

Several variations of wagon were used for freighting. The commonest vehicle used by caravans in the Santa Fe trade between 1820 and 1840 was the Conestoga wagon, originally built by the Pennsylvania Dutch in the Conestoga Valley of Pennsylvania.[20] The Conestoga wagon could carry more freight than pack animals and could handle a load of two or three tons. The so-called "Pittsburg wagon" was a modified version of the Conestoga wagon. The Murphy wagon, which was very similar, was built by Joseph Murphy, a wagonmaker in St. Louis. These wagons had wheels six feet high and eight inches wide, with a bed sixteen feet long and about six feet deep that could carry up to 7,000 pounds of freight.[21] By the 1860s giant military supply wagons could carry up to five tons, or 10,000 pounds, of freight. At the end of the journey, the wagons were often sold in Santa Fe, as eastbound freight was often smaller and lighter and more easily transported on horses or mules. Each mule could carry a load of up to 300 pounds.

As well as being able to carry a large load, the shape of the beds of these wagons made the freight inside remain stable when going up and down hills. The top was heavy-duty canvas waterproofed with paint or linseed oil. From a distance the covered wagons with their billowing canvas tops looked like a fleet of ships at sea (in this case on a sea of grass), which gave them the common name of "prairie schooner."

The rear wheels of the wagons were six feet in diameter and the front wheels four feet across. The front wheels were smaller than the rear ones to allow sharp turns, as larger wheels would have hit the body of the wagon. The wheels were flared slightly outwards in a dish shape to give greater strength. The axle was a tapered conical shape to allow the bottom of the wheel to align itself vertically on the ground in order to bear the greatest load. The use of large wheels allowed the wagons to ride easily over humps and depressions in roadless areas of the Trail. Wide rims helped prevent them from sinking into sand and soft ground.

Muleteers (mule drivers) and bullwhackers (as ox drivers were known) were employed to drive the wagon caravans to New Mexico. Wagons for crossing the prairie were usually drawn by eight mules. Some had as many as ten to twelve animals to pull a heavy cargo. The driver of mule teams was also known as a muleskinner.

Mules were considered to be superior for speed and oxen were best for economy. Oxen could plod fifteen miles each day and mules could move faster at twenty miles a day. Oxen were sturdy, could pull heavier loads than mules, and could survive on the grass that grew alongside the trail. Oxen had stronger legs and could pull better in soft earth, and could even be eaten in an emergency if food supplies ran low. Mules, on the other hand, required a supplement of expensive grain. Mules tended to easily develop sore feet if they were not properly shod.

Capt. Randolph Marcy, writing in the army guide of 1848–1860, claimed that mules could travel faster and endure summer heat better than oxen, if the journey was less than 1,000 miles. If the trip was 1,500 to 2,000 miles over sandy or muddy roads, he felt that oxen would do better than mules. Perhaps more important from a business standpoint, he added that a team of six mules cost $600, whereas an eight-ox team cost only about $200.[22]

He also warned in his 1859 book *The Prairie Traveler* that "on long and arduous expeditions, men are apt to become irritable."

Mules had the disadvantage of being very stubborn if the mood struck them. Trader Josiah Gregg commented on this behavior when he said, "It is sometimes amusing to observe the athletic wagoner hurrying an animal to its post—to see him 'heave upon' the halter of a stubborn mule, while the brute obstinately 'set back,' determined not to 'move a peg' till his own pleasure thinks it proper to do so." He added, "I have more than once seen a driver hitch a harnessed animal to the halter, and by that process haul 'his mulishness' forward, while each of his four projected feet would leave a furrow behind."[23]

If mules or oxen developed tender feet from pulling freight wagons across the prairies, they were sold at the end of the trip to local traders in Santa Fe. The traders kept them for thirty to sixty days to allow their feet to heal, then they re-shod them and sold them back to the freighters. The traders typically bought them for $25 to $35 each and sold them back at $100 to $125. A nice profit indeed.

The front animals of a team of oxen were called the Leaders, and were the most experienced animals. Behind them were the Swing Leaders or Swingers, the most inexperienced animals. Directly ahead of the wagon were the Wheelers, which were usually the oldest and heaviest animals. The largest animals were put next to the wagon as they could pull the most load. The wagons were initially pulled by oxen, but by the end of the trail era, they were primarily pulled by mules. Both mules and oxen were shod.

As horses were traditionally mounted from the left side, the driver walked beside or rode the left rear animal (the Wheeler). He controlled the team with a jerk line, which was a rein that went to the left side of the lead animal's bit. A steady pull on the jerk line turned the animals to the left. Several short jerks turned them to the right.

The driver also encouraged his team with yells and the popping of a bullwhip that was eighteen to twenty feet long. He did not whip the animals themselves, but cracked it just above the animals so as not to cut their skin, using just the sound of the snapping whip over their heads to make them do what he wanted. He also yelled and cursed at them. One Indian term for a freighting wagon was a "goddamn," because bullwhackers frequently used that expression while urging on their ox-drawn carts.

Oncoming traffic typically passed so that each driver could see the other vehicle. This started the tradition of driving on the right side of the road. Other authors have theorized that drovers traveled on the righthand side of the road because Conestoga wagons tended to drift to the right in traffic.

The trip to Santa Fe consisted of long days of plodding travel that tended to be dull and routine, with only buffalo, pronghorn (often, technically, erroneously referred to as antelope or pronghorn antelope), prairie dogs, and the endless horizon disappearing into the distance. Dust, mud, mosquitoes, and heat were constant aggravations. The mosquitoes were more than just a pest as they spread malaria, which was a serious disease without a cure at the time.

Basic meals on the Trail consisted of biscuits, bacon, and coffee made from beans that were roasted fresh each day over a campfire. This monotonous menu was supplemented by wild game, such as buffalo, pronghorn, or wild turkey hunted on the trail. Salt pork might be taken as a supplement and fried or stewed. When salt was in short supply the ingenious men sprinkled a little gunpowder on the meat to add some seasoning and flavor.

Wagon trains might encounter hailstorms, blizzards, or occasional wildfires on the prairie. River crossings could be difficult and could pose a serious obstacle that might include injury to the driver and his stock, and damage to the goods. Though the endless prairie appeared to be deserted, it was the home of roving bands of Comanche, Kiowa, Southern Arapaho, and Southern Cheyenne. Early encounters between freighters and Indians were mostly friendly, but the increasing stream of travelers eventually led to violent confrontations and theft of stock. Livestock theft was prevented by circling the wagons at night to surround the animals.

The constant possibility of Indian attacks forced traders to travel as large well-armed groups. Indians hardly ever attacked a well-organized and armed wagon train on the Santa Fe Trail, and only eight men died during the Trail's first ten years of use.

The men rose at dawn to hitch the animals and prepare for the day's journey. The caravan stopped at noon for the big meal of the day and to rest the team. A typical meal consisted of biscuits or bread, bacon, coffee, beans, and dried apples. The work was not over when the caravan stopped for the night. The stock had to be tended, night guards posted against Indian attacks, and any repair work performed on the wagons. The wagons required constant maintenance, such as greasing the wheels, and repairing yokes and harnesses. The wagons were oriented with the tongues pointing to the North Star when making camp, in order to know the correct direction in the morning. This practice became known as "following the tongue." After all the chores were done, the teamsters could relax for a while before going bed and starting the process all over again the next morning.

There being a lack of firewood on the trail, travelers often had to cook their food over a fire fueled by dried buffalo dung. These pasture pastries were euphemistically known as "buffalo chips" or "meadow muffins" or "prairie coal." When the wagons stopped for the night, large sacks and baskets were filled with the largest and driest chips to make the campfire, as these burned the hottest and cleanest. One traveler claimed that, "Where wood was scarce, dried buffalo dung made for a hot, fast-burning fire. Meat roasted on a spit over such a fire took on a peppery taste."[24] About three bushels were required to cook the evening meal and a bushel could be collected in about a minute. In his recollections of travel in the early West, photographer Robert Taft remembered, "I observed two of our men approaching over a slope, holding between them a blanket filled with something; curious to know what it was, I hailed them, and found they had been gathering 'dried buffalo chips,' to build a fire with. This material burns like peat, and makes a very hot fire, without much smoke, and keeps the heat a long time; a peculiar smell exhales from it while burning, not at all unpleasant. But for this material, it would be impossible to travel over certain parts of this immense country. It served us very often, not only for cooking purposes, but also to warm our half frozen limbs. I have seen chips of a large size—one I had the curiosity to measure, was two feet in diameter."[25]

Bent's Fort

One of the important landmarks and a major stopping point on the Mountain Branch of the Santa Fe Trail was Bent's Fort, located near present-day La Junta, Colorado, on the north bank of the Arkansas River. In the 1830s this was the biggest and most important fort west of the Mississippi. At the time, it was the largest building between the Mississippi

The interior courtyard at Bent's Fort. Miscellaneous workshops and storage rooms were located around the perimeter of the courtyard on the ground level, with sleeping rooms and a small saloon (upper center on second story) on top. The device in the center of the plaza was a fur press used to compact skins for shipment into bales for ease of transport back East.

and the Pacific Coast. Indians, Mexicans, and American fur trappers all did business with the Bents.

The fort was built with adobe walls that were between two-and-a-half and four feet thick, fourteen feet high, in the shape of a square that opened into a large open courtyard that measured 137 feet by 178 feet. A large fur press in the courtyard was used for compacting beaver skins and buffalo hides into ninety-pound bales for easier transport to the East. The courtyard was large enough that an entire wagon train could be pulled inside its protective walls. The only entrance was an opening at the front that was seven feet high and nine feet wide and only large enough for a freight wagon to be pulled through. The opening was in the form of a tunnel with a door reinforced with metal at each end. The inside door could be closed yet still allow trade with the Indians through a side window set in the tunnel between the two doors, without allowing undesirables to enter the interior of the fort. On top of the wall over the tunnel was a cannon that was used to provide protection and could fire for a mile or so out onto the prairie. Over the front gate was a watchtower with a telescope to detect approaching travelers or Indians. Eighteen-foot-high towers, each with a six-pounder cannon, stood at the northeast and southwest corners. The tops of the walls had loopholes for riflemen to defend the fort and two round towers at diagonal corners to allow observation and protection of the outside walls from anyone trying to scale them.

The Bents typically employed between forty and sixty people, though the fort could house up to 200 men and 300 animals. The amenities included warehouses, wagon sheds, clerks' offices, a blacksmith shop, a carpentry shop, meeting rooms, living quarters, kitchen, an arsenal, workshops, storage rooms, and guest rooms. There was a shallow well in one corner of the interior courtyard in case the fort was surrounded by hostiles and it was not possible to fetch water from the nearby river. Two years of provisions were stored at the fort in the unlikely event of a protracted Indian siege.

The fort contained about twenty-five rooms, approximately fifteen feet by twenty feet in size, that lined the inside of the courtyard. The trading and storage rooms were slightly larger. On the upper level was a small saloon that boasted imported French wines and a billiard table.

This outpost of civilization, built during 1833 and 1834 in the middle of nowhere, was not a fort owned by the military, but was a major civilian center for the fur and Indian trade. This lonely outpost of civilization on the Santa Fe Trail grew to be the largest and most important trading post west of the Mississippi, and was at the center of a huge trade and mercantile empire run by the Bents. The fort was also a hospitable stopping-point for travelers. Caravans on their way to Santa Fe stopped at the fort to re-supply with flour, sugar, coffee, cloth, tobacco, weapons, and whiskey. The army used it as an unofficial storage depot and staging point.

Charles Bent was the son of a judge in the Louisiana Territory and a successful fur trader in the 1820s who provided supplies for Northwest fur posts. Bent had originally partnered with a former clerk for a St. Louis mercantile firm, Ceran St. Vrain, and opened a trading store in Santa Fe on the south side of the plaza, opposite the Palace of the Governors. They opened another store in Taos and were later joined in business by Charles' younger brother William.

By the late 1820s, increased competition and excess trapping of beaver streams left the Rocky Mountain fur trade barely profitable. There was also an eventual decline in the demand for skins as fashions changed and gentlemen's silk hats replaced beaver hats. But there was still a demand for buffalo hides. The three partners decided that money could be made in the Indian trade along the Arkansas River, which was then the international boundary between the United States and Mexico. To achieve this, in 1832 they started to build a huge adobe trading post at the edge of a large grove of cottonwood trees on the north bank of the Arkansas River. The location was about fifteen miles east of where the Purgatoire River entered the Arkansas River and eight miles northeast of La Junta, Colorado.[26] The fort was completed 1834 and soon became a hub of activity for the area's fur trappers, hunters, Indian tribes, and passing visitors. The completed fort was originally named Fort William, in honor of William Bent, but the trappers and traders in the area always called it Bent's Fort, so the original name quickly fell into disuse.

The Bents and St. Vrain traded weapons, trinkets, beads and abalone shells, iron for arrowheads, axes, kettles, and tools for Indian blankets, furs, and buffalo hides. The Bents spoke several Indian dialects, as well as French, which was useful for trading with French trappers. They were respected by the local Indians for their honesty, which was unusual among traders. They still made a profit, though. Bent bought buffalo hides for 25 cents at the trading post and sold them in St. Louis for $5 or $6.[27]

Behind the main fort was a large corral surrounded by low walls. These were only six to eight feet high, but were topped with live cactus with long spines to prevent cattle and horse thieves from climbing over them. In the spring the cactus bloomed red and yellow, and added splashes of color to the tan adobe walls. Outside the walls was an adobe icehouse. Ice was cut from the nearby Arkansas River in winter and stored in the icehouse to keep meat cool and for drinks.

When the Santa Fe Trail and trade with the Indians declined, William Bent tried to sell the fort to the army. When they couldn't agree on a price, in a fit of depression Bent set fire to the fort and moved thirty-eight miles downstream to build another fort. The fur trade never recovered and Bent's new business soon failed.

The Character of Santa Fe

In 1824, when wagon caravans started to arrive in Santa Fe in large numbers the population was about 3,000 to 4,000 people. When these traders reached the end of the Trail, they found a town unlike any they had previously encountered. The finest building, the Palace of Governors, was only a plain, mud-covered building that contained government offices, living quarters, a guardroom, a prison, and glass windowpanes. In front was an open ditch (*acequia*) that brought water for drinking and washing from a nearby swampy area. The town had no sewer system.

Many of the buildings had evolved from the classic Indian pueblo style, with flat roofs and walls of thick adobe brick to keep out the cold of winter and the heat of summer. Indian designs were blended into Spanish furniture, clothing, and blankets striped with bright bold colors. In the early 1800s, one textile introduced by the Spanish was *colcha* ("bedspread") embroidery. The base was a woven cloth made from the wool of churro sheep, then dyed in colors from a variety of natural plants and sewn with silver and silk threads. Designs included geometric patterns, birds, and flowers. After the end of Spanish rule and the relaxation of trade barriers, cotton cloth was used for the base material.

The character of the Plaza in Santa Fe was the tinkle and clang of caravan bells, the braying of burros, the clatter of covered wagons, the cries of peddlers hawking their wares and traders arguing, accompanied by the crack of whips and the shouting of the wagonmasters. Oxen with yokes lashed to their horns pulled *carretas* full of sacks of grain, chilis, and corn shucks to be used for stuffing mattresses. Business men traded shawls, socks, ladies' hose, handkerchiefs, shirts, and calico cloth from the East.

For the teamsters who had just finished three months on the trail, Santa Fe provided safety and large profits, and offered a hint of adventure in a strange, romantic place. On the other hand, Englishman H.M. Powell, who visited Santa Fe in 1852, described it as "a miserable hole, gambling and drinking in all directions."[28] Indeed, drunken brawls and knife fights occurred everywhere. When George Ruxton visited Santa Fe, he later recalled in his book detailing his travels that "Every other house was a grocery, as they call a gin or whiskey shop, continually disgorging reeling, drunken men, and everywhere filth and dirt reigned triumphant."[29]

The early Americans who reached Santa Fe were fascinated by the local women, who

Trade on the Santa Fe Trail brought mass-market American goods at reasonable prices to New Mexico. Traders could now supply tobacco, rifles, haberdashery, rope, metal goods, tools, liquor, hardware, cloth, tinned goods, and many other items that were in high demand at the end of the trail. These items were traded for skins, furs, or Spanish silver. Many merchants returned to St. Louis far richer than they were before.

were unlike the women they had known back in the States. They had dark, exotic complexions, silky dark hair worn in long braids, and were decked out in heavy silver bracelets and necklaces, with large earrings dangling alongside their faces. They commonly coated their faces with flour paste, clay, or starch against sunburn and painted crimson berry juice on their cheeks, the combination of which gave them an unusual appearance. Gregg thought the habit to be disgusting. He said that they had handsome figures, though he also noted with a little dismay that they were not laced up in corsets, as were proper American women in the East.[30]

American traders thought it was scandalous that these women smoked cornhusk cigarettes, and indeed felt it was even more scandalous that they smoked at all. Unlike proper American women of the time, the women of Santa Fe often went barefoot. And—heavens above!—they wore calf-length skirts that offered a daring display of ankle to men used to American women of the times who dressed in floor-length skirts that showed nothing at all. The Yankee traders were also appalled by the behavior of the priests, some of whom drank, gambled, and womanized like the rest of the residents.[31]

Gambling was probably the most popular pastime for both men and women, and to keep them occupied keno, monte, and other games of chance were popular in saloons and gambling halls. One of the most famous gamblers was Gertrudes (or Gertrudis) Barceló, also known as La Tules, which was sometimes simplified to Madam T.[32] Tradition had it that she was born in Spain, lost her mother in New York, came West to Taos, then moved to Santa Fe. Other, more convincing evidence shows that she was probably born in Sonora around 1800 and lived in Valencia, south of Albuquerque, in 1815.[33]

She had a neat figure and red hair, but was not described as a beauty, though she was handsome and intelligent, with free-spirited manners. She started as a professional gambler in 1825 in local villages. By 1833 she was living in Santa Fe and making her living from cards. In the early 1840s she was running a bordello and gambling saloon on Burro Alley, Santa Fe's red light district located between San Francisco Street and Palace Avenue. Her establishment was open almost every evening, and she was a successful gambler who became wealthy dealing *monte*. Her added skills as a businesswomen allowed her to invest in trading, real estate, livestock, and finance.[34]

As ties between New Mexico and *Los Estados* ("The States") became stronger, traders settled in Santa Fe, married local women, and entered into business partnerships with New Mexicans. New Mexico was changing again.

El Camino Real

Before Mexican Independence in 1821, *El Camino Real de Tierra Adentro*, the Royal Road to the Interior, to Mexico City, was New Mexico's only legal trading and communications route to the outside world. After traders started arriving from Missouri, Santa Fe enjoyed increased economic activity due to its successful American and Mexican trade. Large quantities of manufactured goods arrived in New Mexico from the eastern United States on the Santa Fe Trail and from Mexico on *El Camino Real*. For a while New Mexicans were buying larger quantities of manufactured goods from the Americans than from the Chihuahua merchants because they were better in quality and priced lower. Santa Fe, however, was still a small town with a limited population, so it quickly became saturated with goods for sale. After reaching Santa Fe, some merchants continued south to trade with Mexican cities in the interior, such as Chihuahua, Parral, Durango, Zacatecas, and Mexico City itself. As a result, *El Camino Real* later became known as the "Chihuahua Trail."

The significance of *El Camino Real* was not just that it was a highway for carrying goods between Mexico and New Mexico, but it also served as a cultural passageway along which ideas, languages, religion, philosophies, and artistic traditions traveled back and forth. It was the conduit along which European ideas and culture flowed and intermingled with the Pueblo culture and ideas of the northern province.

Early transport of goods along the trail was done in *carretas*, the small two-wheeled carts drawn by oxen. This type of cart could carry up to a ton of cargo. After the war with Mexico and trade boomed, these small carts were inadequate to handle the large loads of traders so pack trains and large wagons became common. Mule trains consisted of anywhere from one or two pack animals led by a rider to fifty or more animals driven in a string, each mule carrying up to 300 pounds of freight. One disadvantage to mules over *carretas*

Crude two-wheeled *carretas* were used to carry goods around Santa Fe and between villages. These primitive wagons were noted for the noise they made as the rimless wooden wheels rolled around dry wooden axles. Tallow was sometimes used as a lubricant to try to quiet the racket.

was that each mule had to be unloaded, unsaddled, and cared for each night, and then loaded up again the next morning. This additional time lengthened the trip.

The very largest of the freight wagons were pulled by teams of eighteen or twenty mules or oxen. The string of animals attached to each wagon might stretch for 100 feet, making control of the animals difficult. Transportation by wagon was expensive (around $350 per ton) and slow, traveling only about twelve to fifteen miles in a day. However, before the arrival of the railroad, this was still the most effective way of transporting heavy loads.

The Old Spanish Trail

The third important trade route that developed out of Santa Fe was the Old Spanish Trail between New Mexico and Mission San Gabriel, a few miles east of Los Angeles. Using this trail, traders from New Mexico were able to travel overland to do business with frontier settlements along the Pacific Coast. Those trading with California carried locally produced New Mexican merchandise, such as serapes, blankets, ponchos, socks, hats, shawls, quilts, and a variety of hides, such as buffalo and bear skins and beaver pelts, to exchange for

Californian mules and horses. Petroglyphs found in the desert show that these mule caravans were witnessed by American Indians.

This route had previously been pioneered by missionaries, fur trappers, and Indians. Early Spanish explorations had provided the basic knowledge about the territory and cultures to be found between Santa Fe and Los Angeles. As a result, New Mexican traders were somewhat familiar with routes gained from previous expeditions.

The first trade caravan of sixty men and a hundred pack mules was led by Antonio Armijo, who traveled from Abiquiú, northwest of Santa Fe, to Mission San Gabriel, northeast of Los Angeles, in November of 1829. He took with him woolen rugs and blankets produced in New Mexico to trade for horses and mules. He generally followed the route of the earlier Dominguez-Escalante expedition northwest to the San Juan River and then skirted the Utah-Arizona border as it turned west. At the Colorado River (then named the Grand River), he used the Crossing of the Fathers cut into the canyon wall by Dominguez and Escalante, and crossed the desert to Las Vegas, Nevada. From there he descended across the Mojave Desert to the Mojave River, and down to Mission San Gabriel. The trail went through today's town on Aztec in northern New Mexico, Kayenta and Page in northern Arizona, Fredonia in Utah, south of Las Vegas, Nevada, to Barstow and San Bernadino in California, and then on to Mission San Gabriel and the nearby village of Los Angeles. The trip took him twelve weeks to journey there and six weeks to return.

Commerce along the Old Spanish Trail started with barter for horses and mules. Some unscrupulous individuals, however, found it easier to steal horses and mules in California and take them back for trade in New Mexico. The authorities in California tried to catch horsethieves, but were never able to fully control the illicit trade.

The rugged terrain of the Old Spanish Trail discouraged the use of wagons, so it was always a pack route using mules. Their small, hard hooves were ideal for carrying heavy loads over rocky trails. Mules had prodigious strength and endurance, and survived better than horses where water was scarce and forage was poor. The route, however, was tough, with challenging terrain and an arid climate. Historians Ann and LeRoy Hafen called the Old Spanish Trail with some justification "the longest, crookedest, most arduous pack mule route in the history of America." An important concern was where to find adequate supplies of water and forage for the pack animals, who often suffered in the harsh desert environment and severe mountain weather. Caravans lost their way, animals and men suffered from thirst, and the drovers were sometimes forced to eat their pack mules when food supplies ran out.

The mule caravans left New Mexico in the late summer or fall and returned from California in the spring. Slightly different routes were used at different times. In the fall, early snows often blocked the high mountain passes, so travelers had to choose their route accordingly. In the spring, trails might be blocked by late snows and flooding rivers.

As trading opportunities expanded, traders used the quickest and safest route. One alternate route pioneered in 1826 by Jedediah Smith and a party of fur trappers was a trail used by Indians and Spanish explorers that wound 188 miles across the Mojave Desert. Another, the so-called Northern Route, was pioneered by William Wolfskill and George C. Yount in 1831. This variation went north from Abiquiú, through southern Colorado around Durango, then to Moab in eastern Utah and across central Utah. It dropped down to the southwest to Las Vegas, Nevada, and joined up with Armijo's route. This trail avoided the rugged canyons of the Colorado River and had better water and pasturage in central Utah. Another branch went even further north, through the Rio Grande Gorge to Taos, and then into southern Colorado through the San Luis Valley. This trail followed the Gunnison River from Gunnison to Grand Junction in Colorado, then joined the Northern Route at Green River in Wyoming.

The routes all came together at Fork of Roads, east of present-day Barstow in the Mojave Desert, then crossed Cajon Pass between the San Gabriel and San Bernadino Mountains, went down to San Gabriel Mission, and on to Los Angeles.

Merchants trading with California were many and varied. In 1834 José Avieta and 125 men arrived at Los Angeles carrying 1,645 serapes, 314 blankets and other woolen goods to trade. In 1839 José Antonio Salazar arrived in California at the head of a group of seventy-five men. Francisco Quintana carried domestic goods worth $78.25. In 1842 Francisco Estevan Vigil took 4,150 animals back to New Mexico. In 1843 Juan Arce carried merchandise worth $487.50. In 1844 Francisco Rael transported domestic goods and sheep worth $1,748.

Starting in the mid–1840s, new routes carried troops fighting in the Mexican War, pioneers bound for California, and ever more traders. By 1869 the railroad carried most of the traffic and the Old Spanish Trail fell into disuse.

Chapter Eleven

The Americans Take Over

Changes came again to New Mexico and the Spanish Southwest as the opening of the Santa Fe Trail brought an influx of Anglo-Americans. Santa Fe was a dusty frontier town with a mix of Spanish colonial families, arrivals from Mexico, displaced Indians and slaves, and a growing number of Americans. Some were traders and merchants who lived in New Mexico part-time, while others settled permanently and brought with them their skills as carpenters, trappers, blacksmiths, gunsmiths, and whiskey distillers. They brought new industries, new ideas, and new American customs and ways of thinking to the old Spanish province.

More than 1,000 miles to the west, the Pueblo de la Reina de Los Angeles was an even smaller town. It consisted of little more than a church, a plaza, a few homes, and some government buildings, but it was still the largest Mexican community in the area.

War with Mexico

The continued presence of American traders in Santa Fe and an ongoing unrest in the New Mexican province were two of the factors that eventually led to war between Mexico and the United States.

Internally, the remote provinces felt oppressed by what they saw as excessive tax burdens, regulations, and interference in their lives by a nameless, faceless government in distant Mexico City. These feelings led to a short-lived revolt by a group of farmers and Pueblo Indians against Governor Albino Pérez in 1837. Known as the Chimayó Rebellion, participants in the insurrection overwhelmed the governor's forces and brutally murdered him and his cabinet. The Pueblo Indians cut the head off Pérez's body and used it for a football. They treated other officials equally brutally, including cutting the tongue out of the throat of Santiago Abrevió. In retaliation, former governor Manuel Armijo with a company of soldiers from Mexico ousted the rebels and executed their leader. Though Americans in Santa Fe had not participated in the rebellion, officials in Mexico City were nevertheless suspicious of any foreigners and what they might be doing in the province's capital.

Another incident contributing to war occurred in 1841 when a group from the new Republic of Texas, eyeing the profitable New Mexico trade, decided to visit Santa Fe. Though they statedly had peaceful intentions, the president of Texas may have also had some thoughts about annexing New Mexico to take control of the lucrative Santa Fe trade.[1] Whatever their true intentions were, the Mexican government viewed this as a hostile invasion. Mexico still claimed Texas as a lost province and still disputed the international boundary.

In any case the expedition turned into a comedy of errors. The Texans were attacked by Indians, lost their way on the Plains, and then ran out of food and water. But they still toiled on towards Santa Fe. Armijo and a ragtag army of defenders captured them easily and sent them south to prison in Mexico City.[2]

The 1830s and 1840s saw similar clashes between Spanish and Anglos over Manifest Destiny, which was the concept that Americans had the God-given obligation to spread across and colonize the North American continent, regardless of any existing native cultures.[3] The Americans saw Mexican land as fair game and many Mexicans were forced off their property in the process.[4] Officials in Santa Fe eventually became reluctant to deal with Americans, perhaps because they sensed an impending war between the two countries. Finally, Mexico ordered a brief halt to trade between Mexico and the United States.

A more significant cause for war was that Texas joined the Union on December 29, 1845, as the twenty-eighth state. Unresolved boundary issues between the United States and Mexico, however, caused continued tension along the border. President James K. Polk wanted Mexican recognition of Texas annexation and the boundary to be set at the Rio Grande. The Mexican government, however, refused to recognize either the Independence of Texas or the Rio Grande as the international boundary. One of the puzzles for Polk was how to capture New Mexico without disrupting the lucrative Santa Fe trade.

On January 13, 1846, Polk ordered Brig. Gen. Zachary Taylor and 4,000 troops to Texas to the disputed territory. Taylor proceeded to the Rio Grande and built a fort on the north bank of the river (which eventually became the town of Brownsville, Texas). As anticipated, on April 25, Mexican troops crossed the river and opened fire. President Polk took his case before Congress on May 11, 1846, which led to a declaration of war on Mexico on May 13, 1846. Taylor proceeded south and captured Monterrey, Mexico, in September.

To keep the momentum going, in June of 1846 Col. (later promoted to Brigadier General) Stephen Watts Kearny formed what was called the "Army of the West" at Fort Leavenworth, Kansas, the army's main supply depot for all the West, and prepared to move to occupy New Mexico and California. Kearny left Fort Leavenworth on June 16 with 1,658 men and marched west on the Santa Fe Trail towards Bent's Fort. His army was a mixed lot, consisting of some regular troops, some volunteer cavalry, and some infantry. He was accompanied by a huge supply train consisting of 1,556 wagons and about 19,000 horses, oxen, and pack mules. In spite of the daunting logistical task of moving all these men and their supplies across 900 miles of desolate prairie, he crossed the Arkansas River into Mexican territory on August 1. Traveling as a soldier in the West, however, was not easy. As volunteer soldier Ovando Hollister wrote as they pursued Confederates during the Civil War, "Away into the wee hours of the morning did we tramp, tramp, tramp.... Nothing broke the stillness of the night but the steady tramp of men and the rattle of the wagons.... At length the animals began to drop and die in harness from overwork and underfeed, which forced us to stop."[5]

As Kearny's army moved across the West, successful trader James Magoffin, probably acting under secret orders from Polk, and Captain Philip St. George Cooke went ahead from Bent's Fort to Santa Fe under a flag of truce. The two convinced Governor Armijo that resistance was useless. It may have also been that some money changed hands.[6] Whatever the arrangements were, Armijo put up a good front. He rallied a group of troops and militia, and marched them out to confront the Americans. He boldly claimed that New

Mexicans would resist the Americans to the death. He created a defensive position in Apache Canyon, fifteen miles east of Santa Fe, then suddenly and quietly disappeared. The New Mexican troops waiting for Kearny's arrival subsequently found out to their surprise that their leader, Armijo, had fled south to Mexico.

On August 15, 1846, Kearny reached Las Vegas, New Mexico, then more completely known as *Nuestra Señora de los Dolores de Las Vegas Grandes* ("Our Lady of Sorrows of the Large Meadows"). Las Vegas was similar to Santa Fe in construction. When Ovando Hollister and his fellow soldiers marched through in 1862, he described it like this: "The buildings are not above nine feet high, with flat, dirt roofs, built of adobes and generally plastered with mud. Those surrounding the plaza are ornamented with porticos and thick coats of whitewash in front."[7]

Accompanied by Juan de Dios Maese, the *alcalde* (mayor) of Las Vegas, Kearny addressed the local townspeople from the roof of the *alcalde's* house and announced to the surprised residents that the United States had annexed New Mexico.[8] In his proclamation Kearny boldly said, "Henceforth I absolve you from all allegiance to the Mexican government, and from all obedience to General Armijo. He is no longer your governor. I am your governor." This reportedly caused a great sensation among his listeners. Stating further that he would provide protection for the residents, he went on to say that, "…not a pepper or onion shall be disturbed or taken by my troops without pay…."[9]

In spite of sensationalist false rumors that the invading Americans would destroy the Catholic religion and brand Mexican women on the cheek like mules, the takeover was peaceful. Kearny and his troops faced no opposition from either the local inhabitants or the Mexican army. On August 18, Kearny entered Santa Fe and occupied the city without resistance and without firing a shot.[10] But he stayed busy. Kearny declared that New Mexico was now a territory of the United States, drafted a set of territorial laws, and organized a territorial government. He appointed trader Charles Bent of Bent's Fort, who had a home in Taos, as governor of the new territory.[11]

Similarly, on July 7, 1846, Commodore John D. Sloat, commander of the Pacific fleet, sailed into Monterey Harbor, and raised the American flag over the Customs House. The capital of Spanish (at the time Mexican) California had been occupied without a struggle.

Meanwhile, in New Mexico, Kearny built an imposing fort on top of a prominent steep hill northeast of the Plaza, overlooking Santa Fe, to create an intimidating symbol of United States occupation and to protect the troops in case of an uprising. This became the first United States military post in the Southwest. The fort consisted of a massive earthen embankment surrounded by a ditch, with perimeter walls made of adobe nine feet high and five feet thick. The interior was an area 270 feet long by 80 feet wide.[12] Kearny named the structure Fort Marcy after Secretary of War William L. Marcy.

Much of this was for show, though the fort commanded a panoramic strategic view of the city below. The fort and the United States flag flying over it were intended to be a constant reminder of American military control. In late 1847 soldiers started to transfer out of the fort to the old Spanish military barracks on the Plaza, next to the Palace of the Governors, where their commanding officer had made his headquarters and most of the men lived. This was also the location of the military hospital, storehouses, and gardens. By 1862 Fort Marcy was vacant and all the military administration of New Mexico was carried out from the downtown location.[13] Fort Marcy was officially abandoned by the Army in 1894.

Kearny left some of his troops to maintain the occupation of Santa Fe and continued west with the First Dragoons to complete the final part of his mission by taking over California.[14] He defeated the Mexican army at Los Angeles on March 1, 1847.

Col. Stephen Kearny announced the bloodless takeover of New Mexico from the top of this building on the north side of the plaza in downtown Las Vegas. At the time it was the home of the *alcalde* (mayor), Juan de Dios Maese.

This was the view of the east side of the Plaza in Santa Fe in 1866. The Palace of the Governors was around the corner to the left. The hills to the northeast, at the rear of this view, were where Fort Marcy was located from 1846 to 1851 to serve as a constant reminder to New Mexicans of the presence of American military control (National Archives).

A little more than a year later a treaty was signed in the little village of Guadalupe Hidalgo, a few miles north of Mexico City, and the war officially ended. With the Treaty of Guadalupe Hidalgo, signed on February 2, 1848, Mexico lost over half its territory to the United States. This consisted of the Southwest from Texas to the Pacific, including New Mexico, Arizona, and California, and large parts of Nevada, Utah, and Colorado. In addition, the treaty set the southern boundary of Texas at the Rio Grande. A few years later, the Gadsden Purchase of 1853 (named after James Gadsden, U.S. Minister to Mexico) added slightly over 29 million acres (almost 30,000 square miles) of land south of the Gila River from Texas to California to the United States. The cost was $10 million. With this purchase, the United States borders became what they are today.

This revision of land ownership was not necessarily greeted with enthusiasm by some of those living along the border. At the end of the war with Mexico, many of the Spanish New Mexicans living in this area wanted to remain Mexican citizens, rather than be part of the United States. Mexico agreed to allow them to settle on the southern side of the Rio Grande and many did, happily building homes, planting crops, and resettling their families. Unfortunately, after the Gadsden Purchase, the border changed again, ownership of their land went back to the United States, and they found themselves unwilling U.S. citizens again.

Meanwhile, in northern New Mexico, occasional Indian attacks on outlying settlements and wagon trains still occurred, but with the United States in control of the territory, American traders felt more comfortable about traveling to and from Santa Fe.

When the Southwest became part of the United States, peace did not come immediately. The period between 1850 and 1890 saw the clash of three vital cultures in the West: the Indians, the colonial Spanish of New Mexico, and the Anglo-Americans of the United States. Unfortunately for the Indians there was little improvement in their status with the new owners. The Spanish conquerors were replaced by the Americans, whose philosophy was to exterminate and remove the native population, rather than subjugate them.[15]

Bad American Liquor

One of the American influences that followed the Anglos was liquor. Americans had long had a love affair with alcohol. The earliest settlers on the East Coast in the 1600s brought with them strong spirits and a love of drink. Alcohol at the time was regarded as a healthy and nutritious substance that was essential to well-being.

The Southwest was no different. After the Anglos arrived in northern New Mexico, distilleries were quick to spring up. Canny businessmen produced a raw, fiery liquor called *aguardiente de Taos*. The name came from combining two Spanish words, *agua* and *ardiente*, which mean "fiery water." The liquor was popularly known as "Taos Lightning" and more affectionately by its drinkers as "Old Towse."[16] The raw alcohol was given some flavor with additives such as pepper, chili powder, saltpeter, or even a touch of gunpowder. The drink was said to be somewhat rough and certainly was very potent. During the 1830s and 1840s Taos Lightning was used as a popular trade item for obtaining beaver pelts and other valuable furs. The name was given to it because drinkers felt that after a couple of glasses they had been struck by lightning. Reportedly it was very popular at parties and was drunk by both men and women. Eventually the name *aguardiente* was applied to any kind of raw spirits.

Taos Lightning was first produced in 1824 by Thomas Long Smith (later better-known as mountain man Peg-Leg Smith) and three partners. They constructed a distillery in the upper Rio Grande valley and distilled local corn and grain into a high-proof alcohol. Another man who produced raw alcohol, starting in the 1830s, was an American named Simeon Turley, one of the pioneers in the Taos liquor industry. Turley owned a two-story mill, a granary, barns, and a processing still about two miles west of the town of Arroyo Hondo on the Rio Hondo river, ten miles north of Taos. Turley grew his own grain, ground it in his own mill, and processed it in his distillery. The resulting "whiskey" was a popular drink among the Pueblo Indians and mountain men who lived in the area in nearby Taos. The price was $4 a gallon. Turley also carried five-gallon barrels of whiskey north by wagon into Colorado where he traded it for beaver pelts, buffalo skins, and Indian-made items.

In 1842 Turley established a trading post called El Pueblo in south-central Colorado for the purpose of selling whiskey and bartering for furs with the Indians. The fort was built from adobe bricks on the north side of the junction of Fountain Creek and the Arkansas River, just north of the International Boundary with Mexico.[17] Francis Parkman, a twenty-three-year-old from Boston who traveled the West, described Fort Pueblo in the following fashion. "It was a wretched species of fort, of most primitive construction, being nothing more than a large square enclosure, surrounded by a wall of mud, miserably cracked and dilapidated. The slender pickets that surmounted it were half broken down, and the gate dangled on its wooden hinges so loosely that to open or shut it seemed likely to fling it down altogether. Two or three squalid Mexicans, with their broad hats, and their vile faces overgrown with hair, were lounging about the bank of the river in front of it. They disappeared as they saw us approach...."[18] This down-to-earth type of place was not unusual for the early trappers' forts.

Parkman described Fort St. Vrain in similar fashion. "It was now abandoned and fast falling into ruin. The walls of unbaked bricks were cracked from top to bottom. Our horses recoiled in terror from the neglected entrance, where the heavy gates were torn from their hinges and flung down. The area within was overgrown with weeds, and the long ranges of apartments once occupied by the motley concourse of traders, Canadians, and squaws, were now miserably dilapidated."[19]

Thomas Fitzpatrick, an Indian agent in southern Colorado, writing about Fort Pueblo said: "These villages are becoming the resort of all idlers and loafers. They are also becoming depots for the smuggling of liquors from New Mexico into this country."[20]

Unfortunately, on December 24, 1854, the occupants of Fort Pueblo celebrated Christmas with too much of their own Taos Lightning. In their alcoholic stupor they were overrun and massacred by a marauding band of Jicarilla Apache and Utes under Chief Blanco. The Indians were allegedly retaliating for a smallpox epidemic among the Utes that was blamed on infected goods distributed by the government during the previous summer. Fifteen men and one woman were killed. After the massacre at Fort Pueblo, the Indians crossed into the San Luis Valley and killed more settlers at Costilla.[21] A few years earlier, Turley had been just as unlucky.

The Taos Rebellion

Although the takeover of New Mexico by Kearny had appeared to be uneventful, it had not been entirely peaceful and many of the local inhabitants resented the tide of Anglo-Americans coming in. Local priests and wealthy New Mexicans saw their influence eroding with the American occupation. They agitated for rebellion by spreading rumors and fear that annexation of New Mexico by American outsiders would mean seizure of all the Spanish people's property, destruction of their Catholic religion and traditions, banning of the Spanish language, and violation of Spanish and Indian women.

Some of these erroneous ideas were possibly fomented by fray Antonío José Martinez, an important religious and social leader in the Taos area, who kept firm control over the converted Pueblo Indians, but felt that his power was slipping away after the Americans arrived. As a result, some of the locals plotted a revolt to kill the territorial government. Among the targets was Governor Charles Bent, who had been recently appointed the first territorial governor of New Mexico by Gen. Kearny. Bent was strong-willed and had powerful enemies among the local population, including the Martínez family, and the local Indians who resented Bent trading with their enemies on the Plains. Chronicler George Ruxton, who visited New Mexico just before the Taos uprising, noted that he detected considerable hostility towards Americans.[22]

Based on resentment of the American conquerors and fears of land seizures, a constant stream of oratory and local rabble-rousing against the Anglos finally led to a major rebellion in Taos on January 19, 1847, when the native population rose up and tried to drive the Americans away. A mob of Taos Indians stormed Bent's house, broke down the front door, shot him full of arrows, and scalped him. The others in the house, including three children, Bent's wife Ignacia, and Ignacia's sister, Maria Josefa Jaramillo (Kit Carson's wife), managed to escape into the adjoining house through a hole that they hastily dug in the adobe wall with a poker and a big spoon. Five other prominent citizens who were American sympathizers were also killed. The raiders took cattle, mules and oxen.

Two days later, about ten miles north of Taos, Mexican and Pueblo Indian rebels surrounded and attacked Simeon Turley's Mill in Arroyo Hondo. Turley and eight mountain men escaped by digging a hole from the distillery into the granary.[23] He and the others held out initially, but were overrun on the second day of the siege when their ammunition ran low. The rebels set fire to the mill and killed Turley and six of the other defenders. Two escaped. The dead men were buried in a common grave in Kit Carson Cemetery in Taos. Though the rebels wanted to make their mark on the American colonists, a more subtle reason for the specific attack on the mill may have been due to resentment by local residents over the damaging effects of Turley's whiskey on the local Indian population.

The uprising continued and spread to nearby Santa Cruz and Mora before being suppressed by United States troops. Soldiers under Lt. Col. Sterling Price, who was left by Kearny as military commander in Santa Fe, marched to Santa Cruz, near Espanola, met the rebels, and routed them easily. The rebels retreated and barricaded themselves in the mission church at Taos Pueblo. Taos Pueblo itself was heavily fortified and several Spanish settlers in the area lived inside for protection. On February 4, Price ordered artillery to shell the walls of the church, then his men stormed the ruins. During the fighting, 150 rebels and 7 soldiers were killed. Another major fight between the rebels and American troops under Capt. Israel Hendley took place further north at the village of Mora.

Over the next three months, eleven Mexicans and six Taos Indians were hanged for their parts in the rebellion. Although isolated raiding and skirmishes continued through 1847, there were no more major attacks on the Americans.

Fort Union

After the Americans were firmly entrenched in the Southwest, New Mexico's military installations were turned over to Lt. Col. Edwin Vose Sumner. Sumner had previously received the name "Bull-Head" from his men because a musket ball had bounced off his skull without doing any serious damage.

Sumner traveled to Santa Fe in 1851 and was appalled by the morale and morals of the troops under his command. Sumner felt that the soldiers at Fort Marcy were spending too much time in the bars, fandango houses, gambling dens, and red light houses of the town. In his opinion, Santa Fe was "that sink of vice and extravagance." One of the army officers gave his opinion of the Santa Fe women when he wrote, "They do not seem to know what virtue or industry is, and being almost the slave of the husband, are very fond of the attention of strangers."[24] Most of the local traders and trappers had respected the local women and behaved with politeness towards them, but the new American troops in Santa Fe were not always so polite and incidents of molestation immediately started to occur. This did not go over well with the local Mexican and Pueblo men and had been partly to blame for the Taos rebellion several years earlier.

One of Sumner's first changes was to move his headquarters at Santa Fe to a new eighty-acre location just north of Las Vegas. Fort Union, established in 1851, was close to the junction of the Mountain Branch and the Cimarron Cut-Off on the Santa Fe Trail. It was convenient for the army as much of the traffic over the trail was going to supply the military anyway.

One of Sumner's more bizarre military ideas, proposed by him to save the army money, was to furnish weapons to the Indians and let them fight it out among themselves. His superiors, however, were not amused by his suggestion and this proposal was ignored.[25]

Fort Union grew to be the largest fort in the West and the central storage warehouse depot and stocking point for the distribution of supplies for about half the forts and military in the West. Unlike the wooden Western forts of the movies surrounded by a stockade, or Bent's Fort which was surrounded by a fortified adobe wall, Fort Union had no protective walls, with only a picket marking off its massive open perimeter.

Lt. Col. Edwin Sumner moved the army headquarters from Santa Fe to Fort Union, 100 miles to the north, to guard the Santa Fe trail and keep the soldiers away from what he felt was the poor influence of the gambling halls of Santa Fe. This was the mechanics corral at the fort, where skilled workmen repaired wagons, wheels, and other equipment.

This is all that remains of Julian Baca's combination dance hall, gambling den, and bordello at Loma Parda. This stone pleasure palace provided solace in the form of gambling, drinking, and women for lonely soldiers at nearby Fort Union. There was even wagon taxi service between the fort and the town for those who could afford a dollar.

In all fairness to Col. Sumner, Fort Union was a strategic location. It was located close to where the Cimarron and the Mountain branches of the Santa Fe trail came together and it was a central point to attack the Apache who had had terrorized the Spanish Rio Grande settlements for the previous 250 years. It was convenient for pursuing the Kiowa and Comanche who attacked travelers to the east.

Initially, Sumner's plan succeeded and the hundred or so miles distance of Santa Fe from Fort Union meant that the soldiers stationed there could not conveniently return to engage in gambling and other activities. In this case, however, entertainment followed the soldiers and the small nearby town of Loma Parda, located on the Mora River about five miles southwest of the post, took care of all the amusements and diversions for the lusty young troops. Loma Parda was also known as "Sodom on the Mora," a sly reference to the two wicked towns of Sodom and Gomorrah from the Bible. A wagon ran between the town and Fort Union as a primitive taxi service for $1 for the round trip. For those who could not afford this modest fee, there was also a well-worn pathway. Julian Baca's combination dance hall, gambling den, and bordello featured musical entertainment twenty-four hours a day and provided a local homemade whiskey that was called Loma Lightning (actually Taos Lightning that was shipped in and given a local name).

Ovando Hollister, a soldier in the Colorado First Regiment of Volunteers during the Civil War, remembered drinking at Loma Parda in these terms: "[T]he command ... was scattered ... burying plunder, drinking, fighting and carousing with Mexican women at the Lome, a small 'Sodom' five or six miles from Union. There were a dozen of us too drunk to know friends from foes, consequently most provokingly troublesome. Many came in during the night with rough usage painted on their faces in unmistakable colors."[26]

The Civil War Touches New Mexico

One of the critical battles of the Civil War in the West started at Fort Craig, an adobe cantonment built in 1853 across the river from Valverde in southern New Mexico.[27] The initial purpose of the fort was to protect travelers along the *Jornada del Muerto* ("Journey of the Dead Man"). Travel across the *Journado del Muerto* required plenty of water and the trail was studded with the graves of those who did not take enough with them. The name came from an incident involving a prosperous German trader named Bernardo Gruber. In 1670 he was accused by the Spanish Inquisition of selling magical charms and was jailed at nearby Abo. After twenty-seven months of waiting for a trial and desperate to tend to his starving stock, he escaped and fled down *El Camino Real*. He perished three weeks later in the section of barren desert called *Jornada del Muerto* and his bones were found at a site that became named *El Alemán*, or "The German."[28] Fort Craig was intended to protect travelers from Apache and Comanche along this treacherous segment of desert that stretched for sixty miles along *El Camino Real*, between the towns of Radium Springs and Truth or Consequences. *Parajes*, or rest stops, had previously been established in the desert to ease the journey. Paraje San Diego, Paraje del Perrillo, Las Peñuelas, Paraje del Aleman, and Laguna del Muerto allowed a brief respite from the heat and barren nature of the crossing.

When the Civil War started, some of the officers at Fort Union resigned their commissions to join the South. Among them was Maj. Henry Hopkins Sibley. He was commissioned a lieutenant-general in the Confederate army and took command of the troops in Texas. Sibley and the Confederacy eyed the rich gold fields of Colorado and California as a way to help finance the war. Accordingly, in 1861, Confederate volunteers marched north from El Paso into New Mexico and moved against Union troops stationed at Fort Fillmore near Mesilla.

The main Confederate force under Sibley arrived in January of 1862 and the joint group marched on Fort Craig with 2,600 men. At the time, Fort Craig was occupied by 3,800 Union troops under the command of Col. Edward R. Canby, who had marched down from Fort Union. Sibley tried several times to draw the Union troops out of their fortifications, but they refused to budge. One darkly humorous story of the siege was that the Union troops conceived the seemingly bright idea of loading a couple of mules with howitzer shells, lighting the fuses, and sending them on their way towards the Confederate camp. The mules, however, being mules, had a strong homing instinct and turned back towards their familiar home camp with the fuses still burning. The predictable outcome was that the shells exploded, waking and scaring men on both sides, and left the army with two fewer mules.[29]

Sibley finally chose not to attack Fort Craig directly, but decided to try to sneak by the fort towards Santa Fe, hoping to capture valuable military supplies at Fort Union and then head north for Colorado. Canby, however, sent out troops on February 21, 1862, to challenge and engage the Confederates in what became known as the Battle of Valverde Ford, north of Fort Craig. Sibley had the better force and drove the Union troops back into Fort Craig.

The triumphant Sibley marched north and occupied Albuquerque in March, though the Union troops guarding the supply depot managed to carry off or burn the supplies Sibley had counted on. The Confederates pressed on north towards Santa Fe and Fort Union seeking the replacement supplies that now had become vital for their continued mission.

On March 27, volunteers from Colorado crossed snow covered Raton Pass and confronted the Confederates at Glorieta Pass, east of Santa Fe. The Confederates initially appeared to win the battle that has been called the "Gettysburg of the West." However, during the fight, several hundred troops from the Colorado First Regiment of Volunteers under Maj. John Chivington, an ex–Methodist preacher, worked their way around behind the Confederate troops and completely destroyed their supply train. Without supplies, the Confederates had to retreat back to Texas and the safety of El Paso. This was a major disaster for the South and eliminated any further plans for Confederate expansion into the West.

The Real Spanish Riches

The story of the Spanish in the Southwest started with the search for elusive gold, and it is only appropriate to end by returning to Spanish gold and other riches. Though the original Spanish conquistadors pushed boldly north of New Spain, confident that there was treasure to be found somewhere, they never uncovered the fabled cities of Cibola and Quivira, or any other El Dorado.

Ironically, however, they found natural mineral resources. Silver, for example, was found in large quantities in an area in Mexico's central plateau from Zacatecas to Chihuahua. These rich Spanish silver mines of northern Mexico were partially responsible for the advance of the northern frontier of New Spain. This was the world's richest silver mining country at the time and yielded enormous wealth for the Spanish Crown. The richest silver was at Zacatecas, discovered 300 miles northwest of Mexico City in 1548. A similar rich silver strike was found at Guanajuato in 1554. Eventually dozens of silver mining towns flourished in this area and helped to maintain Spain's riches and power in Europe. The silver went directly from the mines to the government mint.

Unfortunately, this area was also the homeland of various highly aggressive Indian tribes that the Spanish called *chichimecas* after the *Gran Chichimeca*, a vast dry stretch of country of maguey, mesquite, nopal cactus, and spiny underbrush that stretched 500 miles northwards from the city of Zacatecas between the Sierra Madre Occidental and Sierra Madre Oriental mountains. This included today's Mexican states of Durango and Chihuahua. The Spanish used the name *chichimecas* as a generic term for several culturally different native groups (among them Pares, Guamares, and Zacatecos), similar to the Anglos using the generic Old West names of "Apache" and "Indian." These naked, roving, wandering, wild and primitive tribesmen, covered only in body paint, were cruel and barbarous.

They were fierce, independent groups that lived in widely dispersed villages and made war on Spanish travelers in the area.

These Indians had no intention of being dominated by the Spanish or submitting to the Spanish system of *encomienda* and *repartimiento*. Instead, they harassed the mining camps, ambushed supply pack trains, and attacked any Spanish they could. Their weapons were simple stone-tipped arrows. The Indians were known for mutilating living captives, such as skinning Spanish soldiers alive and leaving them hanging besides the roads.[30] Attacks were so bad that for a while the Spanish even considered waging a war of extermination on them, but such a harsh decision was never made.

Part of the ferociousness of the *chichimecas* in battle may have been due to the use of drugs. There is evidence that the Indians of Central America used cohoba, a type of snuff from the *Acacia niopo* plant that was ground up into a powder, mixed with water, and ingested.[31] Users felt that the drug cleared their vision and heightened their senses during hunting expeditions. Spanish missionaries also noted that the natives used a straw to inhale some sort of intoxicating powder (possibly cocaine) up their noses. Friars had previously described the use of coca leaves in South America and peyote among the natives of Central America.[32]

In spite of Indian harassment, though, mining continued to be successful. In 1736 a huge silver deposit was found at Arizonac in Sonora. Instead of occurring in typical veins of silver, though, this deposit was in the form of pure nuggets that were round like balls, many of which weighed up to 500 pounds. The silver in this fabulous mine soon ran out, but the find continued to spark hopes of further rich undiscovered deposits. Had the Spanish only known about the rich bodies of ore that were later found by American prospectors in Colorado, Arizona, and New Mexico, the history of the Southwest might have well been changed. Had they found this gold and silver, the Spanish frontier might have pushed even further north.

Though the hoped-for vast quantities of golden objects waiting to be appropriated, like the earlier Aztec riches, were not found, the Spanish nevertheless were able to find some gold. But it had to be laboriously extracted from the ground. The Spanish knew only how to mine pure gold nuggets, flakes, or dust (as opposed to complex ores), but it had to be separated from the surrounding dirt.

Underground mining was carried out with simple, but effective, techniques. One method of breaking rock apart in an mine below ground level was to build a fire on the ore vein then douse it with cold water. The expansion with heat and then the resultant rapid contraction with cold water fractured the rock into small enough pieces that it could be handled with simple digging tools, such as shovels and iron bars. The more sophisticated mines extracted the ore from the digging surface using a hand operated windlass that hauled up a rope with a bucket made of cowhide on the end. These reinforced leather bags were often carried to the surface by hand, as the mines were typically no more than fifteen or twenty feet deep. The ore was carried up a ladder (often just an inclined log with notches in it), or series of ladders, to the surface by Indian laborers.

One very simple technique used by the Spanish for separating gold dust or nuggets from waste rock was to simply throw the gold-bearing dirt into the air on a windy day. The wind carried away the lighter waste material while the heavier gold particles fell back to the ground and were gathered up. This technique, similar to that for separating wheat from chaff, was called by the same name, or "winnowing." Unfortunately, as one official commented, the process was highly inefficient and a great deal of the gold dust was also blown away and lost.

A simple device used by the Spanish for milling ore was the *arrastra*. This crude crushing mechanism reduced chunks of ore-bearing rock to particles the size of sand. *Arrastras* were cheap, easy to construct, and could be operated by one person. The basic concept was to form a circular basin of rocks, often up to eight to twelve feet in diameter, in the ground. A central post was placed upright in the middle of the basin with a heavy boulder fastened by a rope or chain to each end of a crossbar that rotated on top of the post. Gold or silver ore was shoveled into the basin and the crossbar was rotated to drag the rocks over the ore and crush it. Either a mule or a man walked in a circle around the basin turning the crossbar, though water power was occasionally used.

Ground up waste rock, dirt, and gravel were washed away by water running through the *arrastra*, while the heavier gold dust sank to the bottom of the basin for recovery. After the mid–1500s, quicksilver (mercury) was added to the crushed rock to amalgamate the ore for greater efficiency and to improve the quantity of gold or silver recovered. The amalgamation process increased the efficiency of production by allowing the extraction of silver and gold from ore of poor quality.[33] *Arrastras* were commonly used in mining areas in Spanish New Mexico and California, and later during the American gold rushes of the 1850s and 1860s.

Although Spanish gold and silver mining took place in Arizona and New Mexico, these mines were not as rich as the mines of Mexico. In addition, the cost of transportation and the required 20 percent royalty paid to the crown made mining ventures generally unprofitable. There were exceptions, however. The Spanish "Planches de Plata" strike in 1736 in southern Arizona consisted of slabs of almost pure silver, and the Arivaca silver mines west of Tucson were high grade ore that was easily recovered in shallow diggings. In general, however, large-scale mining was not feasible because of shortages of labor to mine and grow food for the miners, and the danger of Apache Indian attacks. Many small rich surface deposits, however, that required little equipment or manpower, were worked between the arrival of the Spanish in 1541 and the end of the Mexican period.

As well as mining in Arizona and New Mexico, by 1591 the Spanish had prospected in South Park and the San Luis Valley of Colorado, where they established settlements and opened gold and silver mines. A suit of Spanish armor, probably from one of de Anza's soldiers is said to have been found buried in a rock crevice in South Park.[34] In the 1950s, a rancher in Rye, Colorado, found a Spanish ring bit from a horse's bridle.

Legend has it that the Spanish built *arrastras* and mined for gold in central Colorado, and there is indeed an *arrastra* carved out of a boulder in Buckskin Creek near the ghost town of Buckskin. It was reputed to be Spanish, but this is unlikely. There is no evidence that it resulted from any Spanish activity and this particular one appears to have been constructed after 1860 and the influx of Anglo-American miners to the area. There are similar legends that caves on the east side of Buckskin Gulch were the hiding place for Spanish treasure.

Besides gold and silver, several other minerals were found in the provinces. Valuable deposits of cinnabar, for example, were discovered in New Mexico. This ore contained mercury, which was used to process the ore in the silver mines of northern Mexico.[35] Mercury

The Spanish *arrastra* was used to grind ore to extract the gold and silver contained in it. The basic design was a circular basin made of rocks that held the ore to be crushed. The post in the middle had a wooden cross-piece pulled in a circle by a man or a mule. In this way the two large boulders on the end of the chains were dragged around inside the basin and crushed the ore. Water running through the basin washed away waste rock as the heavier gold sank to the bottom for later collection.

was a crown monopoly, thus the supply and price were controlled by the government. A similar situation existed with iron in New Mexico in the 1700s. All raw iron was protected by the crown and iron items had to be imported from Spain in order to protect the Spanish ironworking trades. This made the metal expensive and scarce. This scarcity of iron meant that even simple items, such as hinges and hooks for hanging clothing and implements around the home, which would normally be made from metal, had to be made from wood. Iron reserves in Mexico were not developed until the 1800s.

As well as silver, copper was found in New Mexico. In 1800, a Mimbreño Apache who lived in southwest New Mexico showed Col. José Manuel Carrasco some copper outcroppings twelve miles east of Silver City. Carrasco started a profitable mine and in 1804 sold to Don Francisco Manuel de Elguea. Eventually this mine became the Santa Rita open-pit mine, the largest open-pit copper mine in the world. Most of the early copper ore went to the Royal Mint in Mexico City to be made into copper coins.[36]

A rich deposit of gold was found at nearby Pinos Altos in 1860. In response, the local Apache, offended that the United States had negotiated the Treaty of Guadalupe Hidalgo with Mexico instead of with them, increased their raids on miners, settlers, herders, and travelers. Continued Indian harassment was a major factor in the Indian Wars in the Southwest that lasted until the final defeat of the Apache by the United States army in 1886.

Legends of Lost Spanish Treasure

Stories of lost gold have always been a part of the lore of the West. A few examples are the Lost Adams Diggings in Arizona, the Lost Bonanza in Utah, the Lost Cabin in Montana, and the Lost Cement in California. But none have been more pervasive than the legends of lost Spanish gold and buried treasure in the Old West. These legends started soon after the arrival of the Spanish. For example, Indians in Arizona told Coronado of gold in the Superstition Mountains near Phoenix. Coronado searched for it, but he never found any precious metal. In 1845 Don Miguel Peralta of Sonora, Mexico, supposedly found a gold vein in these mountains; however, the location was lost when he and his miners were massacred by Apache Indians who thought that he was defiling the home of their Thunder God. Repeated stories like these eventually gave rise to the legend of the Lost Dutchman Mine.

Another popular legend was the story of Montezuma's Lost Treasure Caravan. Supposedly the Aztec ruler Montezuma stripped his buildings of gold, silver, and jewels, and sent the treasure north to keep it out of the hands of Cortés. One account said that the caravan traveled deep into Arizona or New Mexico and became lost. Another story placed the treasure trove near Kanab, Utah. A third said that the treasure is still buried in Mexico.[37]

Other stories from Colorado mixed fact and fancy. Legend referred to a mine on Sangre de Cristo Pass that was supposedly opened and worked by the Spanish. A mine in the Culebra Mountains showed evidence of being worked by the Spanish. Spanish *arrastras* for processing ore were found by early settlers on North Arrastra Creek, south of the Great Sand Dunes, and high in the San Juan Mountains near Summitville.[38]

Other legends tell of lost caves and buried Spanish treasure. Early Spanish explorers believed that the Aztecs mined gold somewhere around the Spanish Peaks of southern Colorado and many legends of lost Spanish gold in the area sprang up over the years. One legend said that Spanish conquerors forced Indian slaves to enter deep underground passages and dig out gold, then killed them all and buried the bodies in the abandoned mine to protect the secret of the treasure. Part of this legend described weird wailing noises heard in the vicinity that were supposedly the lonely cries of the unfortunate buried victims. Whatever the real cause of the noises, Indians avoided the area as being haunted.

A similar legend involved the Lost Padre Mine in Arizona. This was supposedly originally an Indian mine that was taken over by Spanish missionaries. The tale of this treasure told that the fathers were worried that miners from the 1849 gold rush that swept California would discover the mine and the gold. So they had their Indian laborers seal off the mine and then buried them deep in the mine with the gold to prevent them from giving away the secret location. Similar stories of similar Lost Padre mines were told in the Rio Grande country in Texas and in Juarez, Mexico. On the Texas side of the river, one local legend told that Governor Oñate of New Mexico buried bars of silver and gold looted earlier from the Aztecs deep at the bottom of an old Lost Padre mine. A group of prospectors set out to clean out the mine and recover the treasure in the late 1880s, but for some unknown reason failed to complete the task, even with the incentive of all the riches.

One intriguing question that has not yet been satisfactorily answered is the presence of primitive gold smelters found by early Spanish exploratory expeditions and the remains of smelted ore in Anasazi country in the Four Corners area. Though Pueblo people enjoyed jewelry, the Spanish did not find any gold or silver among them. If the Anasazi did indeed smelt ore, the questions are why and what happened to it? Did it go back to the Mexico or the Aztecs, or was there some other link that is as yet unknown?

One of the most interesting treasure legends, and one that has never been satisfactorily explained, surrounds *La Caverna del Oro* ("The Cave of Gold"), also known as Spanish Cave. This strange and mysterious cave was located high above timberline at 11,550 feet in the Sangre de Cristo Mountains of southern Colorado. The cave was also called Marble Cave and Marble Mountain Cave because of its location near the top of 13,266 foot Marble Mountain.

The most interesting aspect of the cave was its supposed link to the Spanish. Legend told of heavy doors inside the entrance, behind which was a fortune in Spanish treasure. Spanish Cave has been linked by different legends to being a source of gold for the Aztecs and being part of the riches of the Aztec's wealth before the mine was abandoned and its treasure lost.

After the Spanish arrived, the story goes that three Franciscan friars, Luis de Ureda, Juan de Padilla, and Juan de la Cruz from Coronado's expedition stayed behind. Ureda and Padilla were killed by Indians, but Cruz discovered the mysterious Aztec mine, reopened it, and started to bring out large amounts of gold. As with other mysterious lost mines, Cruz supposedly forced Indians from the Pecos Pueblo to work in the mine, then once the gold he wanted had been extracted, murdered them all and sealed the mine again to hide its entrance. He and his men returned to Mexico and the secret of the Spanish Cave was lost again.

Gold nuggets that were supposedly part of the treasure from Spanish Cave were found along an old trail near Fort Garland, Colorado, by a Mexican traveler named Baca in 1811; however, nothing else was found that might indicate lost treasure.[39] But the legends of the Aztecs still persists. One recent amateur archeologist, after finding odd-looking symbols on a stone wall near the Spanish Peaks, declared that he had found a pool used for sacrifices by the Aztecs and it was full of Aztec treasure. He hired an underwater diver to explore the depths with SCUBA equipment, but the pool was too murky to find anything of value.

As well as being the highest major cave in the United States, experienced cavers say that Spanish Cave is the largest and most dangerous cave in Colorado. The interior contains a maze of 3,500 feet of tight twisting passages that carry a high risk of becoming lost, and a vertical drop inside of almost 700 feet. Access to the entrance requires a long hike to the cave at high altitude, and the interior of the cave has extremely cold year-round temperatures between 34° and 38°F with a high humidity level of 95 percent.[40] Because of the snows of late spring and early winter, the season available to access the cave is limited to only a few months in the summer. Even then snowdrifts usually lie deep around the entrance and ice coats the floor of the entrance. The snowbanks melt around the time that the first snows of the next winter arrive.

The first to stumble on the cave was a man named Elisha Horn in 1869. About ten feet from the entrance he reported that there was a large, very old Maltese Cross about two feet square outlined in red paint. Nearby was a skeleton of a man wearing Spanish armor who had died from an Indian arrow in the back. About 500 yards below the cave entrance, on Hudson Creek, were six rifle pits and the remains of a ruin constructed with large logs that were been theorized to have been part of a Spanish fort built to defend against Indian attacks.[41]

In 1929 Forest Ranger Paul Gilbert led an exploration into part of the cave and found the remains of a crude ladder made of chain and, below it, a wooden ladder. In 1932 another exploratory expedition found the ladder and, further on, an old windlass. Another item found inside by a subsequent expedition was an old shovel. A more questionable newspaper report in Denver's *Rocky Mountain News* on September 4, 1932, told of explorers seeing a skeleton chained by the neck to a rock deep in the cave, which supposedly verified the tale of the Indians forced to work in the mine. A subsequent caving expedition did not find the skeleton, but did recover a hand-forged hammer that dated from the 1600s.

So, what about the legends of Spanish gold and treasure, and their northward quest to find riches? Perhaps the Spanish were right after all and the bonanza of gold is still there. Just waiting to be found.

Postscript

The opening of the Spanish Southwest to Anglo-Americans after the purchase of the Louisiana Territory in 1803 led to a large influx of settlers, farmers, ranchers, and miners who further made their impact on the land as their numbers grew. Estimates of the non-Indian population in the Southwest in 1750 were about 3,000 people. By 1800 this number had risen to 19,000 and by 1900 had increased to 195,000 residents. By 1861 the population of New Mexico (excluding Indians) had grown to 80,000 residents, the majority of whom were of Hispanic descent. By 1900 the population of Santa Fe had risen to 12,000 people.

Many of these Anglo people made their living from the Santa Fe trade. Others pursued agriculture and cattle, or worked at local blacksmithing, weaving, or carpentry. Though early Anglo settlement started in New Mexico after the opening of the Santa Fe Trail in 1821, nothing much changed until after the occupation of the territory by U.S. troops in 1848.

New immigrants came west for a variety of reasons. Some came seeking cheap land for farming and ranching. Others were involved in the fur trade. Some were merchants hoping for business opportunities. Some were soldiers who married local women and settled in Santa Fe and Taos after they left the military. Others were lawyers, merchants, politicians, miners, cattlemen, doctors, cowboys, outlaws, and settlers. Later immigrants came to study, paint, or photograph the remnants of the ancient civilizations that were strewn across the landscape and to enjoy the pleasant climate and the landscape itself.

The Spanish West of New Mexico was considered by many to be remote, unusual, and fascinating. People came for their health, the beauty of the land, and the solitude of wild and undeveloped spaces. Tourism became a large industry. The West had only been tamed relatively recently and many wanted to see American Indians in their own surroundings. The almost-constant daily sunlight, the high, dry air, and the vast landscapes, along with the food and culture of New Mexico, still attracts new residents.

The Spanish colonizers who dominated the Southwest from 1598 to 1821 created a cultural revolution that is still apparent today. As we have seen, in many ways the story of New Mexico and its Spanish ancestry was that of contrasting religions, resulting from the clash between Spanish Christianity and existing native Indian religions. The impact of this Spanish colonization is clearly visible in north-central New Mexico in the architecture, the people, and their customs. Spanish is still a common language of the San Luis Valley of southern Colorado and the Rio Grande valley of northern New Mexico. Many of the villages in these areas have retained the look, cultural flavor, folk customs, and beliefs of their Spanish origins.

The Spanish symbols of Southwestern culture were later marketed by the Santa Fe

Railroad and the Fred Harvey Company. Northern New Mexico and Santa Fe were seen as a unique cultural center in the Southwest and their image was used to boost tourism in New Mexico and Arizona. Houses, hotels, public buildings, and even railroad stations were built in a "Mission Revival" style that became popular in the 1880s. Some of this was an attempt to recreate a past that never was for tourists.

Much of this enthusiasm carried over into the southern California mission country, where the past was reimagined as a picturesque life that was unhurried and gracious, free from care and troubles. Nostalgic elements included the romance, hospitality, and charm of the old Spanish social customs, and the questionable memory of a simple lifestyle peopled with exotic women and friendly men. Never mind that in reality the local men resented the *Americanos* who beguiled away their women and the mission Indians were often abused. The past was sanitized and a less hurried era, full of pastoral values laced with nostalgia for the customs of a simpler time was substituted. The Franciscans were all remembered as kindly Christians administering to devoted Indians. Houses were reimagined as elegant two-story houses with the white stucco walls and red tile roofs that are seen today.

Most of the places described in this book can still be visited today. Some outstanding Anasazi sites have been preserved within the National Park system and are listed in Appendix 2. The pueblos of Hopi, Zuni, Taos, Acoma, and others are still occupied today. Many of the Spanish churches in northern New Mexico are still standing. The missions of the Pacific Coast (Appendix 3) provide a fascinating window into Spanish life in early California. Fort Union and the remains of the mission at Pecos are National Monuments, and the foundations of Fort Marcy in Santa Fe are still visible. Santa Fe itself retains the character of its Spanish ancestry and many of the small villages in northern New Mexico are reminders of as they were when they were originally settled.

The aura of the Spanish past lingers in the Southwest and New Mexico is indeed well-nicknamed *The Land of Enchantment*.

Top: The Hispanic Southwest remains deeply religious, as evidenced by this small roadside shrine in southern Colorado. *Bottom:* The modern Palace of the Governors, facing the plaza in Santa Fe, still serves as a vibrant part of Santa Fe's heritage as a part of New Mexico's state museums. The covered walkway in front of the building is used daily by Indian traders who exhibit and sell handmade jewelry.

Appendix 1

Glossary

The following are some common *Spanish terms* from the Southwest and some of the terms adapted by American cowboys from the Spanish vaqueros.

acequia an irrigation ditch; the main ditch of a town was the *acequia madre* or "mother ditch."
adobe bricks and mortar made from mud mixed with straw or sheep's wool and dried in the sun.
alcalde the mayor and/or local justice of the peace.
arroyo a narrow gully with steep sides, that often acts as a streambed in times of rain, but is otherwise dry; this may also be an *arroyo seco* (dry wash).
barrio a village or part of a town.
bosque a wooded area along a river or stream.
bronco a wild or unmanageable horse
buckaroo a man who herded cattle for a living; from *vaquero*
bulto sculptured wooden carving of a religious subject.
caballero literally a "horseman," in general the name referred to a gentleman.
callaboose jail; from *calabozo*
cantina a tavern.
carreta a long, narrow, two-wheeled cart drawn by mules or oxen.
chaparral dense thorny bushes
chaps protective leather leggings; from *chaparreras*
cienega a marshy area.
cinch strap used to hold a saddle in place on a horse; from *cincha*
concho a silver ornament used on belts and saddles; from *concha*
conquistadores Spanish soldiers and military officers in the conquest of the New World.
convento housing for the Franciscan friars, usually located close to a mission church.
corral a pen for horses or cattle
dally to twist a rope around a saddle horn to anchor it; from *dar la vuelta*
don an honorary title for a Spanish gentleman, used to indicate respect.
encomienda a territory assigned by the Spanish government to prominent individuals for their own use and profit, including the native residents who lived there who were required to provide labor and tribute. In reality this was a private land grant.
encomendero the owner of an *ecomienda*.
estancia a large cattle ranch.
fandango the name was originally used by the Spanish to describe a dance event, but the American Forty-Niners used the term to describe a dance house.
fray used as a respectful title in certain religious orders, such as the Franciscans.
fiesta a social or religious occasion to honor an event or a saint.

hackamore   a rope halter with reins and a lead rope; from *jáquima*
honda   the slip ring or slipknot at the end of a lariat
hoosegow   jail; from *juzgado* (court).
horno   a beehive-shaped outdoor oven.
jacal   a type of construction used for making small one or two-roomed, flat-roofed houses with the walls built by placing small poles upright in the ground and filling the cracks between with earth or adobe.
Journada del Muerto   the eighty mile stretch of barren desert in New Mexico's lower Rio Grande Valley; literally the term means "Journey of the Dead."
jug   jail; from *juzgado* (court)
lariat   long rope with a loop in the end used for catching cattle; from *la reata*
lasso   originally a horsehair rope used to tether animals; from *lazo*
McCarty   reins made from a horsehair rope and attached to a bit; from *mecate*
pinto   a spotted horse
plaza   a public town square surrounded by buildings.
presidio   a garrison or fort used to house soldiers, often built next to or close to a mission to protect it.
ranch   a cattle breeding establishment; from *rancho*
ramada   a structure open on all four sides, made of upright poles with a flat roof made from brush to provide shade from the sun.
remuda   a herd of horses that accompanied cowboys on a trail drive
retablo   pictures of religious scenes and saints that are painted on pine panels.
rio   a river, such as the Rio Grande, or Big River.
rodeo   originally a Spanish cattle roundup, later an American sport
santero   a person who carves religious images, especially of *santos* (saints).
sierra   a range of mountains, such as the Sierra Nevada Mountains.
stampede   a sudden scattering of a herd of cattle of horses; from *estampida*
tank   a device for collecting and holding rainwater for cattle; from *estanque*
torreón   a round watchtower for protection, often placed at the corner or corners of a house, but may also be freestanding.
viga   a ceiling beam or rafter in a house.

Appendix 2

Outstanding Examples of Anasazi Ruins in the Southwest

These ruins are all easily accessible by automobile and represent some of the finest examples of Anasazi culture.

Name	Nearest Town	Outstanding Features
Aztec Ruins National Monument	Aztec, New Mexico	Reconstructed great kiva
Bandelier National Monument	Los Alamos, New Mexico	Hundreds of ruins from many villages
Chaco Canyon National Park	Nageezi, New Mexico	Many large pueblo groupings and kivas
Hovenweep National Monument	Cortez, Colorado	Towers and dwellings perched in and on the canyon rim
Mesa Verde National Park	Cortez, Colorado	The best and largest collections of Anasazi cliff and pit dwellings
Navajo National Monument	Kayenta, Arizona	Some of the largest and best-preserved cliff dwellings, but require a hefty hike with a guide to reach them
Pecos National Monument	Santa Fe, New Mexico	Ruins of an old pueblo with mission church ruins from 1717 built on top of it
Wupatki National Monument	Flagstaff, Arizona	2,000 scattered Indian ruins

Appendix 3

The California Mission Trail

Spanish missionaries built a string of missions along the coast of California to stake a Spanish claim to the territory after being alarmed by the advance of Russian explorers down the California coast from the north. By 1823 there were twenty-one missions strung along the coast. The missions are listed here from south to north as that was the direction of expansion.

Mission	Date Built	Nearest City	Comments
San Diego de Alcalá	1769	San Diego	The first of the California missions
San Luis Rey de Francia	1798	Oceanside	Largest and most prosperous of the missions
San Juan Capistrano	1776	San Juan Capistrano	The ruined church is noted for its migrating swallows
San Gabriel Arcángel	1771	Los Angeles	Distinctive architecture and restored interior
San Fernando Rey de España	1797	San Gabriel	The church is a replica in lath and plaster
San Buenaventura	1782	Ventura	Last mission founded by Junípero Serra
Santa Barbara	1782	Santa Barbara	Known as the "Queen of the Missions"
Santa Inés	1804	Solvang	Restored and well maintained, part original
La Purisíma Concepción	1787	Lompoc	Today a State Historic Park where visitors can see mission life of 200 years ago
San Luis Obispo de Tolosa	1772	San Luis Obispo	Museum with some original paintings and statues
San Miguel Arcángel	1797	San Miguel	Least restored mission with original interior
San Antonio de Padua	1771	near King City	Last restoration in 1949 to almost original
Nuestra Señora de la Soledad	1791	Soledad	Rebuilt 1832 and restored 1954
San Carlos Borromeo de Carmelo	1770	Carmel	Unusual interior stonework, large museum
San Juan Bautista	1797	San Juan Bautista	Original *retablo* painted in 1816
Santa Cruz	1791	Santa Cruz	Present church built 1889
Santa Clara de Asis	1777	Santa Clara	An enlarged replica of the original mission located on the Santa Clara University campus
San José de Guadalupe	1797	Fremont	Redecorated between 1982 and 1985

Mission	Date Built	Nearest City	Comments
San Francisco de Asis (also known as Mission Dolores)	1776	San Francisco	Well maintained with much original interior
San Rafael Arcángel	1817	San Francisco	Originally a sanitarium, a mission in 1822
San Francisco Solano de Sonoma	1823	Sonoma	Today a State Historic Park with a museum

Chapter Notes

Preface

1. Weber, *The Spanish Frontier in North America*, 355.
2. Kessell, *Spain in the Southwest*, 96.
3. King, *First People*, 7.

Chapter One

1. Iberia is the ancient Latin name for the Spanish-Portuguese peninsula.
2. Though not always considered politically correct I have chosen to retain this historical designation.
3. Hine and Faragher, *The American West*, 13.
4. The root of the word "California" comes from the Arabic word *khalifa*, which means "caliph" or "ruler."
5. Thomas, *The Golden Empire*, 299.
6. Johnson, *Baja California*, 24.
7. Dary, *The Santa Fe Trail*, 4.
8. Marrin, *Aztecs and Spaniards*, 64.
9. Restall, *Seven Myths of the Spanish Conquest*, 28.
10. Restall, *Seven Myths of the Spanish Conquest*, 34.
11. Restall, *Seven Myths of the Spanish Conquest*, 43.
12. Placer gold is found in pure metallic form as flakes, nuggets, or gold flour, typically found in the bed of a current or former stream or river. It is extracted by washing away the surrounding dirt and debris to leave pure gold. Other forms of gold occur in complex chemical combinations with other elements that require special mining techniques, such as smelting, to extract the pure gold.
13. Bill Bryson, *The Mother Tongue* (New York: Avon Books, 1990), 210.
14. Marrin, *Aztecs and Spaniards*, 16.
15. The Spanish name of Moctezuma for the Aztec ruler is traditionally translated into English as Montezuma, so I have retained this convention. This particular spelling of his name was also occasionally used by the Spanish in the sixteenth century (Thomas, *The Golden Empire*, xiv).
16. Hine and Faragher, *The American West*, 13.
17. Marrin, *Aztecs and Spaniards*, 78.
18. Innes, *The Conquistadors*, 69.
19. Hine and Faragher, *The American West*, 20.
20. Gutiérrez, *When Jesus Came*, 353; Thomas, *The Golden Empire*, 87.
21. Restall, *Seven Myths of the Spanish Conquest*, 142.
22. Monaghan, *The Book of the American West*, 379.
23. Dary, *The Santa Fe Trail*, 14.
24. Marrin, *Aztecs and Spaniards*, 84.
25. Lilley, *The Importance of Hernando Cortes*, 32.
26. Modern firearms have twisted grooves cut into the bore (the inside of the barrel) to make the bullet spin and give it better stability in flight. Early firearms did not have these grooves and so were referred to as smooth-bore guns.
27. Gunpowder or black powder consists of a mixture of charcoal, sulfur, and saltpeter (potassium nitrate) that is ignited to instantaneously form a large volume of exploding gas that propels the bullet rapidly down the barrel of a gun.
28. Restall, *Seven Myths of the Spanish Conquest*, 143.
29. Marrin, *Aztecs and Spaniards*, 182.
30. Johnson, *Baja California*, 29.
31. King, *First People*, 27.
32. Innes, *The Conquistadors*, 168.
33. Hine and Faragher, *The American West*, 23.
34. Thomas, *The Golden Empire*, 7.
35. Simmons, *New Mexico*, 25.
36. Marrin, *Aztecs and Spaniards*, 177.
37. Marrin, *Aztecs and Spaniards*, 190.
38. Dobie, *Coronado's Children*, vii.
39. Lilley, *The Importance of Hernando Cortes*, 95.
40. Dary, *The Santa Fe Trail*, 4.
41. Dary, *The Santa Fe Trail*, 5.
42. "Mission" in this context is used to mean a religious center where members of the Christian church tried to convert local native people to their religion.
43. Maxwell, *America's Fascinating Indian Heritage*, 104–105.
44. Weber, *The Spanish Frontier in North America*, 101.
45. Scholars still debate whether Esteban was a black African or a dark-skinned Arab. Most of the evidence seems to suggest that he was African.
46. Dary, *The Santa Fe Trail*, 8.

47. Confusion sometimes exists as the word "pueblo" had two different meanings to the Spanish. They named the stepped multistory buildings consisting of many different apartments that were inhabited by groups of native people "pueblos" after the Spanish word for town. They also referred to the inhabitants as "Pueblos" or "townsmen."
48. Gutiérrez, *When Jesus Came*, 39–40.
49. Webb, *The Great Plains*, 102.
50. As a word of clarification about Spanish names, Coronado's full name was Francisco Vásquez de Coronado. Vásquez was his correct surname and Coronado was where he was from. Another example that will be encountered later is Father Silvestre Vélez de Escalante, who explored Utah. Escalante's correct surname was Vélez and Escalante was the name of the birthplace of his father in Spain. However, Coronado and Escalante are their commonly used names, so I will continue to call them by this accepted (but incorrect) terminology in this book. Warner feels that these errors probably came from writers unfamiliar with Spanish names and the manner in which they were put together, thus assuming that the last name written was the family surname (Warner, *The Domínguez-Escalante Journal*, xiv). "Don" was an honorary title applied by the Spanish to any distinguished male as a sign of respect. Originally the title was given only to those of the top ranks of the nobility, but the honor was later extended to all the nobility. The title "Don" was used with the first or Christian name, or with the full name, but never with the surname by itself.
51. Webb, *The Great Plains*, 102.
52. Roberts, *The Pueblo Revolt*, 59.
53. Gutiérrez, *When Jesus Came*, xxvi. The slightly different spellings for the names of some of these pueblos as found in different sources are due to varying attempts to render these names into English.
54. Maxwell, *America's Fascinating Indian Heritage*, 208.
55. Dary, *The Santa Fe Trail*, 16.
56. Dary, *The Santa Fe Trail*, 10.
57. While Coronado was there, he named the area between the towns of Algodones and Isleta as the province of Tiguex.
58. Webb, *The Great Plains*, 103.
59. Kessell, *Spain in the Southwest*, 42.
60. Kessell, *Spain in the Southwest*, 44.
61. Dary, *The Santa Fe Trail*, 17.
62. Roberts, *The Pueblo Revolt*, 66.

Chapter Two

1. There is continuing controversy over whether the name "Anasazi," which may also mean "ancient enemy," is a politically correct designation or not. The first to use this Navajo term was Richard Wetherill, as this was the name he heard used by contemporary Navajo for the people who lived at Mesa Verde. Part of the controversy surrounds whether it is proper to use a Navajo name instead of a more generic Pueblo name. Some scholars object to the implications of calling these people Anasazi and prefer the name "Ancestral Puebloans." Other names sometimes used are "The Old Ones" or "Ancient Ones." At one time these people were called "Aztecs," as they were considered to be a northern branch of the Aztecs of Mexico. In deference to common usage and more than 100 years of previous professional literature, however, I shall continue to use the name Anasazi.
2. This is the only location in the United States where four states meet at one common point.
3. Ferguson and Rohn, *Anasazi Ruins of the Southwest in Color*, 1.
4. Ferguson and Rohn, *Anasazi Ruins of the Southwest in Color*, 1.
5. Mesoamerica included Mexico and Central America north of Mexico City, and extended south beyond Guatemala and Belize into Honduras. Aztec and Mayan civilizations began here around 1500 BCE and ended with the arrival of the Spanish.
6. Hafen, *Colorado*, 29.
7. Ferguson and Rohn, *Anasazi Ruins of the Southwest in Color*, 65.
8. Ferguson and Rohn, *Anasazi Ruins of the Southwest in Color*, 68.
9. Muench and Pike, *Anasazi*, 18.
10. This has been theorized to be the basis for a difference in spatial perception in the prehistoric genders, with the men typically being better at navigation and spatial orientation as they had to roam during a hunt and find their way home, while women were better at using landmarks and remembering where they found plants, berries, and other food, and remembering where their farming plots were located.
11. Ferguson and Rohn, *Anasazi Ruins of the Southwest in Color*, 73.
12. Muench and Pike, *Anasazi*, 142.
13. Ferguson and Rohn, *Anasazi Ruins of the Southwest in Color*, 97.
14. Muench and Pike, *Anasazi*, 138.
15. This is thought to have been the largest "apartment building" in the world until 1882, when a bigger one was built in New York City.
16. Ferguson and Rohn, *Anasazi Ruins of the Southwest in Color*, 200.
17. A macaw is a type of large parrot from Central America with brightly-colored feathers and a harsh voice.
18. Ferguson and Rohn, *Anasazi Ruins of the Southwest in Color*, 211.
19. About ten miles east of Manassa, Colorado, is a large deposit of turquoise that was originally worked by prehistoric Indians. The field was later rediscovered by a man named Israel King. In the 1890s this became one of the world's largest turquoise mines, yielding one impressive nugget that weighed nearly nine pounds (Simmons, *The San Luis Valley*, 192).
20. Ferguson and Rohn, *Anasazi Ruins of the Southwest in Color*, 179.
21. Muench and Pike, *Anasazi*, 143.
22. Ferguson and Rohn, *Anasazi Ruins of the Southwest in Color*, 176.

23. Rock art is found all over the Southwest, including such interesting examples as Newspaper Rock in Canyonlands National Park in Utah and another in Petrified Forest National Park in Arizona. Some of the designs are pictographs and some are petroglyphs. Pictographs (from *picto-* meaning "picture") were painted onto rock. Petroglyphs (from *petro-* meaning "rock") were pictures pecked into the rock surface with another rock. Pictographs of migration stories appear in rocks such as Pictograph Point in Mesa Verde National Park. Symbolic figures, handprints, footprints, animals, and obscure designs are tantalizing images left by the prehistoric peoples of the area.

24. Muench and Pike, *Anasazi*, 145.
25. Muench and Pike, *Anasazi*, 19.
26. Ferguson and Rohn, *Anasazi Ruins of the Southwest in Color*, 241.
27. Simmons, *New Mexico*, 47.
28. The alternative spelling of *katsina* is closer to the pronunciation of the term among the Hopi and will be the preferred name employed here.
29. Ferguson and Rohn, *Anasazi Ruins of the Southwest in Color*, 57.
30. Gutiérrez, *When Jesus Came*, 121.
31. Roberts, *The Pueblo Revolt*, 37.
32. Ferguson and Rohn, *Anasazi Ruins of the Southwest in Color*, 57.
33. Roberts, *The Pueblo Revolt*, 37.
34. The name Apache originally came to the English language from the Spanish as a collective designation for several culturally-related groups of Native American Indians that ranged the Southwest around New Mexico in eastern Arizona, northern Mexico, western Texas, and southern Colorado, rather than the modern application to a specific group of Native Americans.
35. Noble, *Pueblos, Villages, Forts & Trails*, 114.

Chapter Three

1. Hine and Faragher, *The American West*, 32.
2. Weber, *The Spanish Frontier in North America*, 14.
3. Roberts, *The Pueblo Revolt*, 68.
4. Weber, *The Spanish Frontier in North America*, 81.
5. Simmons, *New Mexico*, 37.
6. Ironically, this is essentially the same procedure that Gen. Stephen Watts Kearny followed when he took over New Mexico for the United States in 1846, as will be described in a later chapter.
7. Restall, *Seven Myths of the Spanish Conquest*, 20.
8. Bannon, *The Spanish Borderlands Frontier*, 36.
9. Roberts, *The Pueblo Revolt*, 81.
10. Dary, *The Santa Fe Trail*, 20.
11. Riley, *The Kachina and the Cross*, 93.
12. Gutiérrez, *When Jesus Came*, 105.
13. Simmons, *New Mexico*, 56.
14. Weber, *The Spanish Frontier in North America*, 307.
15. Gutiérrez, *When Jesus Came*, 53–55.
16. Roberts, *The Pueblo Revolt*, 89.
17. Hammond, *Don Juan de Oñate and the Founding of New Mexico*, 121.
18. Riley, *The Kachina and the Cross*, 80.
19. Kessell, *Spain in the Southwest*, 40.
20. Hammond, *Don Juan de Oñate and the Founding of New Mexico*, 123.
21. Kessell, *Spain in the Southwest*, 84.
22. Kessell, *Pueblos, Spaniards, and the Kingdom of New Mexico*, 41.
23. Roberts, *The Pueblo Revolt*, 90.
24. Hammond, *Don Juan de Oñate and the Founding of New Mexico*, 123.
25. Kessell, *Spain in the Southwest*, 84.
26. Roberts, *The Pueblo Revolt*, 145.
27. Roberts, *The Pueblo Revolt*, 104.
28. Warner, *The Domínguez-Escalante Journal*, 141.
29. Dary, *The Santa Fe Trail*, 20.
30. Kessell, *Pueblos, Spaniards, and the Kingdom of New Mexico*, 44.
31. The translation of languages is not precise and especially does not always lend itself to word-for-word translation, thus slightly different versions of the translated inscription will be found in different sources.
32. Kessell, *Pueblos, Spaniards, and the Kingdom of New Mexico*, 41.
33. Roberts, *The Pueblo Revolt*, 95.
34. Weber, *The Spanish Frontier in North America*, 87.
35. Kessell, *Spain in the Southwest*, 98.
36. Loomis, *Old Santa Fe Today*, 8.
37. Albuquerque was not founded until 1706, when a group of Spanish colonists located a plaza on the east bank of the Rio Grande. The name was originally spelled as Alburquerque, named after Francisco Fernández de la Cueva, the duque de Alburquerque. The first "r" was dropped shortly after the American takeover of New Mexico in 1846.
38. Loomis, *Old Santa Fe Today*, 8.
39. Weber, *The Spanish Frontier in North America*, 95.
40. Weber, *The Spanish Frontier in North America*, 242.
41. Dary, *Cowboy Culture*, 343.
42. Riley, *The Kachina and the Cross*, 108.
43. Weber, *The Spanish Frontier in North America*, 194.
44. Chavez, *My Penitente Land*, 108. It was not until after a papal decree in 1897 that brown became the universal color of Franciscan habits.
45. Fray is a contraction of *fraile* (friar) and is used as a title by certain religious orders. Fray is used with the first or full name of a friar, but never with only the surname or apart from the first name. The title "fray" (in lower case) was given to a priest, a member of a mendicant order, or a lay brother. A lay brother was member of religious order, but was not ordained as a priest. The Jesuits were priests, not friars. A Spanish priest or monk was also called a "padre." This book

will follow the convention of "fray" without capitalization.
46. Riley, *The Kachina and the Cross*, 95.
47. Riley, *The Kachina and the Cross*, 93.
48. Roberts, *The Pueblo Revolt*, 113.
49. Dary, *The Santa Fe Trail*, 21.
50. Kessell, *Spain in the Southwest*, 95.
51. Roberts, *The Pueblo Revolt*, 99.
52. Simmons, *New Mexico*, 46.
53. Kessell, *Spain in the Southwest*, 150.
54. Weber, *The Spanish Frontier in North America*, 116.
55. Taos means "People of the Red Willows" in the Tewa Indian language. Some people consider Taos Pueblo to be one of the most beautiful architectural structures in North America.
56. The name "Anglo-American" here is intended to encompass a collective group of people who were not of Native American Indian or Spanish heritage. This included those of European ancestry, particularly those of English, Scottish, and Irish descent.

Chapter Four

1. Weber, *The Spanish Frontier in North America*, 90.
2. Gutiérrez, *When Jesus Came*, 104.
3. Gutiérrez, *When Jesus Came*, 100.
4. Gutiérrez, *When Jesus Came*, 115.
5. Riley, *The Kachina and the Cross*, 133.
6. The origin of the word *acequia* lies in an Arabic word, *al-sáquiyá*, because this type of irrigation ditch was perfected by the Moors (Fisher, *The Spanish Missions of San Antonio*, 3).
7. Gregg, *Commerce of the Prairies*, 147.
8. Riley, *The Kachina and the Cross*, 212.
9. Simmons, *New Mexico*, 102.
10. Riley, *The Kachina and the Cross*, 152.
11. Riley, *The Kachina and the Cross*, 152.
12. Today the ruts of *El Camino Real* in southern New Mexico run generally parallel to modern Interstate 25.
13. Kessell, *Pueblos, Spaniards, and the Kingdom of New Mexico*, 81.
14. Riley, *The Kachina and the Cross*, 136.
15. An excellent remaining example of these haciendas is *El Rancho de las Golondrinas* ("The Ranch of the Swallows") just south of Santa Fe. The land was originally purchased as a ranch by Miguel Vega y Coca in 1710. In 1972 the current owner leased the ranch to a historical group with an agreement that it would be opened to the public. Today, the 200-acre ranch contains excellent displays of original and reconstructed buildings from the original ranch and other historic Spanish colonial buildings.
16. Gutiérrez, *When Jesus Came*, 120.
17. Noble, *Pueblos, Villages, Forts & Trails*, 219.
18. Noble, *Pueblos, Villages, Forts & Trails*, 150.
19. Simmons, *The San Luis Valley*, 250.
20. Horka-Follick, *Los Hermanos Penitentes*, 100.
21. Orfalea, *Journey to the Sun*, 7.
22. Horka-Follick, *Los Hermanos Penitentes*, 79.
23. Carlson, *The Spanish-American Homeland*, 146.
24. Similar mortification and self-punishment was depicted in the motion picture *The Da Vinci Code* (2006) when the fanatical Silas (played by Paul Bettany) scourged himself to atone for his self-perceived sins.
25. Taylor, *Colorado*, 140.
26. Taylor, *Colorado*, 133.
27. Horka-Follick, *Los Hermanos Penitentes*, 57.
28. Carlson, *The Spanish-American Homeland*, 144.
29. Horka-Follick, *Los Hermanos Penitentes*, 70.
30. Gaspar de Villagrá, *History of New Mexico* (Los Angeles: The Quivara Society, 1933), 110.
31. Warren, *Villages of Hispanic New Mexico*, 59.
32. Carlson, *The Spanish-American Homeland*, 144.
33. Chavez, *My Penitente Land*, 218–219.
34. Carlson, *The Spanish-American Homeland*, 144.
35. Horka-Follick, *Los Hermanos Penitentes*, 87.
36. Simmons, *The San Luis Valley*, 99.
37. Carlson, *The Spanish-American Homeland*, 144.
38. Rideing, William H. "A Trail in the Far Southwest." *Harper's Monthly Magazine*, June 1876, 20.
39. Simmons, *The San Luis Valley*, 97.
40. Carlson, *The Spanish-American Homeland*, 146.
41. Simmons, *The San Luis Valley*, 248–249.
42. Carlson, *The Spanish-American Homeland*, 155.
43. Carlson, *The Spanish-American Homeland*, 155.
44. Taylor, *Colorado*, 140.
45. Warren, *Villages of Hispanic New Mexico*, 68–75.

Chapter Five

1. This was the same as the later struggle between the Indians and the U.S. army during the drawn-out Indian Wars in the West that were fought between 1850 and 1890.
2. Hine and Faragher, *The American West*, 14.
3. Weber, *The Spanish Frontier in North America*, 19.
4. Riley, *The Kachina and the Cross*, 105.
5. Weber, *The Spanish Frontier in North America*, 92.
6. Riley, *The Kachina and the Cross*, 157.
7. Gutiérrez, *When Jesus Came*, 40.
8. Hine and Faragher, *The American West*, 35.
9. Riley, *The Kachina and the Cross*, 153. The use of peyote by Native Americans in Texas has been dated back to around 4000 BCE.
10. Gutiérrez, *When Jesus Came*, 71.
11. Gutiérrez, *When Jesus Came*, 72.
12. The "missionary position" was originally named by Polynesians after missionary teaching, because the natives preferred intercourse while squatting (James L. McCary, *Human Sexuality* [New York: Van Nostrand Reinhold, 1978], 169).
13. Gutiérrez, *When Jesus Came*, 212.
14. Weber, *The Spanish Frontier in North America*, 109.
15. Gutiérrez, *When Jesus Came*, 73.

16. Weber, *The Spanish Frontier in North America*, 109.
17. Gutiérrez, *When Jesus Came*, 72.
18. Gutiérrez, *When Jesus Came*, 72.
19. Innes, *The Conquistadors*, 69–70.
20. Roberts, *The Pueblo Revolt*, 116–117.
21. Gutiérrez, *When Jesus Came*, 79.
22. Gutiérrez, *When Jesus Came*, 127–128.
23. Roberts, *The Pueblo Revolt*, 117.
24. Gutiérrez, *When Jesus Came*, 210.
25. Roberts, *The Pueblo Revolt*, 116–117.
26. Gutiérrez, *When Jesus Came*, 210. This gruesome-sounding injury, which has been reported in hospital emergency rooms as a result of accidents, is medically possible if the underlying fascia and blood vessels are so stretched that they are torn.
27. Psychologists confirm that this is an act of domination and masculinity, with the active partner asserting dominance over the submissive, or receiving, partner.
28. Gutiérrez, *When Jesus Came*, 76.
29. Gutiérrez, *When Jesus Came*, 210.
30. Gutiérrez, *When Jesus Came*, 314.
31. Gutiérrez, *When Jesus Came*, 360.
32. Gutiérrez, *When Jesus Came*, 66.
33. Weber, *The Spanish Frontier in North America*, 119.
34. Kessell, *Spain in the Southwest*, 118.
35. Riley, *The Kachina and the Cross*, 104.
36. Kessell, *Spain in the Southwest*, 119.
37. This was a similar concept to the later Indian Ghost Dance of 1890 in which Piute medicine man Wovoka (Captain Jack) prophesied that the Whites would be driven out and prosperity would return to the tribes if certain ritualistic dances were performed.
38. Riley, *The Kachina and the Cross*, 218.
39. Gutiérrez, *When Jesus Came*, xix.
40. Simmons, *New Mexico*, 69.
41. Roberts, *The Pueblo Revolt*, 17.
42. Gutiérrez, *When Jesus Came*, 132.
43. Riley, *The Kachina and the Cross*, 214.
44. One unfortunate side effect of the Revolt was that when fighting swept through Santa Fe in 1680 many local historical documents were destroyed and thus many records of early Spanish settlement were lost.
45. Dary, *The Santa Fe Trail*, 27.
46. Riley, *The Kachina and the Cross*, 225–226.
47. Kessell, *Spain in the Southwest*, xii.
48. Gutiérrez, *When Jesus Came*, 134.
49. Riley, *The Kachina and the Cross*, 214.
50. Roberts, David. *The Pueblo Revolt*, 16.
51. Kessell, *Spain in the Southwest*, 156.
52. Riley, *The Kachina and the Cross*, 214. Today a monument called the Cross of the Martyrs on the hill below the ruins of Fort Marcy, overlooking downtown Santa Fe, is dedicated to the memory of the twenty-one Franciscan friars who were slain in the revolt and contains a list of their individual names.
53. Riley, *The Kachina and the Cross*, 227.
54. Ferguson and Rohn, *Anasazi Ruins of the Southwest in Color*, 232.
55. Michael Wallis, *Heaven's Window* (Portland: Graphic Arts Center Publishing, 2001), 60.
56. Maxwell, *America's Fascinating Indian Heritage*, 214.
57. Kessell, *Spain in the Southwest*, 179.

Chapter Six

1. Gregg, *Commerce of the Prairies*, 273.
2. In a similar manner, the later United States Homestead Act of 1862 was intended to settle the West and Southwest with Americans as quickly as possible, in order to solidify boundaries and claims to the land acquired in the Louisiana Purchase. The Act gave settlers the title to 160 acres of land if they lived on it continuously for five years and made improvements to it, such as farming or building a house.
3. Webb, *The Great Plains*, 86.
4. Weber, *The Spanish Frontier in North America*, 306.
5. Dulle, *Tracing the Santa Fe Trail*, 9.
6. Lavender, *The Great West*, 219.
7. Simmons, *New Mexico*, 26.
8. Trimble, *Arizona*, xx.
9. Simmons, *The San Luis Valley*, 30.
10. Works Projects Administration, *Colorado*, 34.
11. Hafen and Hafen, *Our State*, 69–70.
12. Lavender, *The Great West*, 155.
13. Taylor, *Colorado*, 158–159.
14. There is often confusion about whether to write his name as "de Anza" or "Anza." When he signed his full name, he used the "de" between his first and last names. When he signed only his surname, he signed simply "Anza." I have chosen to follow the convention adopted by the National Park Service and simply call him Anza.
15. Ed Helmuth and Gloria Helmuth, *The Passes of Colorado* (Boulder: Pruett Publishing, 1994), 192–193.
16. Simmons, *The San Luis Valley*, 25.
17. Works Projects Administration, *Colorado*, 353.
18. McConnell, *Bayou Salado*, 26.
19. Parkhill, Forbes. *The Colorado Magazine*. October 1957, 2–3.
20. Ed Helmuth and Gloria Helmuth, *The Passes of Colorado* (Boulder: Pruett Publishing, 1994), 154.
21. Hart and Hulbert, *Zebulon Pike's Arkansaw Journal*, 167.
22. Parkhill, Forbes. *The Colorado Magazine*. October, 1957, 3.
23. Taylor, *Colorado*, 59.
24. Simmons, *The San Luis Valley*, 27.
25. McConnell, *Bayou Salado*, 49. Confusingly Anza's father had the identical name of Juan Bautista de Anza.
26. Noble, *Pueblos, Villages, Forts & Trails*, 220.
27. Running from central to northern Colorado are three broad, flat valleys named North Park, Middle Park, and South Park, that are the feeding grounds for large herds of pronghorn, and originally for buffalo. These three large, open, high-mountain "parks" re-

ceived their names from early French fur-trappers who called them by the French word *parc* ("park"). The fourth "park" is the San Luis Valley in the south-central part of the state. The Spanish name for the San Luis Valley was *Valle Salado* or "salt valley" after the valuable deposits of salt found there.

28. Kessler, *Anza's 1779 Comanche Campaign*, 21.
29. McConnell, *Bayou Salado*, 49–50.
30. Taylor, *Colorado*, 61–62.
31. Weber, *The Spanish Frontier in North America*, 233.
32. Ubbelohde, Benson, and Smith, *A Colorado History*, 18.
33. Simmons, *The San Luis Valley*, 16–17.

Chapter Seven

1. Johnson, *Baja California*, 116.
2. Cabrillo was from Andalusia in southern Spain and was not Portuguese as is commonly stated.
3. Bannon, *The Spanish Borderlands Frontier*, 36.
4. Mora, *Californios*, 33–34.
5. In 1841 a man named William Wolfskill used trees from Mission San Gabriel to start a business growing oranges. This grew into Southern California's nationwide orange industry.
6. Richard Erdoes, *Saloons of the Old West* (New York: Alfred Knopf, 1979), 96–98.
7. Craig MacAndrew and Robert B. Edgerton, *Drunken Comportment: A Social Explanation* (Chicago, Aldine, 1968), 101.
8. Ward, *The West*, 32.
9. Commemorating this famous event is the well-known song "When the Swallows Come Back to Capistrano," written in 1939 by Leon René, and recorded by Glenn Miller, Gene Autry, the Ink Spots, and other popular groups.
10. Hine and Faragher, *The American West*, 95.
11. Dana, *Two Years Before the Mast*, 83.
12. Orfalea, *Journey to the Sun*, 252.
13. Orfalea, *Journey to the Sun*, 234.
14. Weber, *The Spanish Frontier in North America*, 330.
15. Weber, *The Spanish Frontier in North America*, 276.
16. Hine and Faragher, *The American West*, 98.
17. Weber, *The Spanish Frontier in North America*, 265.
18. Dary, *Cowboy Culture*, 54.
19. Dana, *Two Years Before the Mast*, 78. Henry Dana's book contains one of best descriptions of the Old California hide trade. From 1834 to 1836 he sailed in the brig *Pilgrim* from Boston, serving as a common seaman in the hide trade. He went around Cape Horn, then sailed up and down the coast of California for a year as his ship collected hides. His book describing California, first published in 1840, made California life at the time seem like a pastoral paradise.
20. Monaghan, *The Book of the American West*, 81.
21. Mora, *Californios*, 157.
22. Dana, *Two Years Before the Mast*, 196.
23. Dana, *Two Years Before the Mast*, 77.
24. Cordes, *America's National Historic Trails*, 16.
25. Anza's route is today commemorated as the Juan Bautista de Anza National Historic Trail, established in 1990.
26. Quoted in Kessell, *Spain in the Southwest*, 276.
27. The location of their crossing is currently under 500 or so feet of water beneath today's Lake Powell at the west end of Padre Bay.
28. Warner, *The Domínguez-Escalante Journal*, xvi–xvii.
29. Taylor, *Eldorado*, 138.
30. Hine and Faragher, *The American West*, 212.
31. *Robin Hood* (2010).

Chapter Eight

1. Weber, *The Spanish Frontier in North America*, 302.
2. Weber, *The Spanish Frontier in North America*, 311.
3. Carlson, *The Spanish-American Homeland*, 72.
4. Simmons, *The San Luis Valley*, 252–253.
5. Weber, *The Spanish Frontier in North America*, 310.
6. Dary, *Cowboy Culture*, 7.
7. Though the Texas cattle drives of the 1870s are the most famous, several other similar smaller drives had taken place earlier. Before the American Civil War some enterprising cattlemen in Texas successfully drove cattle to market in New Orleans. In the 1840s, cattle drives took place up the California coast to meet the demand for beef in the mining camps of the gold rush country of Northern California.
8. Webb, *The Great Plains*, 57.
9. Davis, *The American Cow Pony*, 5.
10. Dary, *Cowboy Culture*, 4.
11. Webb, *The Great Plains*, 56.
12. Lavender, *Bent's Fort*, 129.
13. The size of a horse is measured in "hands." One hand is considered to be four inches, thus three hands equals twelve inches or one foot. Therefore, a horse that is fifteen hands high is five feet tall from the ground to the top of the shoulders at the withers.
14. To be technically correct, what is commonly called the "buffalo" is the American bison, *Bison bison*.
15. Hafen, *Colorado*, 47.
16. Davis, *The American Cow Pony*, 17.
17. Webb, *The Great Plains*, 57.
18. Monaghan, *The Book of the American West*, 17.
19. Maxwell, *America's Fascinating Indian Heritage*, 167.
20. Maxwell, *America's Fascinating Indian Heritage*, 166. The technique of placing a blindfold over a wild animal's eyes to calm it after capture is still commonly used by wildlife researchers.
21. Lavender, *Bent's Fort*, 122.
22. Dary, *Cowboy Culture*, 53.
23. Monaghan, *The Book of the American West*, 21.
24. Dary, *Cowboy Culture*, 71.
25. Dary, *Cowboy Culture*, 64.

26. Incidentally, the oldtime cowboy lore from fiction and movies that spreading a horsehair rope around a bedroll on the ground so that rattlesnakes would not cross to the sleeper was false.

27. Dary, *Cowboy Culture*, 155.

28. This riding trick was used for audience entertainment by riders in Buffalo Bill's *Wild West*.

29. Susan L. Johnson, *Roaring Camp: The Social World of the California Gold Rush*, (New York: W.W. Norton, 2000), 181–182.

30. Mora, *Californios*, 71–72.

31. The bull trying to toss the bear up in the air and the bear trying to drag the bull down were responsible for the Wall Street descriptions of stock market trends. A bull market goes up, a bear market goes down.

32. Dary, *Cowboy Culture*, 64.

33. Dana, *Two Years Before the Mast*, 128.

34. Hollister, *Boldly They Rode*, 134.

35. Gregg, *Commerce of the Prairies*, 170.

36. Weber, *The Spanish Frontier in North America*, 323.

37. Lavender, *Bent's Fort*, 66.

38. Hollister, *Boldly They Rode*, 133.

Chapter Nine

1. Webb, *The Great Plains*, 87.

2. Weber, *The Spanish Frontier in North America*, 198.

3. Gutiérrez, *When Jesus Came*, 300.

4. McConnell, *Bayou Salado*, 50.

5. Lavender, *The Great West*, 79.

6. George W. Hufsmith, *The Wyoming Lynching of Cattle Kate, 1889* (Glendo: High Plains Press, 1993), 17.

7. Weber, *The Spanish Frontier in North America*, 292.

8. Edward S. Barnard, ed. *The Story of the Great American West* (Pleasantville: Reader's Digest, 1978), 41.

9. Simmons, *The San Luis Valley*, 39.

10. Simmons, *The San Luis Valley*, 39.

11. McConnell, *Bayou Salado*, 51.

12. Simmons, *The San Luis Valley*, 38.

13. Lavender, *The Great West*, 95.

14. Another cause that is often overlooked was the large amount of debt owed to the United States by Mexico.

15. McConnell, *Bayou Salado*, 50.

16. Simmons, *The San Luis Valley*, 105.

17. Simmons, *The San Luis Valley*, 106.

18. Carlson, *The Spanish-American Homeland*, 222–223.

19. Carlson, *The Spanish-American Homeland*, 11.

20. Resentment lived on. In October of 1966, an organization named the *Alianza Federal de Mercedes* (Federal Alliance of Land Grants), headed by Reies Lopez Tijerina, tried to reclaim land grants lost under the Treaty of Guadalupe Hidalgo. They took over Echo Ampitheater park near Abiquiu, New Mexico, and declared it to be the separate state of San Joaquin del Cañon de Rio de Chama. They left peacefully after a few days, but were later charged by the federal government. In June of 1967, they stormed the Rio Arriba county courthouse at Tierra Amarilla and tried to arrest the district attorney. They sprayed bullets in all directions, wounded two officers, and escaped with two hostages. They were caught after a massive manhunt that included the National Guard (Noble, *Pueblos, Villages, Forts & Trails*, 215). In a surprise move, Tijerina was acquitted, but later served a prison sentence for the Echo Campground incident (Simmons, *New Mexico*, 186–187).

21. Taylor, *Colorado*, 53.

22. James E. Perkins, *Tom Tobin: Fontiersman* (Pueblo West: Herodotus Press, 1999), 167.

23. Simmons, *New Mexico*, 80.

24. Dary, *The Santa Fe Trail*, 50.

25. Hafen, *Colorado*, 74.

26. Bannon, *The Spanish Borderlands Frontier*, 218.

Chapter Ten

1. Simmons, *The San Luis Valley*, 47.

2. The memory of the real Santa Fe Trail was later memorialized in fictitious Hollywood movie fashion by the likes of *Santa Fe Trail* (1940), starring Errol Flynn, Olivia de Havilland, and Ronald Reagan, which was more about abolitionist John Brown (Raymond Massey) in Kansas than the real Trail. Another offering was *Santa Fe Passage* (1955), with John Payne and Rod Cameron, about a scout traveling the trail from Missouri to New Mexico. Popular ballads from songsters about the trail included "Down the Santa Fe Trail" and "Along the Santa Fe Trail."

3. Moody, *The Old Trails West*, 186.

4. Lavender, *The Great West*, 169–170.

5. The word "dollar" was originally derived from the Dutch *daler* or German *taler*.

6. Moody, *The Old Trails West*, 195.

7. Moody, *The Old Trails West*, 193.

8. Dulle, *Tracing the Santa Fe Trail*, 6.

9. Dulle, *Tracing the Santa Fe Trail*, 9.

10. Noble, *Santa Fe*, 121.

11. Noble, *Santa Fe*, 126.

12. Dary, *The Santa Fe Trail*, 263.

13. Noble, *Santa Fe*, 117.

14. Dary, *The Santa Fe Trail*, 263.

15. Dulle, *Tracing the Santa Fe Trail*, 6.

16. Poling-Kempes, *The Harvey Girls*, 21.

17. The Gallinas River, which is actually not much more than a creek, runs through Las Vegas east of the Plaza in the Old Town section. This event is commemorated by a bronze plaque at either end of the bridge over the river.

18. Noble, *Santa Fe*, 124.

19. Though not so today, the census of 1900 shows that Las Vegas was the largest city in New Mexico.

20. Pennsylvania Dutch does not mean that these people were of Dutch ancestry. The name is a corruption of the German word *deutsch*, as they were of German descent.

21. Dary, *The Santa Fe Trail*, 165.
22. Dulle, *Tracing the Santa Fe Trail*, 36.
23. Gregg, *Commerce of the Prairies*, 36. Gregg's book contains one of the best accounts of life in New Mexico at the time of the Santa Fe Trail. Dr. Gregg had to abandon medicine due to ill health and became trader. Starting in 1831, he made four round-trip journeys to Santa Fe over the next nine years. He lived for a number of years in Santa Fe and recorded his observations about the natural resources of area, mountains, valleys, rivers, and plains.
24. Kessell, *Pueblos, Spaniards, and the Kingdom of New Mexico*, 78.
25. Robert Taft. *Photography and the American Scene* (New York: Macmillan, 1938), 126.
26. Bent's Fort was reconstructed by the Colorado State Historical Society and completed July 26, 1976. It is now managed by the National Park Service as a National Historic Site.
27. Dary, *The Santa Fe Trail*, 145.
28. H. M. Powell, *The Santa Fe Trail to California, 1849–1852* (New York: Sol Lewis, 1981) 73.
29. George F. Ruxton, *Adventures in Mexico and the Rocky Mountains* (New York: Harper & Brothers, 1848), 190.
30. Gregg, *Commerce of the Prairies*, 153.
31. Simmons, *New Mexico*, 108.
32. She was a women of many names and nicknames. Others she was known under included Señora Doña Gertrudes Barceló, Señora Toulous, Doña María Gertrudiz Barcelo, Lona Barcelo, and Madam Barcelo, but she was most often called La Tules or Doña Tules. Yet other names were Tula, Tulas, Tia Barcelo, Lona Barcelo, Madam Barcelo, Doña Lona, and Doña Julia.
33. Dary, *The Santa Fe Trail*, 160.
34. MacKell, *Red Light Women of the Rocky Mountains*, 251–254.

Chapter Eleven

1. Simmons, *New Mexico*, 114.
2. Lavender, *The Great West*, 218.
3. The term "Manifest Destiny" was coined in 1845 by John L. O'Sullivan, editor of the *New York Morning News*.
4. Hine and Faragher, *The American West*, 212.
5. Hollister, *Boldly They Rode*, 48.
6. Simmons, *New Mexico*, 126.
7. Hollister, *Boldly They Rode*, 56–57.
8. The building is referred to in most books as the Dice Apartments on the north side of the plaza downtown. It is currently the *Casa de Musica*.
9. Quotes from the bronze plaque in the plaza at Las Vegas that commemorates the event.
10. Lavender, *The Great West*, 265.
11. The official New Mexico Territory of the United States was not created until 1850.
12. Loomis, *Old Santa Fe Today*, 45.
13. Noble, *Pueblos, Villages, Forts & Trails*, 245.
14. The Dragoons were the forerunner of the U.S. Cavalry. Dragoons were essentially infantry mounted on horses. The horses allowed them to quickly pursue marauding Indians, then they dismounted for fighting.
15. Muench and Pike, *Anasazi*, 167.
16. Jeremy Agnew, *Alcohol and Opium in the Old West* (Jefferson: McFarland, 2014), 53.
17. The fort has been recreated on the original site as part of a state historical museum in downtown Pueblo, Colorado.
18. Parkman, *The Oregon Trail*, 260.
19. Parkman, *The Oregon Trail*, 255.
20. Taylor, *Colorado*, 363.
21. Simmons, *The San Luis Valley*, 94.
22. Dary, *The Santa Fe Trail*, 197–199.
23. Simmons, *The San Luis Valley*, 51.
24. Moody, *The Old Trails West*, 217.
25. Lavender, *The Great West*, 318.
26. Hollister, *Boldly They Rode*, 55–56.
27. "Cantonment" was originally the name for a temporary military encampment. In 1833 the War Department ordered that all cantonments be called forts.
28. Noble, *Pueblos, Villages, Forts & Trails*, 235.
29. Simmons, *New Mexico*, 144.
30. Simmons, *New Mexico*, 35.
31. Jeremy Agnew, *Medicine in the Old West* (Jefferson: McFarland, 2010), 243.
32. Hine and Faragher, *The American West*, 24.
33. Mercury was mixed with the ore during processing to create an amalgam, which is a substance formed by the reaction of mercury with another metal. This amalgam was heated in a retort to vaporize and drive off the mercury and extract the gold or silver. The mercury fumes were cooled, condensed, and the liquid re-used.
34. McConnell, *Bayou Salado*, 50.
35. Roberts, *The Pueblo Revolt*, 180.
36. Noble, *Pueblos, Villages, Forts & Trails*, 198–199.
37. Interestingly, historians are currently studying possible links between the very early Anasazi and the Aztecs. At some point it is possible that legends of buried Aztec treasure in the Southwest may be found to have some basis.
38. Simmons, *The San Luis Valley*, 26.
39. Works Projects Administration, *Colorado*, 375.
40. Parris, *Caves of Colorado*, 112–116.
41. Kaiser, Bill. "The Treasure of Caverna del Oro." *Colorado Magazine*, Vol. 8, No. 6, May–June 1973, 32–35, 38, 40–41, 93–94.

Bibliography

Bannon, John F. *The Spanish Borderlands Frontier: 1513–1821*. New York: Holt, Rinehart and Winston, 1970.

Barrett, Elinore M. *The Spanish Colonial Settlement Landscapes of New Mexico 1598–1680*. Albuquerque: University of New Mexico Press, 2012.

Baxter, Don J. *Missions of California*. San Francisco: Pacific Gas and Electric, 1970.

Beck, Warren A. *New Mexico: A History of Four Centuries*. Norman: University of Oklahoma Press, 1962.

Carlson, Alvar W. *The Spanish-American Homeland: Four Centuries in New Mexico's Río Arriba*. Baltimore: Johns Hopkins University Press, 1990.

Chavez, Angelico. *My Penitente Land: Reflections on Spanish New Mexico*. Albuquerque: University of New Mexico Press, 1974.

Cordes, Kathleen A. *America's National Historic Trails*. Norman: University of Oklahoma Press, 1999.

Dana, R.H., Jr. *Two Years Before the Mast*. New York: P.F. Collier, 1969.

Dary, David. *Cowboy Culture: A Saga of Five Centuries*. Lawrence: University Press of Kansas, 1989.

_____. *The Santa Fe Trail: Its History, Legends, and Lore*. New York: Alfred A. Knopf, 2000.

Davis, Deering. *The American Cow Pony*. Princeton: Van Nostrand, 1962.

Dobie, Frank J. *Coronado's Children: Tales of Lost Mines and Buried Treasure in the Southwest*. New York: Literary Guild of America, 1931.

Dulle, Ronald J. *Tracing the Santa Fe Trail*. Missoula: Mountain Press Publishing, 2011.

Ellis, Richard N., ed. *New Mexico Past and Present: A Historical Reader*. Albuquerque: University of New Mexico Press, 1971.

Ferguson, William M., and Arthur H. Rohn. *Anasazi Ruins of the Southwest in Color*. Albuquerque: University of New Mexico Press, 1987.

Fisher, Lewis F. *The Spanish Missions of San Antonio*. San Antonio: Maverick Publishing, 1998.

Gavin, Robin F. *Traditional Arts of Spanish New Mexico*. Santa Fe: Museum of New Mexico Press, 1994.

Goetzmann, William H., and William N. Goetzmann. *The West of the Imagination*. New York: W.W. Norton, 1986.

Gregg, Josiah. *Commerce of the Prairies*. Norman: University of Oklahoma Press, 1954.

Gutiérrez, Ramón A. *When Jesus Came, the Corn Mothers Went Away: Marriage, Sexuality, and Power in New Mexico, 1500–1846*. Stanford: Stanford University Press, 1991.

Hafen, LeRoy R. *Colorado: The Story of a Western Commonwealth*. Denver: Peerless, 1933.

_____, and Ann Hafen. *Our State: Colorado*. Boulder: Old West Textbooks, 1976.

Hammond, George P. *Don Juan de Oñate and the Founding of New Mexico*. Santa Fe: El Palacio Press, 1927.

Hart, Stephen H., and Archer B. Hulbert. *Zebulon Pike's Arkansaw Journal: In Search of the Southern Louisiana Purchase Boundary Line*. Colorado Springs: Stewart Commission of Colorado College and Denver Public Library, 1932.

Hine, Robert V., and John M. Faragher. *The American West: A New Interpretive History*. New Haven: Yale University Press, 2000.

Hitt, Jim. *The American West from Fiction (1823–1976) into Film (1909–1986)*. Jefferson: McFarland, 1990.

Hollister, Ovando J. *Boldly They Rode: A History of the First*. Lakewood: Golden Press, 1949.

Horka-Follick, Lorayne A. *Los Hermanos Penitentes*. Los Angeles: Westernlore Press, 1969.

Innes, Hammond. *The Conquistadors*. New York: Alfred A. Knopf, 1969.

James, Harold L. *The Santa Fe Trail*. Globe: Pabsco, 1975.

Johnson, William W. *Baja California*. New York: Time-Life Books, 1972.

Jones, Oakah L., Jr. *Pueblo Warriors and Spanish Conquest*. Norman: University of Oklahoma Press, 1966.

Kessell, John L. *Pueblos, Spaniards, and the Kingdom of New Mexico*. Norman: University of Oklahoma Press, 2008.

_____. *Spain in the Southwest*. Norman: University of Oklahoma Press, 2002.

Kessler, Ronald E. *Anza's 1779 Comanche Campaign*. Monte Vista, CO: Ronald Kessler, 1994.

King, David C. *First People*. New York: DK Publishing, 2008.

Lavender, David. *Bent's Fort*. Lincoln: University of Nebraska Press, 1972.

———. *The Great West*. New York: American Heritage, 1985.

Lawliss, Chuck. *The Old West Sourcebook*. New York: Crown, 1994.

Lilley, Stephen R. *The Importance of Hernando Cortes*. San Diego: Lucent, 1996.

Loomis, Sylvia G. *Old Santa Fe Today*. Santa Fe: School of American Research, 1966.

MacKell, Jan. *Red Light Women of the Rocky Mountains*. Albuquerque: University of New Mexico Press, 2009.

Manns, William, and Elizabeth C. Flood. *Cowboys & The Trappings of the Old West*. Santa Fe: Zon International, 1997.

Marrin, Albert. *Aztecs and Spaniards: Cortes and the Conquest of Mexico*. New York: Atheneum, 1986.

Maxwell, James A., ed. *America's Fascinating Indian Heritage*. Pleasantville: Reader's Digest, 1978.

McConnell, Virginia. *Bayou Salado: The Story of South Park*. Chicago: Sage, 1966.

Mead, Frances H. *Conejos County*. Colorado Springs: Century One Press, 1984.

Monaghan, Jay. *The Book of the American West*. New York: Bonanza, 1963.

Moody, Ralph. *The Old Trails West*. New York: Thomas Y. Crowell, 1963.

Mora, Jo. *Californios*. New York: Doubleday, 1949.

Muench, David, and Donald G. Pike. *Anasazi: Ancient People of the Rock*. New York: Harmony, 1974.

Noble, David G. *Pueblos, Villages, Forts & Trails*. Albuquerque: University of New Mexico Press, 1994.

———. *Santa Fe: History of an Ancient City*. Santa Fe: School of American Research, 1989.

Orfalea, Gregory. *Journey to the Sun: Junípero Serra's Dream and the Founding of California*. New York: Scribner, 2014.

Parkman, Francis. *The Oregon Trail*. Garden City: Doubleday, 1946.

Parris, Lloyd E. *Caves of Colorado*. Boulder: Pruett, 1973.

Poling-Kempes, Lesley. *The Harvey Girls: Women Who Opened the West*. New York: Marlowe, 1991.

Restall, Matthew. *Seven Myths of the Spanish Conquest*. New York: Oxford University Press, 2003.

Riley, Carroll L. *The Kachina and the Cross: Indians and Spaniards in the Early Southwest*. Salt Lake City: University of Utah Press, 1999.

Roberts, David. *The Pueblo Revolt: The Secret Rebellion That Drove the Spaniards Out of the Southwest*. New York: Simon & Schuster, 2004.

Rojas, Arnold R. *The Vaquero*. Charlotte: McNally and Loftin, 1964.

Simmons, Marc. *New Mexico: A History*. New York: W.W. Norton, 1977

Simmons, Virginia M. *The San Luis Valley: Land of the Six-Armed Cross*. Niwot: University Press of Colorado, 1999.

———. *The Upper Arkansas: A Mountain River Valley*. Boulder: Pruett, 1990.

Slatta, Richard W. *Cowboy: The Illustrated History*. New York: Sterling, 2006.

Smith, P. David. *The San Juan Mountains of Southwestern Colorado*. Lake City: Western Reflections, 2013.

Tate, Bill. *The Penitentes of the Sangre de Cristos*. Truchas: privately printed, 1967.

Taylor, Bayard. *Eldorado*. New York: Alfred A. Knopf, 1949.

Taylor, Ralph C. *Colorado: South of the Border*. Denver: Sage, 1963.

Thomas, Hugh. *The Golden Empire: Spain, Charles V, and the Creation of America*. New York: Random House, 2010.

Time-Life Books, ed. *The Spanish West*. Alexandria: Time-Life, 1976.

Trimble, Marshall. *Arizona: A Cavalcade of History*. Tucson: Treasure Chest Publications, 1989.

Ubbelohde, Carl, Maxine Benson, and Duane Smith. *A Colorado History*. Boulder: Pruett, 1976.

Ward, Geoffrey C. *The West*. New York: Little, Brown and Company, 1996.

Warner, Ted J., ed. *The Domínguez-Escalante Journal: Their Expedition Through Colorado, Utah, Arizona and New Mexico in 1776*. Salt Lake City: University of Utah Press, 1995.

Warren, Nancy H. *Villages of Hispanic New Mexico*. Santa Fe: School of American Research Press, 1987.

Webb, Walter P. *The Great Plains*. Boston: Houghton Mifflin, 1936.

Weber, David J. *The Spanish Frontier in North America*. New Haven: Yale University Press, 1992.

Weigle, Marta. *Brothers of Light, Brothers of Blood*. Albuquerque: University of New Mexico Press, 1976.

———. *The Penitentes of the Southwest*. Santa Fe: Ancient City Press, 1970.

Works Projects Administration. *Colorado: A Guide to the Highest State*. New York: Hastings House, 1941.

Index

Numbers in ***bold italics*** refer to pages with illustrations.

abuse of Indians 89–90, 92, 121, 126
acequia 70, 101, 180, 209, 218
Acoma pueblo 27, 49–52, ***50***, 55, 95
Adams-Onis Treaty 160
adobe 37–38, 70–71, ***70***
aguardiente see Taos Lightning
Alamo 103–105, ***104***
alcohol *see* Taos Lightning
Alvarado, Pedro 16, 25
Amazon women 8, 116
Anasazi people 27–28, 27–43, 53, 62, 216; migration 35–37
ancestry *see* mixed ancestry
Andalusia 138, 142–143, 220
annexation methods: American 188, 217; Spanish 46–47, 52, 109
Antilia *see* Seven Cities of Gold
Anza, Juan de 109, 110, 113–114, 129, 199, 219, 220
Apache *see* Plains Indians
Arizona 106–108
Arkansas River 25, 44, 109, 113, 114, 158–160, 164, 177, 179–180, 187, 191
armament, Spanish 12–13, 14–15, 215
Armijo, Antonio 184
Armijo, Manuel 162, 170, 186–188
arquebus 14–15
arrastra 199–200, ***200***, 201
art, religious 78–79
atlatl 30–31
Atsinna pueblo 36, 41
Awatovi 24, 98
Aztec National Monument 42
Aztec people 10–17, ***18***, 19, ***21***, 34, 79, 88, 108, 110, 198, 201–202

Baja California 56, 99, 108, 116–117, 119, 129, 148
Balboa, Vasco de 8
Barceló, Gertrudes 182, 222
basket-maker culture 31
Beaubien, Carlos (Charles) 111, 162–163
Becknell, William 168

Benavides, Alonso de 52, 68, 69, 81, 97
Bent, Charles 160, 179, 188, 192–193
Bent, William 179–180
Bent's Fort 177–180, ***178***, 187, 222
berdache 88
Bering Land Bridge 28, 44
Bernardone, Giovanni 57
Betatakin 34–35
Black Bean incident 105
blood-letting *see* mutilation
border, international 101, 109, 112, 158–160, 165, 179, 186–187, 190, 191
boundary, international *see* border, international
bow and arrow 8, 13, 20, 22, 23, 30–31, 79, 84, 139
Bowie, Jim 104–105
brands, cattle 144
buffalo 21, 25, 44, 63, 65, 76, 113, 138–140, 142, 156, 171, 176–180, 191, 220
buffalo chips 177
bullfights 150–152, 221
bulto see art, religious
Burr, Aaron 158

Cabrillo, Juan 118, 220
Califia 8
California: hide trade 127–128, ***135***; missions 118–127, ***135***; name 215
El Camino Real 75, 77, 99, 119, 124, 168, 182, 196, 218
Canadian River 158
Canyon de Chelly 34–35, 36
Capistrano 123, 132, 220
Cárdenas, García de 24–25
Carmel, California 120
Carmelites 80, 120
carreta de la muerte 79, 83; *see also* art, religious
Carson, Christopher "Kit" 167, 193
carts, wooden 47, 74, 182–183, ***183***
cattle 142–144, ***143***
Caverna del Oro 202–203

Cerillos Hills 34, 45
Chaco Canyon 33–34, 35, ***41***
chaps, cowboy 148
Cheyenne *see* Plains Indians
chichimecas 197–198
Chihuahua carts *see* carts, wooden
Chimayó, New Mexico 77, 81, ***155***
Chimayó Rebellion 154, 186
Chivington, John 197
chocolate 3, 12, 33, 62, 66, 76, 129
churches 76–77
churro sheep 135, 137, 180
Cibola *see* Seven Cities of Gold
Cicuyé *see* Pecos pueblo
Civil War, American 196–197
claims, land *see* annexation methods
Cliff Palace 32, ***32***
Colorado 108–115
Columbus, Christopher 7, 8, 84, 137, 142
Comanche *see* Plains Indians
Conestoga wagon 170, 171–172, ***172***, 175–176
conquest of Mexico 11, 15–18
La Conquistadora 97, ***97***
conquistadors 9–10, 11, 14, 17–21, ***18***, 27, 43, 53, 57, 63, 80, 84, 97, 99, 115, 135, 137, 143, 145, 149, 164, 197
construction, house *see* adobe; jacal
copper 21, 46, 72, 200
copper bells 19, 34
Cordova, Francisco 10
corn, Indian 28, ***29***, ***30***, 31, 38–39, 72
Coronado, Francisco de 23–26, 27, 37, 44, 45, 50, 118, 138, 142, 154, 173, 201, 202, 216
Cortés, Hernán 10, 11, 15, 16–17, ***18***, 46, 56, 116
cowboy, Spanish 127, 141, 142, 144–152; clothing 147–149
crossbow 13
Cuerno Verde see Green Horn
Culiacán 19, 20

225

Day of the Dead *see* art, religious
disease 15, 16, 38–39, 63, 65, 73, 91, 123
dogs 13, 39, 140
dollars *see* Spanish dollars
Dominguez-Escalante expedition 129–132, 184
Dominican Republic *see* Hispaniola
Dominicans 58, 80
Doña Sebastiana see art, religious
Dorantes, Andrés de 20
Drake, Sir Francis 118
drugs, ritual 87, 198

El Cuartelejo 109
El Dorado 18
El Morro 36, 41, 52–53, **54**, **55**, 96, 130
El Sanctuario de Chimayo 77, **155**
encomienda 17, 48–49, 67, 76, 84, 98, 164, 198
Española, country *see* Hispaniola
Espejo, Antonio de 46
Espinoza brothers 163–164
Esplandian 8
Estevan 20, 22, 215

fandango 152–153
Ferdinand, King 7, 58
firearms *see* armament, Spanish
flagellation 80–83, 85, 88, 89, 95, 121
flintlock 15
Florida 7, 19, 20
Fort Marcy 188–189, 190, **193**, 207, 219
Fort Pueblo 191–192
Fort Union 193–196, **194**
Fountain of Youth 7
Four Corners area 27–28, 29, 35, 202, 216
Franciscans 20, 56–57, 60–62, 80, 95
Franklin, Missouri 165, 168, 171
fur trappers and traders *see* trappers

Gadsden Purchase 190
Gila Trail 129
gold 9, 12, 18, 19, 20, 108, 201–203, 215
Grand Canyon 24–25, **24**
grapes 57, 73, 77, 78, 121–123
Great Migration **35**–37
Great Sand Dunes 110, 112–113, 201
Green Horn 113–114, 157
Gregg, Josiah 81, 152, 176, 181
Grijalva, Juan de 10, 11
Gruber, Bernard 196
Guadalupe-Hidalgo, treaty 132, 162, 190, 200
Gulf of California *see* Sea of Cortez

Guzmán, Nuño de 19, 20–21

Haiti *see* Hispaniola
Háwikuh 22–23
Hidalgo, Nicolás 88, 90
Hispaniola 7, 10, 142
Hohokam people 28
Hollister, Ovando 152, 187, 188, 196
Hopi people 24, 26, 27, 28, 35, 36, 37, 39, 40, 42, 43, 51, 63, 85, 86, 87, 89, 93, 98, 99, 130, 135, 157, 207
horno 72, 121
horses 13–14, 91, 137–140, 141, 169, 220
housing 70–73, **73**, 120–121

Iberia 7, 9, 215
Inca Empire 18, 19
Independence, Missouri 168–171, 174
Indians, terminology 4
Indies 7
Inquisition *see* Spanish Inquisition
Inscription Rock *see* El Morro
iron 14, 21, 43, 62, 72, 74, 75, 78, 80, 121, 149, 179, 198, 200
Isabella, Queen 7, 58

jacal 38, 112, 130
Jamestown, Virginia 1, 2, 48
Jaramillo, Josefa 167, 193
Jesuits 15, 56, 80, 106, 116–117, 119, 157, 217
Jicarilla Apache 44, 113, 192
Journada del Muerto 48, 196

katsina (kachina) religion 42–43, 85–87, 89, 91–92, 95, 98, 130, 217
Kayenta region 34–35
Kearney, Stephen 174, 187–189, 192, 193, 217
Keet Seel 34–35
King Mine 115
Kino, Eusebio 106–108
kiva 39–42, **40**, **41**, 95, **131**

LaLande, Baptiste 159, 165
Lamy, Archbishop John 70
land grants 49, 161–164, 221; *see also* encomienda
León, Ponce de 7–8
liquor *see* Taos Lightning
Loma Parda 195–196, **195**
Long, Stephen 160
longhorns *see* cattle
Loreto, Mexico 55, 116
lost treasure 201–203; *also see* gold
Louisiana Purchase 53, 102, 157–158, 160, 165, 179, 203, 219

macaw *see* tropical birds
Mallet brother 164–165

Malonado, Alonso de 20
Manifest Destiny 132, 187, 222
Mason, Charlie 33
matchlock 14–15
matrilineal 38, 88, 89
Maxwell, Lucien 162–163
Mayan people 11, **11**, 12, 216
McCulley, Johnston 133–134
Mendoza, Antonio de 21, 22, 23, 25, 45, 116
mercury 74, 199–200, 222
Mesa Verde 31–33, 35
Mesoamerica 28, 34, 106, 216
Mexican-American War 185, 186–191
Mexican border *see* border, international
Mexican flag 11–12
Mexican independence 65, 154, 160, 165, 167
Mexico City 17; transportation links 75–76, 99
milagro 79
mining, Spanish methods 198–199, 222
mission grapes *see* wine
missionaries *see* Franciscans; Jesuits
mixed ancestry 49, 111
Mogollon people 28
Monterey 118, 120, 125, 127, 129–130, 155, 188
Montezuma 12, 16, **21**, 46, 108, 201, 215
Montezuma Castle **21**
Moors 7, 10, 17, 20, 39, 142–143
morada **82**, 83
Morrison, William 159, 165
Mount of the Holy Cross **114**, 115
mules 175–177, 182, 184
Murrieta, Joaquin *see* social bandits
music 57, 60–61, 62, 66, 74, 125, 152
muskets 14–15, 23, 43, 159, 193
mutilation 12, 51, 80, 89–90, 93

Nacogdoches, Texas 1, 100, 154, 166
Narváez, Pánfilo de 20
Natchitoches 100, 159
Navajo people 27, 35, 62, 65, 70, 84, 87, 89, 91, 96, 135, 160
New Mexico, name 26, 46
Niza, Marcos de 22–23, 45
La Noche Triste 16

Okeh Owingeh pueblo 48
Old Spanish Trail 168, 183–185
Oñate, Juan de 46–48, 50–55, 56, 57, 59, 64–65, 76, 80–81, 85, 99, 138, 154, 201
Ordóñez, Isidro 58
oxen 175–177

Palace of the Governors 68, 76, 94, 96, 109, 179, 188, 190, **206**
Papago people *see* Tohono O'odham
Pecos pueblo 25, **40**, 62–63, 93–94, **94**
penitentes 80–83
Peralta, Pedro de 56, 57–58
pieces of eight 169
Pike, Zebulon 112, 158–159, 165
Pike's stockade 159
pithouses 28, 31–33, 36, 39, 40, 62, 106
Pizarro, Francisco 18, 19, 22
Plains Indians 43–44, 62–63; *see also* individual tribes
Plaza, Santa Fe *see* Santa Fe Plaza
Plymouth, Massachusetts 1, 2, 53
Popé 92–93, 96
population figures 15, 16, 17, 33, 63, 66, 91, 99, 102, 155, 180, 205
Portola, Gaspar de 119–120
Portugal 9, 80, 81
pottery 34, 39
Pueblo Bonito 33–34, 41, **41**
pueblo, definition 27, 84–85, 216
pueblo revolt of 1680 52, 92–97
Puerto Rico 7
Purcell, James 165

Quetzalcoatl 12
Quivira *see* Seven Cities of Gold

Raton Pass 110, 172–174, 197
rebellion, Indian 91–98
Red River 100, 158–159
retablo see art, religious
Rio Grande 3, 25, 27, 35, 36–37, 46–48, 62, 65, 95, 103, 111, 118, 159, 160, 166, 187, 190, 201
roads, royal *see Camino Real*
Robidoux, Antoine 167
Robinson, John 159
Rodríguez, Agustín 45
rope, cowboy 146–147
Royal Road *see Camino Real*

saddles 145–146, **146**
St. Augustine 8, 56
St. Francis cathedral 69–70
St. Francis of Assisi 57
St. Francis, orders of 80
Salinas missions 64–65, **64**
San Acacio 111, **161**
San Antonio 100–102
San Diego 118–120, 125, 128, 155, 157, 166
San Francisco Bay 118, 120
San Francisco Peaks 42, **86**
San Gabriel (New Mexico) 48, 52, 56
San Gabriel Mission 122–123, **122**, 125, 126, 129, 183–185
Sand Dunes *see* Great Sand Dunes

Sangre de Cristo land grant 111, 162–163
Sangre de Cristo Mountains 83, 109, 112, 167
Sangre de Cristo Pass 109, 167, 201, 202
San Juan Capistrano Mission 123
San Luis, Colorado 83, 111
San Luis Valley 110–113, 115, 159–160, 163, 167, 185, 192, 199, 205, 220
San Miguel church 68, **69**, 79, 93, **156**
San Miguel del Vado, New Mexico 105, 173–174
San Xavier del Bac 106, **107**
Santa Anna, Antonio 99–105
Santa Barbara Mission 123, **124**, 132
Santa Fe 48, 51, 56, 58, 59, 66–74, 180–182; trade 164–165
Santa Fe Plaza 68–70, 97, 174, 179, 180, 188, **190**, **206**
Santa Fe Trail 2, 167–180, 221; life on 174–177
santero see art, religious
Sea of Cortez 53, 116
seashells 19, 34, 65
Serra, Junípero 119–120, 123
Seven Cities of Gold 8–9, 19, 21, 25, 37, 52, 108, 197
sexual abuse of Indians 8, 67, 88, 90, 126; *see also* sodomy
sexuality, pueblo 88–89
shields 12, 13, 14, 23, 44, 52, 148
silver 9, 45, 106, 197
Sinagua people **21**, 36, 86, 108
sipapu 40–41, 42–43
slavery, Indian 45, 48–49, 65, 70, 84, 140–141, 160
Sloat, John 188
Smith, Thomas "Peg-Leg" 191
social bandits 132–134
Socorro, New Mexico 36, 48, 77, 118, 166
sodomy 58, 88, 90, 126, 219; *see also* abuse of Indians
Soto, Hernando de 19
South Park 111, 113, 163, 165, 199, 219
South Sea *see* Sea of Cortez
Spanish Cave *see Caverna del Oro*
Spanish dollars 169
Spanish failure 59–60
Spanish Inquisition 58, 59, 67, 90, 196
Spanish Peaks 109, **110**, 201–202
Spanish titles 216, 217
Spanish Trail *see* Old Spanish
Spanish treasure *see* gold
spurs 149–150, **149**
Sumner, Edwin 193–194

Taos fair 65, 160
Taos Lightning 167, 191–192, 195

Taos pueblo 65, 88, 90, 91, 92, 108, 193
Taos Rebellion 192
taxes 9, 61, 66, 143, 155, 163, 167, 170, 173, 186
Taylor, Zachary 187
Tejo 19
Tenochtitlán 11–12, 15, 16
Texas 99–105
Tlaxcalan people 16, 47, 68
Tohono O'odham people 28, 106
Torquemada, Tomás de 58
Tovar, Pedro de 24
trails *see* individual names
trappers, fur 1, 2, 65, 100, 110, 162–167, 171, 173, 174, 178, 179
travois 140
treasure *see* gold
tropical birds 19, 20, 34, 65, 216
Tubac 106, 129
Tumacácori 106–107
Turk 25
turkeys 28, 35, 39, 50, 73, 139, 176
Turley, Simeon 191, 192, 193
turquoise 12, 21, 22, 23, 34, 46, 115, 216

Ulibarri, Juan de 109, 157
Ute people 62, 63, 65, 70, 84, 87, 110, 113, 135, 139, 155, 157, 160, 163, 192

Vaca, Álvar de 20–22, 25, 99
Valverde, Antonio 109, 157, 173
vaquero see cowboy, Spanish
Vargas, Diego 96–98
Velásquez, Diego 10
Villalobos, Gregorio de 137
Vizcaíno, Sebastián 118

wagons, Santa Fe Trail 170–171, **172**
weapons *see* armament, Spanish
West Indies 7, 9
Westport, Missouri 169, 171
Wetherill, Richard 33, 34
whipping *see* flagellation
whiskey *see* Taos Lightning
Wilkinson, James 158–159
wine 61–62, 66, 74, 77–78, 99, 122–123
witchcraft 22, 58, 92
Wupatki pueblo **86**

Yucatán Peninsula 10–11, **11**, 142

Zacatecas, Mexico 46, 47, 75, 182, 197
Zaldívar, Juan de 50, 112, 142
Zaldívar, Vicente de 50–51, 142
Zorro *see* social bandits
Zuni people 22, 28; pueblo 22–24, 27

www.ingramcontent.com/pod-product-compliance
Ingram Content Group UK Ltd.
Pitfield, Milton Keynes, MK11 3LW, UK
UKHW050530150426
5217IPUK00026B/1881